Meditation
and Mantras

by Swami Vishnu Devananda

OM Lotus Publishing Company
243 West 24th Street, New York, New York 10011

By the author of

The Complete Illustrated Book of Yoga

ISBN 0-931546-01-X

Printed in the United States of America

 OM Lotus Publishing Company • New York City
A non-profit company owned and operated by the
International Sivananda Yoga Vedanta Centers, Inc.

Dedicated
to
My Revered Master
H.H. SRI SWAMI SIVANANDA MAHARAJ

And His Chief Disciples
MY VENERABLE GURUBHAIS

Swami Paramananda
Swami Swarupananda
Swami Atmananda
Swami Narayanananda
Swami Chidananda
Swami Krishnananda
Swami Saswadananda
Swami Poorna Bhodh
Swami Visweswarananda
Swami Chinmayananda
Swami Satyananda
Swami Satchidananda
Swami Sahajananda
Swami Govindananda
Swami Purushothamananda
Swami Brehmananda
Swami Vasudevananda
Swami Nijabodhananda
Swami Satchidananda (II)
Swami Nirmalananda
Swami Omkarananda
Swami Harisaranananda

Swami Madhavananda
Swami Sivananda Hridayananda
Swami Vidyananda
Swami Nadabrahmananda
Swami Venkatesananda
Swami Sivapremananda
Swami Chaitanyananda
Swami Dayananda
Swami Nityananda
Swami Saradananda
Swami Sadasivananda
Swami Tejomayananda
Swami Prenavananda
Swami Sadananda
Swami Gyanananda
Swami Raghavananda
Swami Ramananda
Swami Hari Omananda
Swami Premananda (Senior)
Swami Mounananda
Swami Sudhananda
Swami Sredhananda

Swami Jyotirmayananda

And to my revered poorvashram mother and father,
SWAMI SIVACHARANANDA (P. Devaki Amma)
and P. CHATHU PANIKKER.

Master Sivananda

Table of Contents

Preface

This volume is intended to dispel the cloud of confusion that has accumulated around the subject of meditation. Those who are looking for the secret short-cuts, the novel innovations, the exciting new trends and fads in the area of self-development will find nothing here. The methods presented here stem from the classic four paths of Raja Yoga, Karma Yoga, Jnana Yoga and Bhakti Yoga. These are given here in their uncorrupted form, yet with consideration for the Western mind and scientific tradition.

Meditation is a universal tradition which traces its origin thousands of years before the advent of today's civilization. The science of meditation has survived uninterrupted and exhaustive testing as it has passed from generation to generation. It has endured in its original form because the outstanding and fundamental appeals of Yoga have been Tolerance, Universatility, and Simplicity. Within its simple framework are contained the principle teachings and approaches which make up the substance of all known philosophies, religions, and disciplines. If one understands the four paths to meditation, it is possible to unravel the trappings and mysterious elements of any religious or philosophical system.

The shelves of bookstores are overloaded with numerous "new developments", theories, and streamlined approaches to meditation. But many are as blind leading the blind, with no experience to back the methods they tout. There are one-sided fanatics, Mantra hucksters, and outright charlatans. Some promise rapid development of psychic powers. Others are modern spiritual propagandists and con-men. Even the Madison Avenue contingent is well represented. Among all of these there is only a handful of selfless Masters who are teaching the Truth.

Real meditation is liberation from the clutches of the lower senses and mind. By definition it is transcendental, the word not being used as an advertising slogan, but to convey the beauty of meditation, in which all fears, desires, longings and negative emotions are transcended. The meditator reaches the superconscious state in which he or she is able to identify with the all-blissful Self. In this transcendental state there is no awareness of body, mind, or duality, and the knower becomes one with the knowledge and the known.

There is no need for mystery or secrecy about Mantras or any other accessory to meditation. There are no spiritual injunctions against discussing one's Mantra. A Mantra is a mystical energy encased in a sound structure. Its vibrations directly affect the *chakras,* or energy centers of the body. It steadies the mind and leads to the stillness of meditation. Those Mantras which are suitable for meditation are included in this book.

The concoctions of syllables which are currently being peddled in the West as Mantras are obviously bogus. These "Mantras" can lead to deep relaxation but nothing more. So can the repetition of any word or meaningless phrase. One can slow the pulse and breathing as well as lower the blood pressure by sitting still and concentrating on a ticking clock or dripping water tap.

Life in the West has become computerized, compartmentalized and oriented towards instant results. But the tradition from which the four yogic paths stem is a holistic one. It is one where the science, religion, philosophy, psychology, and system of health were all integrated. In the same way, the various classical meditation techniques that have been in use over the ages are based on solid discipline and regular practice. Proper breathing, proper exercise, proper relaxation, proper diet, and positive thinking are the necessary groundwork for successful meditation. These are covered to some extent in the first few chapters that follow, although for a comprehensive view of these and other aspects of Hatha and Raja Yoga, you will want to refer to my previous book, *The Complete Illustrated Book of Yoga.*

If this book clarifies the methods and aim of meditation, it will have served its purpose. The spiritual quest is a thorny path that ultimately must be walked alone. My own path has been blessed by the firm, compassionate, and boundless wisdom of my master, India's late great saint and sage, H.H. Sri Swami Sivananda Maharaj. If, through me as his instrument, the echo of his words and insight can guide the footsteps of seekers in the Western world, I shall have achieved my earthly purpose.

Finally, I wish to gratefully acknowledge the following people whose contributions helped to make this book possible: Dr. Fritjof Capra, for permission to reprint excerpts from his speech "The Yoga of Physics" and the photomontage of dancing Siva in particle tracks taken from his book *The Tao of Physics;* Nicholas and June Regush, for permission to reprint from their book *Mind Search;* Dr. Raymond Moody, Jr., for permission to reprint from his book *Life After Life;* my brother Marcel Vogel, for his great gifts; Dr. Labrosse, Dr. Dionne, M. Blondeau, and M. Forest for the Kirlian photographs; Oh Shinnah, for permission to reprint excerpts of her speech before the New Age Community Center, Vancouver, B.C. on November of 1977; the Association for Research and Enlightenment, for permission to reprint portions of the Edgar Cayce readings from *Edgar Cayce on Atlantis* by Edgar Evans Cayce; Silamata Karuna, for her extensive research and editorial expertise; Silvio Paladini, for the Kundalini Chakra illustrations; Bill Matthias for the deity photographs; and the many disciples and students of the Sivananda Yoga mission for invaluble aid in artwork, editing, proofreading, and typing.

Swami Vishnu Devananda

Val Morin, P.Q., Canada
July 14, 1978

Why Meditate

*Without the help of meditation, you cannot attain Knowledge of
the Self. Without its aid, you cannot grow into the divine state.
Without it, you cannot liberate yourself from the trammels of the
mind and attain immortality.*

*Meditation is the only royal road to the attainment of freedom.
It is a mysterious ladder which reaches from earth to heaven,
from error to truth, from darkness to light, from pain to bliss, from
restlessness to abiding peace, from ignorance to knowledge.
From mortality to immortality.*

— Swami Sivananda
Bliss Divine

Who am I? What is my purpose in life? Why do some people
seem to have an easier time of life than others? Where did I come
from and where am I going?

These are the classic questions that almost everyone muses
over at some time in life. Some struggle their entire lives to find
the answers. Some give up looking, or just put the questions aside
as they get caught up in the routines and details of daily life. But
others discover the answers, and their lives are full and contented.

The meaning of life is found by diving deep, deep within.
But ever distracted by the business of living, people seldom stop,
even for a moment in their busy days, to notice what is going on
inside. It is hardly noticed that the mind is being constantly stim-
ulated by the bombardment of perceptions from the senses. Very
often, it is not until a person reaches a point of great distress that
he realizes it is time to stop and take stock of what is happening
in his life.

Meditation is the practice by which there is constant observation of the mind. It involves setting aside a regular time and
place for the specific purpose of discovering that infinite well of
wisdom that lies within. The chapters that follow give a comprehensive understanding of the philosophy and techniques of medi-

1

tation. First, however, it is best to explore some of the background psychology and terminology that help to explain the purpose of meditation.

MECHANICS OF THE MIND

In man's search for happiness, he invariably turns to external objects and events for satisfaction. He thinks, "If I can just have that car", or "If I were just able to get that job", or "If I only lived in Arizona, then I would be happy". The mind may be stilled and at peace for a short time on attaining the desired object, but eventually it tires of its new toy, and seeks pleasure elsewhere. However, each time the external objects fail to bring happiness. One may acquire new material possessions, a position with more responsibility, and a home in the country, but there always remains the same mind. Contentment is derived from the approach and attitude toward the external world, not from the objects themselves. Every person passes through easier and more difficult periods in his life. When the obstacles in life are confronted with a serene mind, then one lives more happily.

The challenge, then, is to gain control of the internal world. The mind is constantly conversing with itself — replaying past events, rearranging them into a better drama, planning for the future, discussing the pros and cons of this and that. By methodically slowing down its continuous ramblings, the internal dialogue, and focussing on positive and uplifting objects, it is possible to begin to understand the mechanics of the psyche and bring about a more effective life.

But the mind is an elusive animal to tame. So many theories exist as to how it works, yet the human mental process seems to remain intangible. Why does one so often find himself caught in the same frustrations, the same problems? Free will does exist, but only when it is used to break out of the habits that have been developed in life. It is said that this is a free society, but in truth, it is each person's own desires and emotions that bind him. Consider the friend who smokes cigarettes, daily disclaiming them, determined to stop "tomorrow". How many years has he been caught in this charade? He truly wants to be free of the habit, but lacks the necessary control of his own mind.

In a sense, the mind is like a record. It contains grooves, or impressions, called *samskaras* in Sanskrit. These *samskaras* are formed when certain thought waves, or *vrittis,* become habitual.

For example, a man passes a bakery and sees a chocolate eclair in the window. The *vritti* arises in his mind, " How delicious; I will buy that eclair". If he ignores that *vritti,* and turns his mind to something else, then no pattern is formed. But, if he identifies with the thought, he gives life to it. He buys the eclair, looking forward to enjoying it as dessert that evening. Now, suppose he finds he must pass that same bakery every Tuesday and Thursday. Each time he goes by, he recalls that wonderful eclair, and purchases another. Now what was originally just a flash in the mind has become a force in his life, and a *samskara* has been formed.

Samskaras are not necessarily negative. There can be grooves in the mind which are uplifting and those which bring one down. It is the express purpose of meditation to create new, positive channels in the mind, and to eradicate those which are destructive. It is an absolutely scientific process, but at the same time, the goal is spiritual. It is not sufficient to eliminate the negative. There must be a striving to develop love, compassion, a sense of service, cheerfulness, kindness, and the many other qualities which not only make one's own life happy, but which radiate to others.

Everyone wants to be his best. Each person would like to think that he is perfect. Yet despite repeated resolutions, every person finds himself so many times being less than what he would like to be. The cause of this predicament is the *ahamkara,* or ego. Sri Sankara, one of the wisest men of all history, stated in the *Vivekachudamani,* "Calamity is due to being subject to ego, bad agonies are due to ego, desire is due to subjection to ego; there is no greater enemy than ego." This *ahamkara* is the cause of all bondage and is the chief barrier to the experience of inner Reality.

Ego is the self-arrogating aspect of the mind. It is the ego which separates the individual from unity with others and within himself, for the ego asserts "I-ness". *Ahamkara* is the greatest obstacle to tranquility, for it is that which occupies the mind with whether we are better or worse, possess more or less, and have greater or lesser power than others. It is attended by desire, pride, anger, delusion, greed, jealousy, lust and hatred. The ego is the most difficult aspect of the mind to control, for its nature is such that it deludes even while one is striving to overcome it. It is that very part of the being that would not be controlled.

Through meditation, the play of the mind is witnessed. In the early stages nothing more can be done than to gain understanding as the ego is observed constantly asserting itself. But in

time its games become familiar, and one begins to prefer the peace
of contentment. When the ego is subdued, energies can then be
utilized constructively for personal growth and the service of
others.

THOUGHT POWER

Every person projects some kind of vibration to those around
him. Some people are a pleasure to be with. They seem to have a
certain *prana,* or energy, that they share with others. Then there
are those who are negative and depressed, and they seem to actually draw *prana* out of people in their environment. The reason
for this is that there is a power contained in thought. It is very
subtle, yet it does exist and it is extremely powerful. Whether a
person is aware of it or not, he is constantly transmitting and
receiving thoughts. This is why people have experiences of ESP
from time to time. Some wish to call these experiences coincidence,
but they are not. The ability to communicate and perceive thought
is developed to a higher degree in those who are said to be psychic,
or to have great intuitive abilities.

Every thought has weight, shape, size, form, color, quality,
and power. An experienced meditator can see all these aspects
directly with his inner eye. For example, a spiritual thought has a
yellow color, while a thought charged with anger and hatred is
dark red. A thought is like an object. Just as an apple can be given
to your friend, or taken back, so also it is possible to give a useful,
powerful thought to someone and take it back.

Good and evil, friend and enemy, are in the mind only.
Every man creates a world of virtue and vice, pleasure and pain,
out of his own imagination. These qualities do not proceed from
the objects themselves; they belong to the attitude of the mind.
One man's joy is another man's burden. Thoughts control one's
life, mold one's character, shape one's destiny, and affect all other
people. When the potential contained in the power of thought is
realized, it is the beginning of great spiritual growth in the individual and all of humanity.

THE SELF

What is spirituality? The past two decades encompassed
what has been called an age of alienation. Old traditions and religions were rejected. Thousands of "New Age" seekers began to

experiment with a myriad of chemicals and philosophies. There was a pervasive current of feeling that the Truth was someplace close at hand — but where was it? Somehow it seemed necessary to broaden perspectives a little.

In each society, the organized religion contains cultural practices and techniques which are handed down from generation to generation. It is when the means becomes confused with the end that its members begin to search elsewhere. They look for inspiration that is alive, that has a practical and observable effect in their daily lives. Whether a person lives a spiritual life on his own, or is part of an organized tradition, the goal is the same: the attainment of perfection, purity, and peace of mind, or Self-Realization.

There is a Power, an Energy, into which each person can tap if he only knows it is available to him. This Force inspires, encourages, reinforces, and gives strength to all those who seek to grow in a positive direction. Many, however, are unaware of this resource, or they have misconceptions about it. They are like the farmer who moved to a house in the city, and lived in darkness because he did not know what those strange sockets in the wall were. The Light is there and available to all; we need only to connect ourselves with the current.

This source of wisdom is the Self. The Self is not the individual body or mind, but rather that aspect deep inside each person that knows the Truth. It exists in each being, and yet it exists independently also. Some call it God. Others call it Jehovah, Allah, Brahman, Cosmic Consciousness, *Atman,* Holy Spirit, or the Universal Mind. The names and paths are many, but there is one Essence which pervades all beings.

The Self is impossible to understand with the limited senses and intellect. The human mind cannot fathom the Infinite and the Eternal. Therefore a visualization is sometimes used to help one focus on the Supreme. Christians may meditate on the image of a cross, or the form of Jesus Christ. Hindus may picture Lord Siva (that Energy which destroys the old in preparation for renewal) as a very beautiful eternally youthful ascetic meditating atop the Himalayas. Those who conceive of the Absolute in more abstract terms may concentrate on a candle flame, a *chakra* (energy center of the body), or the sound of OM. But these are only partial impressions of the Truth.

Imagine a highly advanced scientist. He knows the theory and mathematics of how large space is, or how minute an atom is, or what the difference is between life and death. He can explain them in detail and at great length. But this is only theoretical knowledge; he can never really grasp the essence of these things. There is no way to define or describe that which is limitless. It is only through *direct experience,* not the intellect or the senses, that Absolute Knowledge can be attained. Through the protracted practice of mediation it becomes possible to still the outgoing mind, develop intuitive abilities, and touch that small part of the Supreme that lies within all.

KARMA AND REINCARNATION

Meditation unleashes the immense potential of every person. We gain mastery of the mind by bringing a halt to its incessant chatter and teaching it to focus in a concentrated manner. Awareness of thought patterns helps to give the power to project thoughts to others. Yet, one must be very careful always to send only vibrant, positive, loving and healing energy. For a complete understanding of why this is so, consider the subjects of Karma and reincarnation.

There is a law in physics that states, "For every action there is an equal and opposite reaction." Expressed popularly, it is said that "What goes 'round, comes 'round". Jesus taught, "Do unto others as you would have them do unto you." These are all expressions of the law of Karma, of cause and effect. It works something like a boomerang. Whatever thought or deed comes from a person will be returned to him. It may not come in the same form, but sooner or later each will confront the results of his own actions. A joyous and giving person immediately draws a response of warmth and love. If a person is hateful, he will be disliked — until he removes this negative quality. This is the law.

Karmic reactions are not always experienced immediately. Sometimes lessons are not easily learned, and negative patterns may be continued for many years. A single lifetime is not sufficient for anyone to attain Perfection. So each person reincarnates again and again. This is the reason for the apparent inequality between people. One is poor and another rich, one is healthy and another crippled, one is cheerful and another depressed. It is neither cruel fate nor a distant and unconcerned God that set the stage for these situations, but one's own Karma.

Here it can be seen why one must not be fooled by those who would sell magic mantras and instant insight. These quick-realization gurus will bring nothing but disappointment, for ultimately we must reckon with the effects of our own deeds. Each man's life is his own responsibility. To blame difficulties on unfortunate circumstances or parents who weren't well enough versed in psychology is to beg the question. Only when we realize that we are caught in our own web and begin to spiritualize our lives, do we break out of the wheel of births and deaths, and find peace and union in the Self.

Reincarnation is not an exclusively Eastern precept. It is a fact of life, and is contained in some form in almost every major religion and mystical philosophy. Research indicates that it was an accepted doctrine, at least in some quarters, at the time of Christ, and is still an integral part of some sects of the Jewish tradition. The Bible contains no condemnation of the principle of reincarnation, and in fact, when Christ was asked when Elijah would return, he answered that Elijah *had* returned, referring to John the Baptist. Origen, of the early Christian Greek Church, wrote extensively regarding the pre-existence of the soul, and this concept was basically accepted in the Church until the fourth century B.C. More recently, Pope Pius XII named Origen a Doctor of the Universal Church, indicating a tolerance if not an actual embracing of his teachings.

But reincarnation is not merely an abstract principle. All have experienced recollections from past lives at some time or another. It is called déjà vu. It is not unusual to meet someone for the first time, yet experience an uncanny sense of familiarity. This is because that person was known in previous lives. Occasionally there may be a place or scene that stirs memories deep inside. It will seem as if one has been there before, and in fact, that is the case. At times one will awake from a dream that is strangely familiar, even though it bears no relationship to the present life and environment; it is a segment of an earlier lifetime that has surfaced in order to help work out present Karma.

WHAT DOES YOGA HAVE TO DO WITH IT?

The methods are many for eliminating these karmic debts. Through one form or another of meditation one learns to understand how the mind operates and thus is able to begin the growth process. Exactly what techniques are used depends on the nature of the individual. In Yoga, which means "union", there are four main paths. Raja Yoga is a psychological approach focussing on concentration and meditation. Karma Yoga is the path of eliminating the ego and attachments through selfless service. Jnana Yoga is the method by which the intellect is used to negate bondage to the material world. Bhakti Yoga is the way of union through conversion of the emotions to devotion.

There are, as well, a number of other forms of Yoga. They include Hatha Yoga, which is actually the aspect of Raja Yoga that works with the energies of the astral body through exercises, or postures, and *kundalini* meditation. Here the meditator concentrates on a specific Sanskrit phrase for the purpose of stilling the mind and evoking positive energy.

It is said that the paths are many but the Truth is One. Each person must travel his own road to union with the Source. It should be borne in mind, however, that by placing all of one's energies into only one form of Yoga, there is a danger of imbalance, even fanaticism. For stable and consistent progress, the meditator should choose a preferred path, but always draw from the techniques and wisdom of the other methods. Only through a synthesis of Yogas is an equilibrium maintained.

In meditating regularly, the mind becomes clearer and clearer, and motives become more and more pure. The subconscious releases hidden knowledge that allows understanding of the ways in which each binds himself in daily habits. The ego is slowly eradicated by concentration on a broader awareness of the universe and one's relation to it. Ultimately the superconscious, or intuitive forces, are released, leading to a life of wisdom and peace.

The Basics of Meditation

O aspirants! Struggle hard. Make sincere efforts. Meditate
regularly and systematically. Never miss a day in meditation.
There will be a great loss if you lose even a day.
No more words! Enough of discussions and heated debates.
Retire into a solitary room. Close your eyes. Have deep silent
meditation. Destroy the imaginations, thoughts, whims, fancies
and desires when they arise from the surface of the mind.
Withdraw the wandering mind and fix it on the Supreme. Now
meditation will become deep and intense. Do not open your eyes.
Do not stir from the seat. Dive deep into the recesses of the heart.
Enjoy the silence now.

— Swami Sivananda
Concentration and Meditation

Much has been said and written about meditation, yet it
takes years to understand its nature. It cannot be taught, just as
sleep cannot be taught. One may have a king-sized posture-pedic
mattress, an air-conditioned room, and the absence of all disturbances, but sleep may not come. Sleep itself is not in anyone's
hands. One falls into it. In the same way, meditation comes by
itself. To still the mind and enter silence requires daily practice.
Yet there are certain steps that one can take along the way to
establish a foundation and thus insure success.

Before beginning meditation, it is best to have a proper environment and attitude. One's place of meditation, schedule, physical health, and mental state should all reflect a readiness to turn
inward. Many of the most difficult obstacles are removed merely
by creating a setting which is conducive to meditation.

GUIDE TO MEDITATION

The following are certain practical points regarding the basic
techniques and stages of meditation. They are primarily intended
for the beginner, although even the most experienced meditator

9

will find a review of them useful.

1. Regularity of time, place and practice are very important. Regularity conditions the mind to slow down its activities with a minimum of delay. It is difficult to focus the mind, which wants to jump about as soon as one sits for concentration. Just as a conditioned reflex is a response to established external stimuli, so the mind will settle down more quickly when time and place are established.

2. The most effective times are early dawn and dusk, when the atmosphere is charged with special spiritual force. The preferred time is *brahmamuhurta,* the hours between 4:00 and 6:00 a.m. In these quiet hours after sleep, the mind is clear and unruffled by activities of the day. Refreshed and free of wordly concerns, it can be molded very easily, and concentration will come without effort. If it is not feasible to sit for meditation at this time, choose an hour when one is not involved with daily activities and the mind is apt to be calm. Regularity is the most important consideration.

3. Try to have a separate room for meditation. If this is impossible, screen off a portion of a room, and do not allow others to enter it. The area should be used only for meditation, and should be kept free from other vibrations and associations. Incense should be burned morning and evening. The focal point of the room should be a picture or image of the chosen deity or inspirational figure, with the meditation mat placed before it. As meditation is repeated, the powerful vibrations set up by it will be lodged in the room. In six months the peace and purity of the atmosphere will be felt, and it will have a magnetic aura. In times of stress one can sit in the room, do repetition of Mantra for half an hour, and experience comfort and relief.

4. When sitting, face north or east in order to take advantage of favorable magnetic vibrations. Sit in a comfortable steady posture, with spine and neck held erect but not tense. This helps to steady the mind, and encourages concentration. Just as important, the psychic current must be able to travel unimpeded from the base of the spine to the top of the head. It is not necessary to place the legs in *padmasana,* the classic lotus posture. Any comfortable cross-legged posture will do. A cross-legged position provides a firm base for the body, and makes a triangular path for the flow of energy, which must be contained rather than dispersed in all directions. Metabolism, brain waves and breathing will slow down as concentration deepens.

5. Before beginning, command the mind to be quiet for a specific length of time. Forget the past, present and future.

6. Consciously regulate the breath. Begin with five minutes of deep abdominal breathing to bring oxygen to the brain. Then slow it down to an imperceptible rate.

7. Keep the breathing rhythmic. Inhale for three seconds and exhale for three seconds. Regulation of breath also regulates the flow of *prana,* the vital energy. If a Mantra is being used, it should be coordinated with the breathing.

8. Allow the mind to wander at first. It will jump around, but will eventually become concentrated, along with the concentration of *prana.*

9. Do not force the mind to be still. This would set into motion additional brain waves, hindering meditation. If the mind persists in wandering, simply disassociate from it, and watch it as though you were watching a movie. It will gradually slow down.

10. Select a focal point on which the mind, like a bird in need of a perch, may rest when it tires. For those who are predominantly intellectual, the object of focus should be visualized in the space between the eyebrows. For those who are more emotional, it should be visualized in the heart plexus. Never change this focal point.

11. Focus on a neutral or uplifting object or symbol, holding the image to the place of concentration. If using a Mantra, repeat it mentally, and coordinate the repetition with the breathing. If one does not have a personal Mantra, *OM* may be used. Those who prefer a personalized diety may refer to the chapter on Mantras, or use *RAM* or *SHYAM*. Although mental repetition is stronger, the Mantra may be repeated aloud if one becomes drowsy. Never change the Mantra.

12. Repetition will lead to pure thought, in which sound vibration merges with thought vibration, and there is no awareness of meaning. Vocal repetition progresses though mental repetition to telepathic language, and from there to pure thought. This is a subtle state of transcendental bliss with duality, where there remains awareness of subject and object.

13. With practice, duality disappears and *samadhi,* or the superconscious state is reached. Do not become impatient, as this takes a long time.

14. In *samadhi* one rests in a state of bliss in which the Knower, Knowledge and Known become One. This is the superconscious state reached by mystics of all faiths and persuasions.

15. Begin the practice of meditation with twenty minute periods, and increase to one hour. If the body is overcome by jerking or tremors control them and keep the energy internalized.

HEALTH FOR MEDITATION

A healthy body is essential to the development of one's full potential. If the physical machinery is not in optimum condition, it will not be a fit instrument for one's daily work, meditation, and service to others. Some think a yogi should be emaciated in the name of self-discipline. But in fact, excessive physical austerities indicate an over-concern with the body. Others believe that those on the spiritual path need not concern themselves with matters of the body as their energies are directed towards loftier things. Yet these are both extreme points of view, for one must always keep a balance in life.

Proper exercise, proper breathing, proper relaxation, proper diet, and positive thinking are the requisite attendants of meditation. In order to remove distractions from the mind, a healthy body and psyche are necessary. When there are disturbances of a physical or emotional nature, meditation is not possible. Let us consider each of the above aspects that lead to a healthy, dynamic, and effective existence.

Proper exercise is not muscle building, nor is it a short set of strenuous calesthenics for the purpose of reducing one portion of the body which has taken on extra weight due to poor living habits. The entire physical system, internal and external, should be kept constantly in tune. This is the purpose of Yoga exercises, or *asanas*. Sometimes called postures, these *asanas* involve systematically stretching muscles rather than contracting them. The effect is to tone the muscles of the body, release tension, and insure excellent circulation, digestion, assimilation and elimination. The body is kept supple, and at the same time concentration and serenity are developed.

Yogic breathing is called *pranayama,* which actually means control of the vital energy. One can live without food, water, sunlight, and sleep for fairly extended periods of time, but the body cannot survive without oxygen beyond several minutes. *Prana,* the vital force, or energy of the body, makes the difference between life and death, and its primary source is the breath. The quality and quantity of .air, and the timing of the breath have a direct effect upon the brain and its function. This is an area which Western

At the Sivananda Yoga Camp Headquarters

scientists are just beginning to investigate. There are certain *pranayamas* or breathing exercises that increase the amount of energy in the body, cleanse the lungs, reduce the amount of sleep needed, calm the nerves, still the mind, heat and cool the physical system, and even help raise the *kundalini,* or spiritual energies of the body.

Proper relaxation is also needed to maintain mental, spiritual, and physical health. The yogic *asanas* and *pranayama* mentioned above include special techniques for relaxation. These techniques also emphasize the conservation and efficient use of the energies which are contained in the body. Many think that relaxation involves leaving home for some exotic place where the mind and body are ceaselessly pumped with stimulants and depressants and a full range of other damaging delights. It is no wonder one hears so often, "I just couldn't wait to get home from my vacation so I could relax!" True relaxation comes from removing the stimuli — visual, edible and otherwise — and tuning in to the inner awareness.

Like any piece of sturdy machinery, man's physical and mental bodies can take quite a bit of abuse before giving any signs of protest. Unfortunately in the West it has become a practice to ignore the basic rules of health, and to think that a pill here or there which relieves symptoms will actually bring about well-being. Quite the opposite is true. Pain in the body is a warning, like a red light on the instrument panel of a car. Taking this or that compound of chemicals to remove the symptoms is the same as taking a hammer and breaking the red light. It does nothing to solve the problem, and in fact may make it worse, while only giving the appearance of helping. Many of the chemicals ingested are not useful to the body, cannot be eliminated, and are therefore merely stored. These medicines accumulate, along with the food additives that are eaten in such abundance (on the average of 25 pounds per person, per year), and they combine with each other to literally poison the system. The effects may not be felt for many years.

Man is just beginning to be aware of the collection of illnesses that are partner to a technologically advanced society. That is not to say that there is no need for modern medicine, but often doctors are considered to have some form of absolute knowledge. Too often, frequent visits to the local GP, specialist, or psychologist are substituted for living a healthy life. Most of the diseases of the mind and body can be eliminated by following the five basic points. 1) Proper exercise, 2) proper breathing, and 3) proper relaxation all come under the realm of Hatha Yoga, and are covered extensively in my first book, *The Complete Illustrated Book of Yoga.* We will now take a closer look at the other two points, 4) proper diet and 5) positive thinking and meditation.

A PEACEFUL DIET

What goes into the human body correlates directly to the efficiency with which the brain functions. Recent studies show that certain red food coloring creates hyperactivity in children, and that refined sugar can cause emotional instability. These are just two examples of the substances that are often heedlessly consumed without understanding of their effect on the body and mind. A person who meditates regularly must be particularly aware of these substances, for even on a day by day basis, diet affects the quality of meditation.

The optimum diet for a meditator is a bland one. This is not to say that meals should not be appetizing, but there should be an absence of those foods which affect the mind. Hot and pungent spices, garlic, onions, salt, coffee, black tea, and meat agitate the mind, and hence control of the thoughts becomes difficult. Then there are those foods which dull the mind, rendering a state of sleepiness instead of concentration. These include all pre-cooked and overripe foods, as well as the obvious, alcohol. Marijuana and cigarettes, though not taken as foods, also fit into this category.

Of course a good portion of the above items are on most people's list of favorite indulgences. It is not expected that every person will be able to make an immediate radical change in his diet, but those who are sincerely interested in meditation should promptly begin to phase out meat and cigarettes. (Hatha Yoga will make this much easier.) If there is an awareness of the goals, many of the detrimental habits will fall away of themselves in time simply due to the change of consciousness that occurs in meditation. One should start by shopping and cooking with a greater degree of awareness. There are many natural foods which are easy to prepare, and snacks such as fruit and nuts are as available as a candy bar or a martini. Buy fresh fruits and vegetables. Read all labels and avoid additives, pre-cooked and processed foods, and canned goods wherever possible. Explore the local health food store. Buy a few good books on nutrition and vegetarian diet. Within a few months a great change will take place.

Ten years ago vegetarianism was, in a sense, an underground

practice. One always eyed a person who refrained from eating meat with a certain amount of curiosity, if not suspicion. Today it is quite a different story. Health food stores and vegetarian restaurants are prevalent, even in the smallest of towns. There is a growing awareness that our health is directly affected by what we eat. Almost any disease can be cured by either a change in diet, or a short period of fasting, and with no medications at all. This is not only true of physical disorders, but of many mental difficulties as well. It is particularly important that pregnant mothers have this awareness, for too often they do not realize the effect of their diet on the developing fetus.

Contrary to the popular concept, it is not vegetarians who do not get enough protein, but rather meat-eaters who take in an excess of protein. Animal protein contains a high concentration of uric acid, which is a nitrogen compound similar to ammonia. It is not water soluble and cannot be broken down by the liver. Thus, though a certain amount is eliminated, the greater portion of uric acid is deposited in the joints. The result of this is referred to as arthritis.

Hardening of the arteries and heart disease are two of the most common maladies in the West, where the greatest amount of meat is consumed. The culprit is cholesterol, which also cannot be eliminated from the body, and thus forms fatty deposits along the walls of the heart and arteries, gradually thickening until they are clogged and inflexible. Some think that by merely switching from butter to margarine will solve the problem, but in fact any oil that has been hydrogenated is equally as harmful. The major source of cholesterol, however, does not come from occasional butter on your toast in the morning but from the hundreds of pounds of animal tissue and its fats that each person consumes each year.

Heart disease, hardening of the arteries, and arthritis are common infirmities, but the one that strikes the most fear in the hearts of Westerners is cancer. Many substances have been found to create cancer in animals, but results always seem to indicate that the amount consumed by the average person is insufficient to create cancer. What is not revealed is that the accumulation of these poisons over a period of years *does* create cancer.

And what are these substances? Innumerable chemicals are fed and injected into animals; these increase weight to yield more dollars per animal. Nitrites, food coloring, artificial hormones, and even arsenic are among the chemicals contained in animal flesh by the time it goes on the supermarket shelf. These, plus the many other additives consumed by members of an industrialized society, collect in the body and are stored in the tissues. Cancer occurs when the cells react to these excessive toxins by, in a sense, mutating into cells which reproduce uncontrollably.

So much for the horrors of the meat industry. There are several other interesting physical and spiritual reasons for not eating meat. One is that it takes four times as much grain to feed animals than for man to consume it directly. This raises a moral question in regard to sharing our resources with poorer peoples. Plants are the original source of energy for all living things, as they store the energy of the sun through photosynthesis. Vegetarians not only take their nourishment from the original source, but their diet is more economical with regards to cost and the best utilization of available land.

It is also noteworthy that man's digestive system is not one of a carnivore. His teeth are designed for biting and mashing vegetables, not tearing flesh, which is why man ages, tenderizes, and cooks his meat. The human liver is proportionally smaller than that of a meat-eating animal and is not built to handle the filtering of animal poisons. Also the alimentary canal, which is short in carnivorous animals to speed poisons through the body quickly, is quite long in man, as it is in any vegetarian animal.

For a yogi, though, the main consideration in not eating meat is the basic principle of *ahimsa,* or non-injury. "Thou shalt not kill." Animals have feelings and a consciousness, just as humans do. The mass breeding and slaughter is as much cruelty as throwing stones at the neighbor's dog. In India, a cow is regarded with great respect for the service it renders to man. It tills the fields, provides milk and all its by-products for nourishment, and its dung is used for fuel and building houses. An Indian farmer would no more think of cooking up his cow for dinner than his pet cat.

There is no doubt that, "You are what you eat". A subtle part of what is consumed becomes the consciousness. Animals live, eat, sleep and procreate. Their awareness is not much higher than this. The vibrations of a plant are extremely subtle, and those who have changed from a meat to vegetarian diet notice a corresponding change in consciousness. There is a certain grossness that disappears, and the awareness becomes finely tuned. This is, of course, extremely conducive to meditation. The purer the diet, the more easily the mind is controlled. Then, with time and practice, success in meditation is assured.

KARMA YOGA

Meditation is a continuous dehypnotizing of oneself from identification with body, mind, name and form. It starts in one's everyday life. If one cannot be detached from the day to day activities, then it is not possible to close the eyes and enter into meditation. If there is continuous identification with one's activties, then those same activities will go on even when the body is sitting still. The eyes may be closed, hands clasped and feet crossed, but the mind is not checked. It plays the part, and there remains identification with the mental play. Activitiy or inactivity makes no difference. The mind plays its part in all conditions.

In order to sit for meditation, the mind must be detached and withdrawn from day to day concerns. The first step is Karma Yoga, or selfless service. It is the fundamental step on which meditation is built, and no meditation is possible without it. Through service to others without thought of personal gain, positive thinking is also practiced in daily life.

A true Karma Yogi is continuously meditating. When he helps others his attitude is "Lord, I am working, worshipping and serving You through this particular person. Thank you for giving me this opportunity." He also detaches himself from the effect of the action, whether good or bad. Whether working in the kitchen, worshipping in the temple, or mowing the lawn, the Karma Yogi knows that he is different from the work, and that the work is only a way of achieving the Supreme.

Detachment is learned through service. Until it is acquired and one is able to renounce emotional ties to one's labor, no meditation is possible. As the detachment increases, it becomes easier and easier to disassociate from activities. Then, when the eyes are closed, the mind will remain unperturbed, for in daily activities it has been trained to focus inwardly at all times. Others will see a Karma Yogi and think he is just another person working; they will not know the secret of his inner peace. Only he can touch and feel it.

A true meditator is circumspect. Outwardly he appears to be an ordinary man, but inside he is a fathomless ocean. He has touched infinite peace, nothing can change him inside. Karma Yoga leads to that peace which, once tasted, can never be described. Time and patience are necessary to reach it.

Detachment from action does not mean shirking one's responsibilities. A haphazard life is not yogic, for it engenders to steadiness of mind. When a yogi takes on a job, he finishes it. His mind does not waver, and that is the secret of his success. If he assumes a responsibility, his mind is focussed steadily on it until completion. Because it can be focussed at all times, the yogic mind is powerful. The average person does a little here and a little there, keeping several projects going at once and finishing nothing. There is no meditative state of mind.

A person who meditates can turn out more work in less time. He has peace within. His actions are all on a pure level, and those who come in contact with him are uplifted. In his dynamic presence even the laziest people find strength and encouragement. They are inspired to perform actions that they could not otherwise do. Lethargy vanishes in the presence of a true yogi.

Through Karma Yoga, the path of selfless service, one can learn detachment is one's everyday life. This is the first essential step of meditation. One should not be misled by promises of instant meditation. It is a long and disciplined path. The goal, however, can be reached by all who make a determined effort.

Concentration: Theory

In man's struggle to achieve any desired end, there is no necessity for him to turn to external forces. He contains within himself vast resources of inherent power lying untapped or only partially used. Because he has scattered his faculties on a hundred different things, he fails to achieve anything substantial, despite inherent potentialities. If he intelligently regulates and applies them, concrete results are ensured. To use his existing forces rationally and effectively, he need not wait for the invention of new methods for guidance. Nature itself abounds in instructive lessons.

— Swami Sivananda
Concentration and Meditation

The world is the materialization of the thought forms of Divine Intelligence. It exists as vibration. Just as there are waves of heat, light, electricity and energy, there are also thought waves. Thought has tremendous power. Everybody experiences it to some degree. It could be used a thousand times more effectively if one had a comprehensive understanding of the workings of thought vibration, the techniques for controlling them, and the method of transmitting them to others at a distance.

Hidden psychic and occult powers are awakened by understanding and realizing the powers of the mind. One can see distant objects, hear distant sounds, send messages to any part of the universe, heal people thousands of miles away, and move to distant places in no time. There is no limit to the power of the human mind when one has learned to merge it with the Cosmic Mind.

POWER OF CONCENTRATION

When flowing loosely over a wide area, every force in nature moves slowly and with less power than if gathered in one mass and directed through a single restricted outlet. Dammed and accumulated, the once sluggish and leisurely flow of a river rushes out with amazing force through the sluice. The warm rays of the sun focussed through a magnifying glass become hot enough to burn objects. Such is the power generated by the concentration of force.

This natural law is also applicable to man in all branches of his activities. Mental concentration is the fixing of the mind for an extended period of time on one external or internal point. There can be no concentration without something on which the gathered rays of the mind can rest. It must be a single object or idea.

People sometimes pride themselves on being able to think of two things at once. The mind does not work in this way; its oscillating waves are merely bouncing back and forth with lightning velocity between the two ideas. Mind can do only one thing at a time. Those who imagine that a mundane chore such as dishwashing goes faster if they are thinking of palm trees and a sunny beach are fooling themselves. Their mental waves are moving between the daydream and the task at hand. The attention actually given to the work is thus slowed down because of the constant interruptions, and the hands slow down, too. How much better to keep the mind one-pointed and finish the job in half the time.

If you are deeply engrossed in a book or television show, you hear no outside noises, not even your own name being called. If somebody approaches you, you do not see him. Nor do you smell the fragrance of the roses on the table by your side. This is concentration or one-pointedness of mind fixed firmly on one thing.

Everybody possesses the ability to concentrate to some degree. Conscious practice of this innate ability strengthens the thought currents, clarifies ideas and utilizes some of the immense latent power of the mind. What has once been cloudy and hazy becomes clear and definite. What has been difficult, complex and confusing becomes easy. One is able to work with greater efficiency, to turn out more work in less time, and to increase one's earning capacity.

Concentration can also prevent or minimize the problems of senility. After the age of thirty, man's brain cells die off at the rate of 100,000 per day and are not replaced. It is vital to strengthen and make the best use of one's waning capacity. He who practices concentration retains clear mental vision.

With utmost concentrated attention the surgeon operates on his patient. Deepest absorption marks the state of the technician, engineer, architect or painter engaged in drawing the minute details of a plan, chart or sketch in which accuracy is of the highest importance. The same concentration is necessary on the spiritual path, where the aspirant must deal with the internal forces. For progress to be made, it must be developed to a very high degree. Practice demands patience, will, untiring persistence and regularity. There are no shortcuts along the spiritual path.

In Yoga, as in other spiritual disciplines, concentration is the first stage of meditation, which in turn leads ultimately to experience of God. What most people think of as meditation is, in fact, concentration. The focussing power of the mind is brought to bear on one abstract or uplifting symbol. When all extraneous waves are stilled, one goes straight to the Source like a truly shot arrow. There are many streets leading to the heart of a city. One reaches it by following one of them, not by wandering from route to route.

All of creation is God, according to *Adwaita,* or monistic Vedanta. Intense concentration on any symbol can, therefore, eventually lead to God-Realization. However, abstract symbols, because they are not emotional, and symbols that uplift the mind are more effective than those that are emotionally colored and drag the mind downward.

Although the mind is controlled during concentration, the point at which it becomes meditation cannot be controlled. One falls into meditation much as one falls into sleep. Meditation is the continuous flow of one thought of the Supreme. It is the identification of the individual with God, and is experienced like a constant flow of oil from one vessel to another.

PLEASURE AND THE MIND

It usually takes years before this shift in consciousness occurs during practice. Wordly people are ruled by the senses. When the mind is distracted by passion and desires, it is difficult to concentrate on anything. Sense objects and desires are externalizing forces. They encourage the mind's natural tendency to run outward. When it is externalized, it engages itself with the unending rush of fleeting events. The mental rays scatter and energy is dissipated. To concentrate, these mental rays must be gathered and turned toward the Self. When they are concentrated, illumination begins.

Proper application of the senses can help internalize the mind. Of the various methods employed to curtail the innate oscillatory tendency of the mind, those using sight and sound are the most effective. These two senses are the strongest. They are able to capture the attention and still the thought waves.

The hypnotist subdues the subject's mind by capturing his

gaze and repeating suggestions in a rhythmic, monotonous way. The teacher's sudden "Look here!" when he wants special attention to what he is saying is significant. By fixing the student's gaze, he also fixes the attention of their minds upon his teaching.

Similarly, in the course of spiritual discipline the methods of developing concentration rely on sight and sound. One may gaze steadily at an abstract symbol, the image of a favorite deity (covered in the sections on Japa Meditation), the sky, a rose or any concrete object. As an alternative to visual concentration, with regular rhythm and intonation one may repeat a Mantra, the Lord's name, OM or certain chants. By these means the mind gradually becomes focussed inward. As the inward state deepens, one slowly looses awareness of material surroundings. The next step is meditation, in which body awareness is also lost. When perfected, meditation brings about *samadhi,* the ultimate state of Self-awareness or God-Realization.

Wordly pleasures intensify the desire for greater and greater enjoyment. The mind can never be satisfied, no matter how many pleasures it is fed. The more it possesses, the more it wants. Without knowing it, people are exceedingly plagued by the insatiability of their own minds. In order to remove this sort of trouble, the craving for sensory stimulation must be removed. Once the mind has been stilled and concentrated, it no longer presses one to seek further pleasures.

When the senses are controlled and the outgoing tendencies stopped, the mind will no longer pose a threat to successful meditation. During the times of meditation, the mind must be introspective, turning inward to explore its own mysteries. The senses can be controlled through reduction of wants and activities. Dietary discipline is essential. Further, one should avoid undesirable company as well as stimulants and depressants. Television, cinemas and newspapers, which agitate the mind, should be reduced and replaced with periods of sitting in silence and solitude. By witnessing and tempering desires and emotions, the qualities of egoism, anger, greed, lust and hatred are eradicated.

For trained yogis, distinctions between withdrawal of the senses (*pratyahara*), concentration (*dharana*), meditation (*dhyana)* and the beginning of the superconscious state *(samadhi)* are blurred. When they sit to meditate, all the processes occur almost simultaneously, and they reach the meditative state very quickly.

Neophytes first experience withdrawal of the senses. Then concentration begins. Only after that does true meditation slowly

come. Before the superconscious state manifests itself, the mind
usually becomes impatient and tired, for it has not been trained
to bear the strain of prolonged attention and wants to give up.
Success in achieving *samadhi* depends on constant and intense
practice, knowledge of the workings of the mind, awareness of the
pitfalls and willingness to make sacrifices to overcome the obstacles.

BEST FRIEND: WORST ENEMY

The mind is its own worst enemy as well as its own best
friend. According to yogic thought, the mind has five different
manifestations of behavior. In the *kshipta* state, it is fragmented,
distracted and scattered on various objects. It is restless and jumps
from one thing to another. In the *mudha* state it is dull and for-
getful. *Vikshipta* is the gathering mind. It is occasionally steady and
at other times distracted. This is its condition during practice as it
struggles to become focussed. In the *ekagrata* or one-pointed state
there is only one idea present. In the *niruddha* state full control is
achieved.

The greatest impediment to concentration is restlessness and
tossing of the mind. When a beginner sits for practice, the thoughts,
unaccustomed to this new game and freed from their usual grooves,
leap about in an uncontrolled way. To remove tossing and other
obstacles to one-pointedness, one should adamantly fix the mind
on one object alone. When it runs away, as it naturally will, it must
be pulled back again and again. It will want to create hundreds of
alternate thought forms. But it must be disciplined, or no progress
can be made.

It is necessary to introspect and watch the mind carefully.
Bubbling thoughts must be silenced and the emotions calmed, for
the purpose of concentration is the stilling of mental waves. One
should not allow the mind to dissipate its energy uselessly — on
vain thoughts, worries, imagination and fears. Through constant
practice it will hold to one thought form for half an hour, and then
it is possible to increase the time to several hours. When the mental
vibrations are collected and focussed in concentration, one eventually experiences Bliss from within.

The mind is attracted to pleasing or favorite ideas. Therefore,
one should concentrate on something that is appealing. Because of
its natural externalizing bent, in the beginning it should be trained
to concentrate on gross objects. A flame, the moon or a concrete
spiritual symbol can be concentrated upon with open eyes. Later

one can successfully concentrate on subtle objects and abstract ideas. With the eyes closed, the aspirant concentrates on the space between the eyebrows, the heart, or on any of the *chakras,* or centers of spiritual energy.

By manipulating the mind, one is able to bring it under control and compel it to concentrate its powers. However, one must not wrestle with it. Struggle only sets more mental waves into motion. Many beginners commit this grave error in their impatience to succeed. They may develop headaches or sometimes feel the need to urinate, because of irritation set up in the spinal cord. As a clever cook notes which foods are most enjoyed and makes a point of serving those foods, so the aspirant notes the conditions that precede progress in the attainment of the goal. In duplicating and fulfilling those conditions, he moves forward along the path.

Sometimes spiritual aspirants leave off the practice of concentration, as they find it difficult. They make a great mistake. In the initial struggle to overcome body consciousness, practice may well be troublesome. There is physical restlessness attended by an overabundance of emotions and thoughts. In due time. however — often only after many years — the mind becomes cool, pure and strong, and immense joy is derived from it.

The sum total of all the pleasures in the world is nothing compared to the bliss derived from meditation. One should not give up the practice at any cost. There should be an attitude of patience, cheerfulness, and tenacity. Success will eventually come. By serious introspection, it is possible to discover the various impediments to concentration. They are removed with patience and effort. They can be nipped in the bud through discrimination, right inquiry and meditation.

The more concentrated the mind is, the more power is brought to bear on one point. The purpose of life is to fix the mind on the Absolute. When it is so fixed, one becomes calm, serene, steady and strong. In concentration the senses cease to function, and there is no longer awareness of the body and surroundings. As it deepens, one experiences great joy and spiritual intoxication. Concentration opens the inner chambers of love and, as it leads to meditation, is the sole key to the realm of Eternity.

Concentration: Practice

*It is difficult for man to establish a control over his own
mind. For gaining mastery over his own mind, he has to know what
the mind is, how it works, how it deceives him at every turn and
by which methods it can be subdued. As long as the mind restlessly
wanders about amidst objects, ever fluctuating, excited, agitated and
uncontrolled, the true joy of the Self cannot be realized and
enjoyed. To control the restless mind and bring all thoughts and
cravings to a stillness and sublimation is the greatest problem of
man. If he has subjugated the mind, he may be said to be,
in his subjective freedom and power, the Emperor of emperors.*

— Swami Sivananda
Conquest of Mind

Scientists estimate that man has conscious control of only
about ten per cent of his brain power, while the rest lies hidden
like the bulk of an iceberg floating beneath the surface of the
water. There are vast resources lying untapped below the surface
of man's conscious mind. The practice of concentration opens the
gates of these latent resources and releases them for man's use.
A proper foundation must be laid before the practice of concentration can be taken up in earnest, for the powers of the mind are
elusive and unpredictable. This foundation is built of right conduct,
a healthy body and steady posture, breath regulation and withdrawal of the senses. Only if it is firm will the superstructure of
concentration and meditation be successful.

THE EIGHT STEPS

The blueprint for this base is found in the *ashtanga,* or eight
limbs, of Raja Yoga. These eight progressive steps are *yama*
(abstentions), *niyama* (observances), *asanas* (postures), *pranayama*
(breath control), *pratyahara* (withdrawal of the senses), *dharana*
(concentration), *dhyana* (meditation), and *samadhi* (superconscious

26

state). The first five steps form the basis for concentration.

Yama is a series of injunctions similar to the Ten Commandments. They are non-injury to any living thing; truthfulness in thought, word and deed; non-stealing, which includes non-covetousness; and sublimation of sexual energy. *Niyama* is the cultivation of such virtues as cleanliness of body and environment, contentment, austerity or control of senses, study of spiritual books, and surrendering to the Divine Will. Together, the *yamas* and *niyamas* foster high moral character and ethical conduct. The mind is uplifted and purified for deep meditation.

A healthy and strong physical system is also essential. Steady mind presupposes steady posture. Concentration is impossible if one is plagued by aching knees, backache and other attendant woes of prolonged sitting. To attain one-pointedness of mind, one must be able to forget the body altogether. The nerves must be strong enough to withstand various mental phenomena and disorientations that can occur during practice. In the process of turning the mind inward, old negativities are surfaced; on rare occasions they may even appear symbolically in the form of visions. A frail person may discontinue his practice of concentration rather than confront these aspects of his subconscious. Concentration is successful only when the body and mind are kept healthy. *Asanas* keep the body and nervous system strong and flexible, and help to ensure that the flow of vital energy is unimpeded.

Just as steady posture is mandatory, so also is breath control. Consider what happens when a person concentrates very hard to hear an indistinct whisper. The breath stops. The mind and breath are as inseparable as the two sides of a coin. When the mind is agitated, the breath becomes irregular. Similarly, when the breath is slow and regular, the mind responds by becoming calm. *Pranayama*, the yogic system of breath control, is designed to steady and prepare the mind for concentration.

To reduce the outward flow and waste of mental energies, the senses must be subjugated. One fourth of one's energy is diverted to the digestion of food, which is often eaten for the pleasure of the taste buds rather than for sustenance. Additional mental and physical energy is squandered in useless idle talking. Follow a wholesome, natural, vegetarian diet and eat frugally. Learn control of the tongue by observing silence for an hour or two a day. Our senses have been habitually overfed and geared to gluttony. One should examine all worldly habits and curtail them sharply.

Pratyahara, or withdrawal of the senses, is a kind of fasting for the mind. The thoughts are weaned from attachment to the many fleeting sensations that they feed upon. The senses do not convey experience without the cooperation of the mind. *Pratyahara* is that by which the senses do not come in contact with their objects. For example, if certain music or television programs are found to leave the mind in an agitated state, they should be eliminated. By withdrawing the mind, the senses are also withdrawn. *Pratyahara* in its most graphic form is symbolized by the *yoni mudra,* which itself is a concentration exercise. To execute it, the eyes, nose and mouth are closed with the fingers of both hands and the thumbs block the ears. Distractions are thus blocked out, and the attention is freed to be fixed on the only thing that remains, the internal or *anahata* sounds.

When some degree of attainment has been reached in these five steps, one may proceed to the practice of concentration, which is the springboard for meditation and *samadhi.* Practice should not merely be confined to an hour or two in a quiet room. It can and should pervade all aspects of life.

ATTENTION

In everyday situations, one should develop the faculty of attention. Concentration itself is a narrowing of the field of attention. The entire attention is thrown into whatever is being done. The individual becomes lost in the job at hand. One must concentrate on the work and rigorously shut out all other thoughts, doing nothing haphazardly or hastily. No work can be done successfully without calmness and concentration. In this way the mind becomes one-pointed.

Failure is a stranger to work done with perfect attention. When one sits for meditation, there should be no thought of office work. When doing office work, household chores never enter the mind. In training the mind to attend only to the work at hand, there will also be a development of will power and memory. A person with good concentration can accomplish a task in half the time and with twice the accuracy that it would take the average person.

It is easy to pay attention to what is pleasant, for the mind is naturally attracted to what pleases it. A beneficial exercise is to fix the attention on unpleasant tasks from which one may have previously shrunk. Under scrutiny, they become interesting and interest reduces the unpleasantness. Similarly, the attention can be fixed on uninteresting objects and ideas, if they are held before the mind and examined. Interest slowly manifests. Many mental weaknesses and blocks vanish. The mind and will power become stronger.

As a preliminary exercise in concentration, retire to a quiet room and sit in a comfortable cross-legged position. Sitting on a pillow helps to bring the knees to the floor so that the body may relax properly. Close the eyes and notice what occurs when concentrating on an apple.

At first, there may be thoughts of its color, shape, size and different parts such as stem, skin, pulp and seeds. Next, one may think of its effects on the digestive system and blood. Through the law of association, ideas of other fruits may also try to enter the mind. Soon, extraneous ideas pop in. The mind begins to wander about. It may think of meeting a friend at 4 P.M. It may think of buying a towel or a can of beans. It may review an embarrassing happening of the previous day.

There must be an attempt to follow a definite line of thought, without any break in it. Extraneous thoughts that are not connected with the object at hand must be continuously banished. This demands persistence. The mind will try its best to run in the old familiar grooves. The attempt to concentrate is somewhat like going uphill, but each small success is greatly rewarding.

Just as laws of gravitation, cohesion, etc. operate in the physical world, so also do laws of thought, such as the law of continuity, operate on the mental plane. Those who practice concentration should thoroughly understand these laws. They must be aware that when the mind thinks of an object, it also thinks of its qualities and parts; when it thinks of a cause, it thinks of its effects. Awareness of the workings of the mind is developed by training it to concentrate on various subjects, gross and subtle, and of various sizes. In the course of time, a strong habit is formed.

A classic yogic exercise in concentration is *tratak,* or steady gazing. It can be done with a candle flame, an OM symbol, a picture of one's favorite deity, or any other suitable object or symbol. Sit in front of it. Concentrate on it with open eyes until tears come. Then close the eyes and visualize the object. Repeat and gradually increase the period of time for the gazing and visualization. It should be possible to visualize the object of concentration very clearly, even in its absence. With practice comes the ability to conjure up the mental picture at a moment's notice. *Tratak* and visualization steady the wandering mind and help greatly in concentration.

Practice the exercise for only one minute on the first day,

gradually increasing the length of time each week. Do not strain the eyes. In some people who have weak capillaries, the eyes may become red. There is no cause to be alarmed, for the redness will pass quickly. An excellent preliminary concentration exercise, *tratak* should be practiced for six months. It is necessary to be regular and systematic about it. If there is a break in practice, the time should be made up. *Tratak* can be effective in preventing or eliminating many ailments of the eye.

Tratak utilizes the sense of sight. Sense, object and mind are captured in the gross concrete world and then internalized to the subtle plane. Sound, also, when expressed on the subtle level, can draw the mind inward. But unlike the visualization exercise, concentration on the *anahata,* internal, sounds begins and ends on the subtle plane.

Sit in the most comfortable cross-legged posture. Close the eyes, and close the ears with the thumbs, earplugs or cotton. Try to hear the inner mystic sounds. It may be possible to hear various kinds of sounds, such as flute, violin, kettledrum, thunder, conch, bells and the humming of bees. If several sounds are heard simultaneously, hold the mind to the loudest one. Generally they will be experienced in the right ear, sometimes in the left. Concentrate only on the sound in the right ear. This practice develops one-pointedness of the mind, which is achieved by focussing on sound vibrations.

ESTABLISHING THE PRACTICE

In establishing the regular practice of concentration, the beginner should choose a pleasing object or symbol and stay with it. If he is on the spiritual path, he should fix the mind on the image or Mantra of his chosen deity. Sitting in a comfortable cross-legged position, he should close the eyes and make the breathing regular. Three seconds inhalation and three seconds exhalation is recommended. Once the breathing pattern is established, withdraw the mind from it; the body will automatically carry on that rhythm. The object of focus is visualized in the space between the eyebrows, *ajna chakra,* or in the heart, *anahata chakra.* Generally speaking, the *ajna chakra* is best for those of an intellectual nature, while the heart area is better for emotional types. Once the center of concentration is chosen, it should not be changed.

Avoid tension anywhere in the body or mind. Think gently of the object in a continuous manner. When the mind wanders, as it will, gently pull it back, but do not wrestle with it. If emotions cause disturbance during practice pay no attention. They will soon pass away. If there is an attempt to drive them away, more mental waves and strain are created. Keep an indifferent attitude. If emotions and mind-wandering fail to fade out of there own accord, do not identify with them. Detach and observe as a witness, as though watching a motion picture. The Self is neither body nor mind. In detaching from physical and mental activity, one experiences one's true nature.

The main aim of concentration is to bring the mind to the same point or object again and again by limiting its movements in the beginning to a small circle. When meditating on an object, summon all thoughts connected with that object and dwell on those thoughts alone. Do not allow any other thought related to any other subject to enter the mind. There should be one line of thought. There may be several ideas connected with the one subject, but this does not matter. The number of ideas can eventually be reduced to one.

A time will come when the mind will stick to one point alone, like the continuous sound of a church bell. This is meditation, the fruit of constant and protracted practice of concentration. The joy will be indescribable. When this one idea also dies, the superconscious state, *samadhi*, is attained. With the fading out of the one idea, there is a stage of mental vacuity or thoughtlessness. Rising above this blank state, one identifies with the Supreme, the silent, motionless witness of everything. Then and then alone does one reach the highest goal of life.

The practice of concentration may seem tedious in the beginning, while new grooves are being formed in the brain. Yet after a period of practice, real interest develops. As the aspirant advances and realizes some of the benefits, he finds he does not want to abandon the practice. If he neglects it even for a day, he becomes restless. Concentration brings supreme joy, inner spiritual strength and infinite eternal bliss. It plumbs the depths of profound knowledge and intuition, and leads to communion with God.

Meditation

Put a piece of iron-rod in the blazing furnace. It becomes red as fire. Remove it. It loses its red color. If you want to keep it always red, you must always keep it in the fire. So also, if you want to keep the mind charged with the fire of Brahmic wisdom, you must keep it always in contact with the Brahmic fire of knowledge through constant and intense meditation. You must keep up an unceasing flow of the Brahmic consciousness. If you can meditate for half an hour, you will be able to engage yourself with peace and spiritual strength. Such is the beneficial result of meditation. As you have to move with different minds of peculiar nature in your daily life, get the strength and peace from meditation. Then you will have no trouble or worry.

— Swami Sivananda
Practice of Yoga

Meditation does not come easily. A beautiful tree grows slowly. One must wait for the blossom, the ripening of the fruit and the ultimate taste. The blossom of meditation is an inexpressible peace that permeates the entire being. Its fruit is the bliss of the superconscious state, and is indescribable because one becomes It, leaving no one to say anything about It. Wherever one may wander, from the lowest to the most exalted of places, the mind is nowhere truly satisfied except within, when it withdraws from the world and touches the inner silence.

MIND: MASTER OR SERVANT?

We rush about in search of unknown experience, but every place in the world is the same. The only place where a difference can really be found is in the mind, which accompanies us wherever we go. Only after years of continually withdrawing the mind from the external world may one attain a glimpse of ineffable peace. There is no easy way to reach it. It cannot be attained in ten easy lessons as is often expected in the West today.

Many Western scientists do not fully understand the theory of mind over matter. Too often they equate control of the mind with mental institutions, drugs, and bio-feedback techniques. They do not realize that the soul stands above both mind and body, which it uses for its expression and evolution. Until the power of the soul over all animate and inanimate objects is understood, there will be more and more confusion in the scientific world. Both body and mind have to adapt and adjust to new environmental situations as well as new levels of awareness in order for man to evolve and achieve his final freedom.

In the Western tradition, behavior of the body is often related only to the accepted laws of physical nature. Such experiences as astral projection, seeing without eyes, hearing without ears, communicating telepathically, or bending a spoon with thought waves are commonly considered to be beyond the pale of rational acceptability. However, for the meditator who practices intunement with his intuitive faculties, these natural phenomena are occasionally experienced and are more easily accepted. They are no more miraculous than the projection of sight and sound to distant places by means of radio waves. Voluntary control over the heart and what are regarded as involuntary functions as well as extrasensory perception, astral travel, the astral body and its *nadis, prana* and *kundalini* are commonly accepted facts of life in the Eastern way of living and thinking.

The mind is a hard taskmaster if one succumbs to its control. It insists that we jump when it says jump, that we eat when it says eat. If it wants a cigarette, it cons us into going out for one, however inconvenient it may be. Its desires are insatiable, and one fulfilled desire can spawn a hundred more.

There was once a monk who retired to a cave in the Himalayas. He had only two possessions — the loincloth that he was wearing and an extra one. Returning one day from a distant village where he had gone to beg food, he found that the spare loincloth had been chewed up by a rat. He bought another cloth and the same thing happened. So he bought a cat to get rid of the rat. The cat disposed of the rat, but it had to have milk. It is difficult to buy milk in an Indian village, and as daily expeditions for it would have been too time-consuming, the monk bought a cow. It is also difficult to feed and milk a cow, look after its needs, tend to a cat and pursue intensive spiritual practice. Needing help, the renunciate got married, and everything that he had renounced came back to him.

One must always be wary. One desire can multiply and destroy the best intentions. The secret of conquering the tyranny of the mind is not to play the game. By continuously controlling the thought waves, or by observing but not identifying with them, one can reduce and eventually stop them. When the thought waves are stilled during meditation, the true Self is revealed, and one experiences Cosmic Consciousness. The realization of the Oneness of all existence, manifested and unmanifested, is the goal of human life.

Unity already exists. It is one's true nature but has been forgotten through ignorance. Removal of the veil of ignorance, the idea that we are confined within body and mind, is the chief aim of any spiritual practice. If a pot containing a lamp is broken in a dark room, the darkness is instantly dispelled, and the entire room is illuminated. If identification with body and mind is broken through constant meditation on the Self, ignorance is destroyed, and the supreme light of *Atman* is seen everywhere.

To realize unity, the idea of diversity must be given up. The idea that each person is all-pervading and all-powerful must constantly be nourished. In unity there is neither desire nor emotional attractions and repulsions; there is only steady, persistant, calm, eternal bliss. Spiritual liberation means attainment of this state of unity.

The desire for liberation in itself is meaningless because infinite freedom already exists as man's real essence. There can be no desire to gain that which is one's very nature. All desire for progeny, wealth and happiness in this world or in the next, and even the illusory desire for liberation itself, must eventually be abandoned whether in the present or in a future lifetime. By pure and disinterested will, all actions should be guided toward the goal. Therefore, the fruits of meditation should not be pursued impatiently. It take many months before the mind is sufficiently ripened and purified to make any visible progress.

The constant attempt to feel that you are the All can and ought to be practiced in the midst of intense activity. Let the mind and body work, but feel that you are above them as their controlling witness. Do not identify with them. If the senses are under full control, perfect peace and solitude can be found even in the noisiest and most crowded places of a large city. If the senses are turbulent and you have not sufficient power to withdraw them, there will be no peace of mind even in a solitary cave in the Himalayas.

In the beginning one must consciously sit and meditate to experience the feeling of unity. The steadiness of posture and mind makes the effort comparatively easy. In the midst of activity, it is more difficult. The practice, however, must be kept up at all times. Otherwise, progress is slow. A few hours spent meditating on identification with the All, while identifying with body and mind for the rest of the day does not bring about rapid or substantial progress.

FROM THE UNREAL TO THE REAL

Meditation is an experience that cannot be described, just as colors cannot be described to a blind man. All ordinary experiences are limited by time, space, and the law of cause and effect. Normal awareness and understanding do not transcend these bounds. Finite experience cannot be transcendental, for it is measured in terms of past, present and future. These concepts of time are illusory, for they have no permanence. Immeasurably small and fleeting, the present cannot be grasped. Both past and future are non-existent in the present, and therefore are unreal. We live in illusion.

The meditative state transcends all such limitations. In it there is neither past nor future, but only the consciousness of I AM in the eternal NOW. This consciousness is only possible when all of the mental waves are stilled and there is no mind. The closest analogous state is deep sleep, in which there is neither time, space nor causation. Meditation, however, differs from deep sleep, which embraces an experience of the void. It is, rather, a state of intense, pure awareness, and it works profound changes in the psyche. For the same reasons, and because it operates on the super-conscious rather than the subconscious level, it is not to be confused with a hypnotic state.

Meditation is the source of real rest. True deep sleep is a rare occurrence. Even during dreams the mind remains active although working subtly. Hence, there is little true rest during sleep. It is secured in meditation when the mind is fully concentrated, far away from objects and near the *Atman,* the Self. It is a lasting, spiritual, blissful rest, which must be experienced. Once it can be achieved in meditation, the time normally devoted to sleep can gradually be reduced to as little as three or four hours.

On the purely physical level, meditation helps to prolong the body's anabolic process of growth and repair and to reduce the catabolic, decaying process. Ordinarily the anabolic process predominates until the age of eighteen. Between eighteen and thirty-five the catabolic process sets in. Meditation significantly reduces this decline because of the innate receptivity of body cells to its benign vibrations.

Only recently have scientists become aware of the relationship between mind and cells. A few years ago they reacted with extreme skepticism to yogic demonstrations of mental control over such supposedly involuntary functions as heart beat, respiration and circulation. They believed the autonomic nervous system to be independent of any conscious mental process. Biofeedback techniques, however, now prove that most bodily functions can be controlled by concentration.

Modern research substantiates the fact that the mind can control the activity of a single cell, as well as groups of cells. Each of the body cells is governed by instinctive, subsconscious mind. Each has both individual and collective consciousness. When thoughts and desires pour into the body, the cells are activated, and the body always obeys the group demand.

Meditation is a powerful tonic. During meditation there is generally a tremendous acceleration of energy to the individual cells. Just as negative thoughts can pollute them, positive thoughts rejuvenate them and retard decay. Penetrating all of the cells, the vibrations can prevent and cure diseases. Meditation is also a powerful mental and nervine tonic. The soothing waves that arise exercise a favorable effect on mind and nerves, resulting in a prolonged, positive state of mind. Thus the interior world takes direction from the mind and promotes physical health, mental acuity, and tranquility.

Every individual possesses inherent potentialities and capacities. From past reincarnations he brings to this life a storehouse of power and knowledge. During meditation these unsuspected faculties emerge. New changes also take place in the brain and nervous system as new currents, channels, vibrations and cells are formed. In addition to new sensations and feelings, one acquires new modes of thinking, a new view of the universe, and the vision of unity. Negative tendencies vanish, and the mind becomes steady. One enjoys perfect harmony, undisturbed happiness and abiding peace.

With meditation comes freedom from fear of death. Most people think that death is the end of existence, but, in fact, death means only the extinction of the present name and form. The greater the identification with name and form, the greater the fear.

Above: Sivananda Yoga Farm.   Below: Sivananda Yoga Camp

The practice of meditation induces detachment from name and form. It makes one aware of the ever-changing nature of the body and of all phenomenal existence. In recognizing the ephemerality of it all, one realizes the impossibility of holding on to anything, including one's cumbersome ego-identity. When this need to grasp disappears, when the fear of losing what one never has really possessed vanishes, immortality is within reach.

One who meditates regularly develops a magnetic and dynamic personality. Those who come into contact with him are influenced by his cheerfulness, powerful speech, lustrous eyes, healthy body and inexhaustable energy. Just as a grain of salt dropped into a basin of water dissolves and is distributed throughout the water, so the spiritual aura of the meditator infiltrates the minds of others. People draw joy, peace and strength from him. They are inspired by his words, and their minds are elevated by mere contact with him. The advanced yogi who meditates in a solitary cave in the Himalayas can help the world more than can somebody preaching fine words from a platform. Even as sound vibrations travel in space, so the indestructible spiritual vibrations of a meditator travel an infinite distance, bringing peace and strength to thousands.

WILD HORSES

To achieve the meditative state takes time, for the mind is like a wild horse resisting all attempts at control. Discipline, order and specific techniques, as well as perseverance, are necessary to insure progress. At first the mind will resort to tricks, dodges and rebellion, making progress slow and difficult. One should therefore have an understanding of its workings. As part of the progress of self-inquiry and control, preliminary practise can be done on the subconscious level.

One means of counteracting the many tricks of the mind is by training the subconscious mind, potentially one's most obedient servant. This wonderful power can be utilized by everybody if the effort is only made. Because it cannot reason, it awaits training by command. Trust is the most important factor in developing it. Indeed, any doubts about the power of the subconscious mind will impede its effectiveness. This inherent power, which can be destroyed and polluted by drugs and alcohol, has generally gone unrecognized as a practical tool. Swami Sivananda realized its latent possibilities, and wrote in his book *Concentration and Meditation:*

The subconscious mind never rests. Even during sleep it is sifting, analyzing and comparing information, and carrying out commands. A great deal of the subconscious mind is bundles of submerged experiences, which can be drawn up to the surface of the conscious mind by means of concentration. It is the repository of memories, not only of this life but also of past lives. All that you have inherited, all that you have seen, heard, enjoyed, tasted, read or known in this life and past lives is hidden in it. By mastering the technique of commanding the subconscious mind, all of this knowledge can be tapped and extracted.

When you are unable to solve a problem, whether personal, philosophical or scientific, tell your subconscious to do it for you. Approached with full trust and confidence it will provide the right answer. The command must be couched in very clear, explicit terms, with no ambiguity. If the solution is not elicited after a night's sleep, repeat the command at the same time each day, until the response is forthcoming.

As well as a source of knowledge, the subconscious mind can be a faithful servant. It can be trained to awaken you at a particular hour. It needs only a positive suggestion or clear command before you go to sleep. As a preliminary exercise, give it one of these simple tasks. By making further use of its potentialities, pressure will be taken off the conscious mind, which will then be freed of some of its customary clutter.

The practice of concentration and constant vigilance help to prepare and discipline the conscious mind for meditation. There are two basic modes of meditation — *saguna* meaning with qualities or concrete, and *Nirguna,* without qualities or abstract. Meditation on a picture or other external object is concrete. Meditation on an idea or concept, such as love or beauty, is abstract. Because it is easier to hold the mind to a concrete image than to an abstract idea, *saguna* meditation must be practiced for a long time before the mind is ready to handle an abstraction. There is no problem in visualizing a rose and considering its various aspects — its color, aroma, thorns, various uses, etc. The mind moves in a specific orbit. But to meditate on Divine Intelligence? One can exhaust the mental energy in wandering down a thousand byways.

Needless to say, beginners should practice concrete meditation. It does not ultimately matter what the object is. Meditation on a dot can lead to the same result as meditation on the Christian Cross, although it might take much longer. In either case the mind exhausts itself by thinking all possible thoughts about the object,

or it may keep to one or two ideas about it, and rigidly exclude
all other ideas. What matters is not the object, but the stilling of
the mind.

Because of this, however, the task is made easier if the object
is neutral, with no emotional or mental connotations that might
trigger additional mental waves. A dot on the wall is a preferable
object to one's sweetheart, for instance; meditation on the latter
would be like opening Pandora's box. Although it creates mental
waves, an uplifting spiritual symbol, image or Mantra is beneficial
and mandatory for spiritual aspirants. The vibrations of such a
symbol do not excite the lower mind, but lift one up to the higher
planes of consciousness. In concrete meditation the devotee considers himself to be separate from the object of meditation. He wants
to experience it, just as one experiences the taste of honey. He holds
back from actually merging with the object.

With practice and purification through *saguna* meditation,
the mind becomes well-trained and disciplined. One can then move
on to abstract meditation, which is a natural progression from the
concrete mode. In fixing on an abstract idea, the mind slowly
melts, expands, loses its own consciousness and becomes one with
the formless Absolute. Instead of just tasting the honey, the meditator merges and becomes the honey itself.

Evolving out of concentration, meditation is a continuous
flow of perception or thought, like the flow of water in a river.
During concentration one keeps a tight rein on the mind; during
meditation the rein is no longer necessary, for the mind stays of
its own accord on one single thought wave. For the spiritual
aspirant, it is just keeping up an unceasing flow of God-consciousness. Jesus said, "Empty thyself and I shall fill thee." This
corresponds to Patanjali's teaching, *"Yogas chitta vritti nirodha"*
(Yoga is the restraint of all mental modifications). This emptying
process, in which the modifications are reduced to one, is a trying
discipline. Continued intense practice, however, will bring success.

In addition to the practical suggestions outlined for concentration, there are a few other points for the serious Yoga aspirant
to bear in mind. The first is the necessity of having a separate
area for meditation. A small room kept under lock and key is best.
If this is impossible, then the corner of a room can be set apart
from the rest of the room with a curtain or screen. It is important
that the meditation room be kept separate from other areas and
not be used for any other purpose so that the mental vibrations
put out in that place will continue to be pure. The front of the

room should be decorated with pictures of saints, sages, prophets and world teachers. Incense and candles should be burned in the morning and evening. Do not allow anybody else to enter the room and disturb its vibrations. It should be regarded as a temple of God, and should be entered with reverence. No wordly talk or thoughts should be indulged in. No word that is uttered, thought that is cherished, nor deed that is done is lost. They are reflected on the subtle layers of ether encircling the room, and invariably affect the mind.

Because of the many strains and pitfalls on the yogic path, a guru is essential. If an aspirant meditates upon his guru, even from far away, a connection is established between them. In response to his thoughts the guru radiates power, peace and joy to the student. The stream of spiritual magnetism flows steadily from the preceptor to his disciple, just as oil flows from one vessel to another. The student draws from the teacher in proportion to his degree of faith. When he sincerely meditates on the teacher, the latter actually feels the thought current touching his heart. He who possesses inner astral sight can clearly visualize a thin line of bright light between disciple and teacher, which is caused by the movement of pure thought vibrations.

ADVANCED MEDITATION

While meditating, various experiences will manifest from time to time. An aspirant may notice a light appearing in the center of the forehead, or small fiery balls moving about before the mind's eye. Sometimes various *anahata* sounds may be heard more clearly. Occasionally beings or objects from the astral world manifest. There may even be brief sensations of bliss. These phenomena are covered in more detail in the chapter on spiritual experiences.

When these extraordinary experiences of meditation occur, one should not be frightened. Nor should the mistake be made that *samadhi* has been attained simply because some lights and a little rising above body consciousness have been experienced. Do not cling to these visions. Simply accept them for what they are — encouragements to keep the aspirant on the path and to convince him of the existence of superphysical realities.

During deep meditation, the aspirant forgets the external world first, and then the body. The idea of time disappears. He hears no sounds and is unaware of his surroundings. The feeling of rising up is a sign of going above body consciousness. In the beginning this feeling will last for only a minute. It is accompanied by a peculiar sensation of bliss. As the meditation deepens, body consciousness is lost. The loss of sensation usually occurs first in the legs, then the spinal column, back, trunk and hands. When this happens, the head feels suspended in air, and mental consciousness reigns supreme.

Should there be a disinclination for work and a desire for meditation only, one should lead a life of complete seclusion, living on a diet of milk and fruits. There will be rapid spiritual progress. When the meditative mood vanishes, work should be taken up again. Thus by gradual practice, the mind will be molded.

In time the awareness of ego gradually vanishes, and reasoning and reflection cease. A higher type of indescribable peace descends. However, it takes a long time to transcend the body completely, to merge with the object of meditation, or to receive a true spiritual experience. *Samadhi,* the superconscious state, is the highest goal to be attained through meditation, and is not achieved merely through a little practice. To attain the ultimate state of merging with the Divine, one must also observe celibacy and strict dietary restrictions, have purity of heart and be completely devoted to God.

After prolonged and steady meditation, Cosmic Consciousness is first experienced as a glimpse, and then becomes natural and permanent in realized souls. Therefore, when there is a flash of illumination, do not be frightened. It will be a new experience of intense joy. Do not turn away or give up meditation. It is a glimpse of Truth, a new platform but not the whole experience. Do not stop. Keep ascending until the final goal is reached.

Similarly, different minds are comfortable with different kinds of meditation. As the various techniques and approaches work differently for each person, one should experiment with a variety of methods, and then stay with the one that seems most comfortable.

It cannot be stated too strongly that all of the systems arrive at the same destination, despite differences. Which method is easiest — Raja, Mantra, Kundalini, Jnana or Bhakti Yoga? Each has its own problems and temptations. In Raja Yoga there is the danger of identifying with one's purity, and building up egoism because of pride in one's mental control. In Hatha Yoga one may spend years awakening the *kundalini*. By the time it happens, a few spiritual powers have manifested, and one may be side-tracked. Despite asserting their identify with Brahman, Jnana Yogis tend to be attached to the intellectual sheath. When a Bhakta Yogi surrenders to the Lord, he will encounter severe tests to see if his surrender is complete. Whatever the means, terminology and techniques employed, the basic concepts are the same, and the methods often overlap. There are no sharp lines of definition or fundamentally distinct concepts. All Yogas culminate in the merging with the Absolute.

The state of Cosmic Consciousness is sublime beyond description. The mind is most inadequate to grasp and describe it. It inspires awe, joy, and freedom from pain, sorrow and fear. It bestows enlightenment, and places the experiencer on a new plane of existence. One experiences a sense of universality, an awareness of eternal life. There is not merely a conviction; it is an actual experience of knowledge. Although this knowledge is an inherent natural faculty of man, training and discipline are necessary to awaken it. Because of ignorance, it is non-functioning in the majority of people.

The Absolute can be experienced by all through regular practice of meditation with a pure heart. Abstract reasoning and study of books do not suffice. Direct experience is the source for this higher intuitional knowledge, or divine wisdom. The experience is superconscious and transcendental; senses, mind, emotions and intellect are at perfect rest. It is not an imaginary revery of a visionary dreamer, nor is it a hypnotic trance. It is absolute Truth, cognized through the spiritual eye, the eye of intuition.

The little ego melts, and the differentiating mind vanishes. All barriers, sense of duality, differences, separateness and distinctions disappear. There is no time or space; there is only eternity. The experiencer has the feeling that he has obtained all of his desires and that there is nothing more to be known. He feels perfect awareness of the superconscious plane of knowledge and intuition. He knows the whole secret of creation.

There is neither darkness nor void; all is light. Dualities vanish. There is neither subject nor object. There is neither meditation nor *samadhi*. There is neither meditator nor the meditated upon. There is neither pleasure nor pain. There is only perfect Peace and Absolute Bliss.

Japa Meditation: Theory

Mantra Yoga is an exact science. Mananat trayete iti
Mantrah — *"By the constant thinking of Mantra, one is protected
and released from the round of births and deaths." A Mantra is so
called because it is achieved by the mental process. The root
"man" in the word Mantra comes from the first syllable of that
word meaning "to think" and "tra" from "trai" meaning
"to protect or free" from the bondage of the phenomenal world.
A Mantra generates the creative force and bestows eternal Bliss.
A Mantra when constantly repeated awakens the consciousness.*

— Swami Sivananda
Japa Yoga

A Mantra is mystical energy encased in a sound structure.
Every Mantra contains within its vibrations a certain power. Upon
concentration and repetition of a given Mantra, its energy is elicited
and takes form. Japa, or Mantra Yoga, is that practice by which
the power contained within Mantras is applied for specific purposes.

Each Mantra is constructed from a combination of sounds
derived from the fifty letters of the Sanskrit alphabet. Sanskrit is
also known as *Devanagari,* or language of the gods. The ancient
sages, who were intuned to higher levels of consciousness, were
well aware of the inherent power contained in sound, and they
utilized combinations of sounds to set up specific vibrations. These
vibrations applied systematically could literally move mountains. In
fact, one theory on the building of the pyramids suggests that it was
the highly developed science of manipulating sound vibrations that
enabled the early Egyptians to sculpt and move stones of such
enormous proportions.

Whether such feats can be attributed to the control of sound
is a question modern science has not yet covered. Yet there is no
doubt that sound does have a definite and predictable effect on the
human psyche and body. An obvious example is the difference

44

between classical and rock music. The first tends to be relaxing while the other is inclined to excite the senses. On a more subtle level, various Mantras are applied for certain purposes. Most specifically, they turn the mind toward concentration on the Supreme and release spiritual energy in the *chakras* of the body.

There are different types of Mantras. Some, called *bija* or seed Mantras, are such that they have no exact meaning. They act directly on the *nadis,* or nerve tubes of the astral body. They vibrate in the *chakras* along the spine, acting as a subtle massage, releasing blockages and allowing the *kundalini* energy to flow more freely. In these the name and form of the sound are merged and cannot be separated. There are also Mantras that have meaning which can be translated. These *nirguna* or abstract Mantras also set up powerful vibrations in the body, but verbally assert union with unmanifest pure consciousness.

More common, however, is the deity Mantra, in which a specific form with attributes is visualized along with the repetition of the sound. For example, a reclusive person bent on destroying his negative qualities would repeat a Siva Mantra. A family person, whose ideal was to be a loving and responsible husband or wife, might meditate on the name of Rama. An individual who sees God as infinite, all-loving, and even a little playful would build these qualities in himself by repeating a Krishna Mantra.

THE YOGA OF PHYSICS

It is important to understand, however, that the visualizations of deities are only an aid to focussing the mind. Repeating Mantras which are the names of deities internalizes the power of the vibrations that are contained in the name. When the name of Siva is repeated with concentration, the sound actually breaks down one's lower qualities. Long ago, Siva was explained in a mythological way; now, scientists explain that when energy breaks down, it forms patterns, it dances. This is the same as the dance of Siva. Fritjof Capra, author of *The Tao of Physics,* notes the similarity between the Hindu Lord Siva, the Power of Destruction, and the Quantum Theory, which states that matter is never quiet but is always in a state of motion. In the following section entitled "The Yoga of Physics," Dr. Capra explains this relationship. It is an excerpt from his keynote address at the Los Angeles Symposium on *Physics and Metaphysics,* on October 29, 1977.

"What is the nature and origin of the universe? What is the nature of human existence? What is matter made of? What is the relation between spirit and matter? What is space? What is time? Throughout the ages men and women have been fascinated by these questions. Different approaches have been developed in different cultural contexts and at different times.

"Artists, scientists, shamans, mystics — all have their own way of describing, both verbally and non-verbally, the world. We shall focus mainly on two approaches. We shall look at modern Western science, on the one hand, and Eastern mysticism — particularly the tradition of Yoga — on the other. We shall see that they lead to very similar views of the world.

"My field is physics, a science which, in the 20th century, has led to a radical revision of many of our basic concepts of reality. For example, the concept of matter is very different in sub-atomic physics from the traditional idea of a material substance that was held in classical physics. The same is true of other concepts of reality such as space, time, objects or cause and effect. Out of these changes in our concepts of reality, a new world view is emerging. This view turns out to be closely related to the views of mystics of all ages and traditions, particularly the religious philosophies of the Far East — Hinduism, Buddhism, Taoism.

"In the Yoga tradition it is said that there are many paths, all leading to spiritual knowledge and Self-Realization. I believe that modern physics, to some extent, can be such a path. Its view of the universe is in harmony with those of the great yogis and sages. In that sense, I'm going to talk of the Yoga of physics.

"Classical Western physics has its roots in the philosophy of the fifth century Greek Atomists, a philosophical school which saw matter as made up of basic building blocks called atoms. These were believed to be hard, solid, basically passive chunks of matter. This inert matter was said to be moved by external forces of a totally different nature and category, which was identified with the spiritual realm. In this way, a dichotomy was created which became characteristic of Western thinking in subsequent centuries. It gave rise to the dualism between spirit and matter, between the mind and the body.

"In contrast to the mechanistic view of classical Western science, the Eastern view could be called an organic, holistic, or ecological view. Things and phenomena are perceived as being different manifestations of the same reality. The division of the world into separate objects, though useful and practical on the everyday level, is seen as an illusion — *Maya,* as the Indians say. To Eastern mystics, objects have a fluid and ever-changing character. Change and transformation, flow and movement, play an essential role in their world view. The cosmos is seen as one inseparable reality, forever in motion. It is alive, organic, spiritual and material at the same time. A very similar view is now emerging from modern physics.

"In the 20th century Western scientists began probing the atom. They discovered that atoms were not hard and solid, but consisted mainly of empty space. Each atom had a tiny nucleus made up of particles around which whirled other particles. At first, scientists decided that these sub-atomic particles must be the essential building blocks of matter. But they found that this was again wrong. This was shown in the 1920's when Quantum Theory, the theoretical framework of atomic physics, was worked out.

"Quantum Theory showed that the sub-atomic particles have no meaning as isolated entities, but can only be understood as interconnections between various agencies of observation and measurement. Particles are not things but interconnections between things; and these things are interconnections between other things, and so on.

"Quantum Theory thus reveals a basic oneness of the universe. It shows that we cannot decompose the world into independently existing smallest units. As we penetrate into matter, Nature does not show us any isolated basic building blocks, but rather appears as a complicated web of relations between the various parts of a unified whole.

"This network of relations, furthermore, is intrinsically dynamic. According to Quantum Theory, matter is never quiescent, but always in a state of motion. Macroscopically, the materials around us may seem dead and inert. But if you magnify a piece of metal or stone, you realize that it is full of activity.

"Modern physics pictures matter, not as passive and inert, but as continuously dancing and vibrating. This is very much like the Eastern mystics description of the world. Both emphasize that the universe has to be grasped dynamically. It structures are not static, rigid ones, but should be seen in terms of dynamic equilibrium.

"Physicists speak of the continuous dance of sub-atomic matter which goes on all the time. They have actually used the words 'dance of creation and destruction' or 'energy dance'. This naturally comes to mind when you see some of the pictures of particles taken by physicists in their bubble chambers.

"Of course, physicists are not the only one talking about this cosmic dance. Perhaps the most beautiful example of this metaphor exists in Hinduism — the idea of the dancing Lord Siva. Siva is the personification of the cosmic dance. According to Indian tradition, all life is a rhythmic interplay of death and birth, of creation and destruction.

"Indian artists have created beautiful pictures and statues of dancing Lord Siva. These statues are visual images of the cosmic dance, and so are the bubble chamber tracks photographed by modern physicists. They are a modern version of the dance of Siva, obtained by using the most modern and advanced of our Western technological instruments. To me, the effect is as beautiful and as profound as the magnificent Hindu statues. In both cases, we are picturing an eternal dance of creation and destruction, which is the basis of all natural phenomena, the basis of all existence. Therefore, I have put the two together — here you have the 'Dance of Siva' merging the 12th and 20th century versions. You can see that this image of the cosmic dance unifies, in a very beautiful way, ancient mythology, religious art, mystical insight and modern science."

SOUND: THE SEED OF ALL MATTER

"In the beginning was the Word, the Word was God and the Word was with God." The Word of the Bible is the *Sabdabrahman* of the Hindu *Tantra*. Word, sound and Mantra are integral parts of Indian cosmology, and cannot be separated from it. Taking cosmological principles out of the realm of theory, *japa,* or Mantra repetition, puts them to work in a pragmatic way. It is the path from microcosm to macrocosm; it is the vehicle that carries the individual back to the Source.

In the beginning, *Shakti,* the unmanifest Cosmos, floats like an egg in the silent, motionless Void. A mass of latent, undifferentiated energy, it contains the seed power of all the universes. It rests in the Void, alternately flowering as the manifest, evolved Cosmos, and then withdrawing itself in dissolution, *pralaya.* Throughout eternity, like day and night, the universe alternately expands into matter and recedes into primal energy.

During the period of dissolution, *Shakti,* also known as the Divine Power or Cosmic Energy, lies quiescent. Just as the tulip is latent within the bulb, so this universe of names and forms, as we know it, lies enfolded in *Shakti*. Within its heart rest the

Photomontage of Dancing Siva in particle tracks. Reprinted by special arrangement with Shambhala Publications, 1123 Spruce Street, Boulder, Colorado 80302. From the Tao of Physics by Fritjof Capra, p. 224. Copyright © 1975 by Fritjof Capra.

three qualities, *sattwa* (purity), *rajas* (activity), and *tamas* (inertia), whose kaleidoscopic shifting permeates all aspects of the universe.

Cosmic evolution procedes from the unconscious, unmoving, unknowable and unmanifest to the conscious, moving, knowable and manifest microcosm. On the other hand, human evolution is a return journey from the gross physical plane of the microcosm back to the Absolute. In one case the force is centrifugal, in the other, centripetal.

In the Tantric view, sound, as a vibration of undifferentiated Intelligence, is the catalyst that sets into motion the unfolding of the manifest cosmos. A primal shudder disturbs the slumbering equilibrium of *Shakti* and arouses *rajas,* the active principle, to carry out the creation of the manifold universes. The causal vibration, *Sabdabrahman,* is undifferentiated, soundless Sound. It is the wavelength experienced as God.

This great Cosmic Vibration splits *Shakti* into two fields of magnetic force, and projects it as two aspects, *Nada* and *Bindu*. As centrifugal, positive male force, *Bindu* is the ground from which *Nada* operates. As centripetal, negative female force, *Nada* unfolds the manifest universe. They are regarded as Father and Mother aspects of the Supreme Power. The bifurcation of *Shakti* is a duality in unity, not a separation. This duality of poles in the substratum of manifested *Shakti* actually provides the magnetic force holding together in a state of vibration the molecules of the physical world.

Through the medium of time-lapse photography, it is possible to watch a rosebud explode into full flower. Like a rosebud, the universe unfolds and expands. After the first differentiation containing the seed energies of the universe, the vibrating mass of energy continues differentiating and expanding as wavelengths. By the fifth differentiation, the energy is evolved on the gross plane, with the creation of fifty articulate sounds or *varnas. Varna* means color, and all sounds have corresponding color vibrations in the invisible world.

From the combinations and permutations of these root sounds, the universe of forms is created. Sounds, as physical vibrations, are able to produce predictable forms. Combinations of sounds produce complicated shapes. Experiments have demonstrated that notes produced by certain instruments can trace out on a bed of sand definite geometrical figures. In order to produce a particular form, a specific note at a particular pitch must be generated. Repetition of the exact note and pitch create a duplication of the form.

Underlying all the forms of the physical world are the oscillating wavelengths of the fifty primeval sounds in varying combinations. Sound is thus potential form, and form is sound made manifest. Because of the oscillatory nature of matter and of mind as perceiver, the world of manifest forms can only be experienced in distortion as illusion.

Fragmented and fractured, the fifty basic sounds themselves have faded down the corridor of time, and are lost to human memory. The Sanskrit language, however, is directly derived from them, and of all languages it is the closest approximation. Mantras are sound powers evolved from the *varnas* and revealed in Sanskrit syllables to the ancient sages.

SOUND AS ENERGY

The sacred syllables used in meditation by spiritual aspirants are usually Sanskrit names of the Absolute. As divine power made manifest in sound, the Mantra itself is the subtle body of Deity. The theory of *japa* meditation, or Mantra repetition, holds that by repeating the syllables with accuracy and intense devotion, the form of the Mantra's presiding deity will be evoked. Meditation on *OM Namah Sivaya* produces the form of Siva, while *OM Namo Narayanaya* produces that of Vishnu. The vibrations produced by the tones of a Mantra are all important, and pronunciation cannot be a haphazard matter. Through attunement with the wavelength of the Mantra, one is led from the gross plane of articulate sound back through the obscuring veil of the material universe to personalized Deity, and ultimately to the primal undifferentiated energy of the Supreme Power.

At this point it is necessary to consider the microcosm, which is the macrocosm in miniature. It is the vehicle by means of which the return trip from articulate sound to the Causal Power is made. Like the cosmos, the individual continually undergoes the flowering and dissolving of countless lifetimes, the periods of activity and rest. Centrifugal and centripetal forces manifest in him as breath and in the beating of the heart. In man, *Nada,* the vital power of the universe, takes form as *kundalini,* the psychic force lying coiled in astral slumber at the base of the spine. This energy pulsates with the wavelengths of the fifty basic sounds, which eventually reach gross articulation through the vocal chords.

In yogic theory, thought, form and sound are all the same, just as steam, water and ice are all the same substance. They are different aspects of a particular wavelength, or the same vibrational energy as passed through different levels of consciousness. Form manifests in the mind the moment that the name is heard by the ears and transmitted to the consciousness.

Thought and sound manifest in four fundamental states, with sound at one end of the spectrum and thought at the other. *Japa* meditation leads one from the lowest to the highest of these states. *Vaikhari,* the spoken word, is dense, audible sound at its maximum differentiation. It is thought translated into the coded state called language. As the spoken word, it is the most concrete state of thought. In this first stage, thought implies both name and form. The name is the same as the thought wave, and they cannot be separated. When the word "cat" is pronounced, a form is visualized. The reverse is also true. However, the more abstract the word, such as "God," the more difficult is the conceptualization.

The use of language calls for differentiation of thought into word. This process occurs during the second stage, *madhyama.* Through a mental prism clouded by preconceptions, impressions, emotions and other limitations, the speaker or writer selects his words. They are translated back into thought by the listener or reader, whose mind in turn is clouded by his own ideas. The transmission of thought into language inevitably leads to confusion.

Suppose for a moment that a computer is given the job of translating from English to Russian the sentence, "The spirit is willing, but the flesh is weak." In translating a second time, from Russian back to English, the result could very well be, "The ghost is wishing, but the meat is raw." The mechanism of language is extremely crude and inadequate.

Pashyanti, the third stage, is visible sound. It is the telepathic state, in which one can literally feel the form of the thought. It is the universal level on which all thought takes place, whether a person is English or Chinese. There is no differentiation of thought, name and form. An Indian, Eskimo, German, and Bantu can all look at the same flower and experience the thought of it at the same time and in the same non-verbal language.

Para, the fourth and highest state, is transcendental. Formed into no particular wavelength, it is above all names and forms. It is the unchanging, primal substratum of all language and is pure energy, or *shakti.* As undifferentiated potential sound, it corresponds to *Sabdabrahman,* the Divine Vibration that unites all.

Thought cannot be held at the first level of vocal or visual experience. Its vibrations are too rapid, even on the lowest plane.

In the telepathic state, it can travel anywhere instantly. In the transcendental state everything merges together. This state of thought or vibration, which can be reached in meditation, is commonly called God.

USING SOUND VIBRATIONS FOR MEDITATION

Japa meditation is a method of channeling one's consciousness from the lowest to the highest level of pure thought. Repeated verbally or mentally, a Mantra lifts one into the telepathic stage and beyond to the transcendental. "Rama", for instance, has a specific form that merges with the name in the telepathic state. On the fourth level, name, form, and one's own Self as witness are indistinguishable. They unite and a state of bliss prevails. One does not enjoy bliss, but becomes Bliss itself. This is the true experience of meditation.

The power of sound is tremendous. In addition to image and form, it can generate ideas, emotions and experiences. By merely hearing words the mind can undergo pain or pleasure. If somebody shouts, "Snake! Snake!" one immediately jumps with fright. Consciousness of the presence of something considered dangerous has been created. The mind reacts with terror, and the body jumps in fear. When such is the power of the name of an ordinary thing of this world, imagine what power resides in the name of the Lord.

Japa is one of the most direct ways of Self-Realization, or Universal Consciousness. It removes the dirt of the mind, the anger, greed, lust and other impurities that hide the light within. Just as a dusty mirror acquires the power of reflection when cleaned, the mind from which impurities have been removed acquires the capacity to reflect higher spiritual truth. Even a little recitation with feeling and one-pointed concentration on the meaning destroys mental impurities. *Japa* meditation done with faith, devotion and purity augments the power of the aspirant, bestowing on him the virtues and powers of the Mantra's presiding deity. Revealing God to his consciousness, it confers illumination and eternal bliss

The Supreme is not an individual entity. God is an experience realized on a particular wavelength. *Japa* produces in the mind the form of the deity connected with the Mantra. Through constant practice, this form becomes the center of one's consciousness and can be directly realized. The Mantra of the deity, therefore, is the same as the deity. Repetition with concentration on the meaning of the Mantra and on the attributes of the particular deity will bring

God-Realization quickly. However, through sheer vibratory power, *japa* with no knowledge of the meaning will also bring realization, although it will take more time.

INITIATION INTO A MANTRA

If possible, before attempting *japa* one should seek out a guru and receive Mantra initiation from him. Mantra initiation is the spark that ignites the dormant spiritual energy residing in every human heart. Once lit, the fire is kept going by daily *japa* meditation.

Only those who are themselves pure can give initiation to others. Therefore it is important to find a qualified guru. For him to successfully implant the Mantra in the disciple's heart, he must have broken its power himself. Breaking the power of a Mantra means that one has meditated on it until obtaining the mystic experience of God through it, thus making its power one's own. At the time of initiation, the guru arouses the Mantra's *shakti,* or power, in his consciousness and transmits it, along with his own energy, to the disciple. If the disciple is receptive, he receives the radiant mass of energy in his own heart and is immeasurably reinforced and strengthened. Guru, Mantra and disciple are bound together in Divine Power made manifest in consciousness.

There must be psychic affinity between teacher and student, for the spiritual path is a lifetime involvement. The guru continues to guide and purify the aspirant, to prepare and strengthen him for God-Realization, whether it be through *japa* meditation or other means. There are no shortcuts to the goal. Needless to say, the commercial peddlers of instant-mix mumbo-jumbo, which is sold as Mantras, should be assiduously avoided. They are opportunists preying on the spiritual instincts of those who are sincerely looking for Truth.

If no guru can be found, one may select any Mantra that seems appropriate. It should be repeated mentally with faith and devotion every day. This in itself has a purificatory effect, and the realization of God-consciousness will eventually be attained.

Everything in the universe vibrates on specific wavelengths. These wavelengths can be manipulated. For example, when its pitch is increased high enough, a violin note can shatter glass. The various Mantras, although equally efficient, vibrate on different wavelengths. At the time of initiation, a Mantra is selected, either by the guru or by the initiate himself, in accordance with the latter's mental type. The vibrations of the Mantra and those of the disciple's mind must be mutually compatible. The mind must also be receptive to the deity whose form it will eventually assume. The process of attuning body and mind to the Mantra through *japa* meditation is prolonged. When attunement finally is achieved, meditation takes place.

In the state of meditation the flow of inner thought wave, which has been channeled by repetition of the Mantra, is greatly intensified. The deeper the meditation, the more marked the effect. The mind's upward concentration sends a rush of force through the top of the head. Response comes in a fine rain of magnetism which bathes the body in a downward flow of soft electricity. Thus the power of *japa* meditation leads to the Divine Vibration. One experiences that eternal Silence which encompasses all sound.

Japa Meditation: Practice

The efficiency of the Japa is accentuated according to the degree of concentration. The mind should be fixed on the Source. Then only you will realize the maximum benefits of a Mantra. Every Mantra has got tremendous force. A Mantra is a mass of Tejas or radiant energy. It transforms the mental substance by producing a particular thought movement. The rhythmical vibrations produced by repeating the Mantra, regulate the unsteady vibrations of the five sheaths. It checks the natural tendencies of objective thoughts of the mind. It helps the spiritual power and reinforces it.

— Swami Sivananda
Practice of Yoga

Mantras are Sanskrit invocations of the Supreme Being. Reinforced and propelled by *japa* meditation, they pass from the verbal level through the mental and telepathic states, and on to pure thought energy. Of all languages, Sanskrit most closely approaches telepathic language because of its affinity to the fifty primeval sounds. Therefore it is the most direct way to approach the transcendental state.

Mantras cannot be concocted or tailor-made for the individual, despite some current claims. They have always existed in a latent state as sound energies. Just as gravity was discovered but not invented by Newton, Mantras were revealed to the ancient masters. They have been codified in the scriptures and handed down from guru to disciple. Although it is customary for the guru when giving initiation to accept voluntary offerings of fruit, flowers or money, the selling of Mantras is strictly against all spiritual rules.

Neither Mantra, deity nor guru, once chosen, should be changed. There are many paths up the mountain. Perseverance on one alone will bring the aspirant to the top faster than if he were to spread his energies in exploring all the alternative paths.

SAGUNA MANTRAS

Mantras used by spiritual aspirants to achieve God-Realization are called deity Mantras. They are *saguna,* with qualities or form-producing, and aid the conceptualization process, just as do visual symbols. In time, recitation gives rise to the actual form of the particular deity.

As a specialized sound-body of consciousness, the Mantra is the deity itself. The form of the deity manifests as the visible portion of the sound. The Mantra, therefore, must be repeated in the proper way, with attention to the syllables and rhythm. If translated, it ceases to be a Mantra because sound vibrations newly created in translation are no longer the body of the deity, and therefore cannot evoke it. Only the rhythmical vibrations of the Sanskrit syllables properly recited can regulate the unsteady vibrations of the worshipper and permit the form of the deity to arise.

Westerners are prone to think that the various Mantras refer to different gods, and that there is a wide diversity in the culminating experience. It must never be forgotten that the deities are aspects of the one Divinity whose grandeur is too vast for the mind to comprehend at the beginning of spiritual practice. To use again the analogy of the hill, the many paths to the top can be viewed as the worship of the various aspects of God. The hill itself is one hill, and the summit is the same. After reaching the pinnacle, one will have the vision to encompass the totality.

Every true Mantra fulfills six conditions. 1) It was originally revealed to a sage, who achieved Self-Realization through it and passed it down to others. 2) It has a presiding deity and 3) a specific meter. 4) It possesses a *bija,* or seed, investing it with a special power that is the essence of the Mantra. 5) It also has dynamic divine power, or *Shakti.* 6) Lastly, there is a plug that conceals the pure consciousness hidden in the Mantra. As soon as the plug is removed by constant prolonged repetition, pure consciousness is revealed, and the devotee receives the vision of his deity.

All devotees are really worshipping the same Supreme *Atman.* Differences are only the differences in worshippers. These differences arise from the need for multiplicity in approach to Godhead. Various temperments are attracted to particular manifestations of the Divine. Some people are drawn by silence, others by activity; some lose themselves in nature, others in intellectual abstractions. One can approach God more easily if there is a compatible relationship with the most suitable manifestation. Harmony between aspirant and chosen deity is most essential. However, the goal will be reached only when one can see his chosen deity in all deities and in all beings.

At the time of initiation by a guru, one's deity, or *ishta devata,* is chosen. Every person has worshipped some deity in his previous lives, and the impressions of this worship are imprinted in the subconscious mind. These impressions have influenced the mental vibrations and have helped to form the particular mentality. Worship of Lord Siva in a previous birth would incline one to Siva worship in this life also, and would impart certain mental characteristics, such as stoicism and love of solitude. One who choses Siva as his *ishta devata* would be most drawn to abstract forms of thought, and meditation as his method of worship.

The householder to whom family, responsibility, order and ideals are important is drawn to Rama, the ideal son, husband and law-giver. Krishna attracts most people, particularly devotional types and active, balanced extroverts who are concerned with the welfare of others. As the mischievous baby, a young man engaged in divine play in the fields and forests of Vrindavan, and inspired giver of the wisdom of the *Bhagavad Gita,* His range is all inclusive. Those who feel reverence for the mother aspect as divine universal energy might worship Durga. If one cannot discover his own natural inclination, the guru will choose the deity in accordance with his insight.

Once the deity and appropriate Mantra have been selected, and the aspirant has received initiation from his guru, he works with the Mantra until reaching enlightenment. The Mantra becomes his theme song, so to speak. He makes its vibrations his own, and to the extent that he can do this, he is drawn closer to God.

Other deity Mantras can also be used in a supplementary way, such as for acquiring particular attributes. Repetition of *OM Aim Saraswatyai Namah* bestows wisdom, intelligence and creative achievement. *OM Sri Maha Lakshmyai Namah* confers wealth and prosperity. The Ganesha Mantra removes obstacles in any undertaking.

The *Maha Mrityunjaya* Mantra prevents accidents, incurable diseases and calamities, and bestows longevity and immortality. It is also a *moksha* Mantra, bringing liberation. Those who do *japa* of it daily will enjoy health, long life and ultimate enlightenment. The translation of this most powerful Mantra is: "We bow to that three-eyed Lord (Siva) who is full of sweet fragrance, who nourishes human beings. May he free me from the bondage of births and deaths, just as the ripe cucumber is separated from the vine, and may I be fixed in immortality."

The *Gayatri* Mantra is the supreme Mantra of the *Vedas*. It is the one Mantra that can be commonly prescribed for all, for *Gayatri* is the mother of the universe, *Shakti* herself, and there is nothing she cannot do. Her Mantra purifies the mind; destroys pain, sin and ignorance; brings liberation; and bestows health, beauty, strength, vitality, power, intelligence and magnetic aura.

Repetition of the *Gayatri* Mantra, *OM Namah Sivaya, OM Namo Narayanaya,* or *OM Namo Bhagavate Vasudevaya* 125,000 times, with feeling, faith, and devotion secures for the devotee the grace of the presiding deity. *OM Sri Ramaya Namah* and *OM Namo Bhagavate Vasudevaya* enable one to attain realization of God with attributes first, and subsequently realization without attributes.

MANTRAS FOR JAPA

1. ॐ श्रीमहागणपतये नम:

OM Sri Maha Ganapataye Namah

Prostrations to the great Lord Ganesha

OM is the original, most powerful Mantra sound. It is a part of almost every other Mantra, and serves to invoke pure supreme vibrations. *Sri* is a title of reverent respect. *Maha* means great. Ganapata is another name for Ganesha who is symbolized as the elephant-headed god, representing strength and fortitude. He is the remover of obstacles and bestower of success.

2. ॐ नम: शिवाय

OM Namah Sivaya

Prostrations to Lord Siva

Siva is the lord of ascetics and recluses. He is part of the Hindu Trinity. Brahma and Vishnu, the other two parts, are associated with creation and preservation, respectively. Siva, known as the Cosmic Dancer, presides over the destructive energies which break up the universe at the end of each age.

This is the process of the old making way for the new. In a more personal sense, it is Siva's energy by which one's lower nature is destroyed, making way for positive growth.

3. ॐ नमो नारायणाय

OM Namo Narayanaya

Prostrations to Lord Vishnu

Narayana is a name of Vishnu, the Preserver of the world. After the Creation, it is the energy of Vishnu which puts order to the universe. It is Lord Vishnu who regularly takes on a human life and incarnates on the earth to benefit mankind. People who are closely involved with the running of the world and maintaining the harmony of life are drawn to this aspect of God.

4. ॐ नमो भगवते वासुदेवाय

OM Namo Bhagavate Vasudevaya

Prostrations to the Lord God, Vasudeva

Bhagavan means Lord, referring to Vishnu. Vasudeva, meaning "He Who abides in all things and in Whom all things abide," is a name of Krishna. Krishna is one of the most loved of all deities. He is considered to be a world teacher for he is the source of the *Bhagavad Gita,* one of the most well-known of all Eastern religious texts. People are drawn to Krishna because of his playfulness and joyful nature.

5. हरि ॐ

Hari OM

OM Vishnu

Hari is another name for Vishnu. It is that aspect which forgives the past actions of those who take refuge in Him and destroy their negative deeds. Thus Hari is a redeemer and a guide to personal salvation as well as the World Preserver.

6. ॐ श्रीरामाय नम:

OM Sri Ramaya Namah

Prostrations to Lord Rama

Rama, an incarnation of Vishnu, took life on earth for the purpose of upholding righteousness and rewarding virtue. His life is the subject of *The Ramayana*. Rama lived the life of perfection and responsibility. Rama and Sita epitomized the devotional relationship between husband and wife. They are the model for all householders and people with family duties.

7. ॐ श्रीदुर्गायै नमः

OM Sri Durgayai Namah

Prostrations to Mother Durga

Supreme Divinity is without qualities or attributes, and as such it contains all qualities and attributes. The masculine principles are important yet, of necessity, they must be balanced with the feminine principles, for masculine and feminine are but obverse and reverse of the same coin. Durga represents the motherhood aspect of God. She is the force, or *shakti,* through which Divinity manifests, for Durga is power. She is the protector and benefactor. According to Hindu mythology, the *chaitanya,* or pure consciousness, of Brahma, Vishnu and Siva was united to form the being of Mother Durga. She is commonly pictured riding a tiger and having eight arms with which she carried flowers and weapons of protection and gives the gesture of blessing.

8. ॐ श्रीमहालक्ष्म्यै नमः

OM Sri Maha Lakshmyai Namah

Prostrations to the great Mother Lakshmi

Lakshmi is the bountiful provider. As Vishnu's consort, She aids in the preservation of the three worlds by bestowing wealth and abundance of a material and spiritual nature. She is pictured as a beautiful lady standing on a lotus blossom with her arms open and giving.

9. ॐ ऐं सरस्वत्यै नमः

OM Aim Saraswatyai Namah

Prostrations to Mother Saraswati

Aim is the *bija* of Saraswati who, in this aspect, bestows all learning, and knowledge of the arts and music. She is Brahma's consort and is involved with the creation of new ideas and things. She is responsible for bestowing wisdom and knowledge. She is often worshipped by people in the creative arts.

10. ॐ श्री महा कालिकायै नमः

OM Sri Maha Kalikayai Namah

Prostrations to Mother Kali

Kali is that divine aspect which is responsible for the violent destruction and eradication of negative qualities in this world. She is the transformative power of Divinity which dissolves the individual into cosmic union. Maha Kali is one of the most fearsome of all the expressions of Divinity. Because of the intensity of her purgative nature, very few people are initiated into this Mantra.

11. ॐ श्रीहनूमते नमः

OM Sri Hanumate Namah

Prostrations to Blessed Hanuman

Hanuman is the perfection of devotion. He is the greatest and the most selfless devotee of Lord Rama. In the Hindu tradition, he is considered to be a semi-deity, for he is the son of the wind-god. He possesses great strength and courage.

12. हरे राम हरे राम राम राम हरे हरे
    हरे कृष्ण हरे कृष्ण कृष्ण कृष्ण हरे हरे

Hare Rama Hare Rama, Rama Rama Hare Hare;
Hare Krishna Hare Krishna, Krishna Krishna Hare Hare

My Lord, Rama! My Lord, Krishna!

Hare is a glorified form of address for calling upon God. Rama and Krishna were two of the best known and most beloved incarnations of Vishnu. They took human birth on this earth to lead mankind to eternal salvation. This is the *Maha Mantra*, the easiest and surest way for attaining God-Realization in this present age.

13. ॐ श्रीराम जय राम जय जय राम

OM Sri Rama Jaya Rama Jaya Jaya Rama

Victory to Rama

Jaya means "victory" or "hail".

14. श्रीराम राम रामेति रमे रामे मनोरमे
सहस्रनाम तत्तुल्यं रामनाम वरानने ॥

Sri Rama Rama Rameti, Rame Rame Manorame;
Sahasranama Tattulyam, Rama Nama Varanane

*All these sacred names of Rama are equal to the highest name
of God*

This Mantra cures gossiping and back-biting, and makes up
for time lost in idle chit-chat.

15. ॐ त्र्यम्बकं यजामहे सुगन्धि पुष्टिवर्धनम् ।
उर्वारुकमिव बन्धनान्मृत्योर्मुक्षीय माऽमृतात् ।

OM Tryambakam Yajamahe Sugandhim Pushtivardhanam
Urvarukamiva Bandhanan Mrityor Mukshiya Mamritat

*We worship the three-eyed Lord (Siva) who is full of sweet
fragrance and nourishes human beings. May he liberate me
from bondage, even as the cucumber is severed from the vine.*

This is the *Maha Mrityunjaya Mantra*. It removes diseases,
prevents accidents and bestows liberation. It should be repeated daily.

16. ॐ नमोऽस्तु ते महायोगिन् प्रपन्नमनुशाधि माम् ।
यथा त्वच्चरणांभोजे रतिः स्यादनपायिनी ॥

OM Namo 'stute Mahayogin Prapannamanusadhi Mam
Yatha Twachcharanam Bhoje Retih Syadanapayini

*Salutation to thee, O great Yogi! Pray direct me that have
fallen at Thy feet, so that I may find unfailing delight at Thy
lotus feet.*

This is the Mantra for self surrender. It should be repeated
with a pure heart free of personal desires.

Lord Siva

Lord Vishnu

Lord Krishna

Left: Lord Rama; right: Hanuman worshipping Rama

Sri Lakshmi

Divine Mother in different aspects. Clockwise from upper left:
Sri Saraswati, Maha Kali, Maha Lakshmi, Sri Durga

Top: Ganesha; left: Jesus Christ; right: Master Sivananda.

GAYATRI MANTRA

ॐ । भूर्भुवः स्वः । तत् सवितुर्वरेण्यम् ।
भर्गो देवस्य धीमहि । धियो यो नः प्रचोदयात् ॥

OM Bhur Bhuvah Swah, Tat Savitur Varenyam
Bhargo Devasya Dheemahi, Dhiyo Yo Nah Prachodayat

We meditate on that Ishwara's glory, Who has created the universe, Who is fit to be worshipped, Who is the embodiment of Knowledge and Light, Who is the remover of all sins and ignorance. May He enlighten our intellects.

ॐ . . . . *OM* . . . . .Symbol of the Para Brahman
भूः . . . . *Bhur* . . . . Bhu-Loka (Physical plane)
भुवः . . . . . . *Bhuvah* . . . . . .Antariksha-Loka (Astral plane)
स्वः . . . . *Swah* . . . . .Swarga-Loka (Celestial plane)
तत् . . . . *Tat* . . . . That; Transcendent Paramatman
सवितुः . . . . *Savitur* . . . . . .Ishwara or Creator
वरेण्यम् . . . *Varenyam* . . . .Fit to be worshipped or adored
भर्गः . . . . . . *Bhargo* . . . . . . Remover of sins and ignorance; Glory
Effulgence
देवस्य . . . . . *Devasya* . . . . . Resplendent; Shining
धीमहि . . . . *Dheemahi* . . . .We meditate
धियः . . . . . *Dhiyo* . . . . Buddhis; Intellects; Understandings
यः . . . . *Yo* . . . . .Which; Who
नः . . . . *Nah* . . . . .Our
प्रचोदयात् . . *Prachodayat* . . Enlighten; Guide; Impel

GAYATRIES OF DIFFERENT DEITIES

Gayatri is a verse of specific length and meter. Although the Gayatri described above is one of the most sacred of the Vedic Mantras, and is called "Mother of the Vedas," this verse form is also used to praise and invoke many of the deities.

1. श्रो३म् एकदन्ताय विद्महे वक्रतुण्डाय धीमहि ।
तन्नो दन्ती प्रचोदयात् ॥

OM Ekadantaya Vidmahe Vakratundaya Dheemahi, Tanno Danti Prachodayat

This is the Gayatri of Ganesha

2. ॐ३म् नारायणाय विद्महे वासुदेवाय धीमहि ।
   तन्नो विष्णु: प्रचोदयात् ॥

   *OM Narayanaya Vidmahe Vasudevaya Dheemahi, Tanno
   Vishnuh Prachodayat*

   This is the Gayatri of Vishnu

3. ॐ३म् तत्पुरुषाय विद्महे सहस्राक्षाय महादेवाय धीमहि ।
   तन्नो रुद्र: प्रचोदयात् ॥

   *OM Tatpurshaya Vidmahe Sahasrakshaya Mahadevaya
   Dheemahi, Tanno Rudrah Prachodayat*

   This is the Gayatri of Siva

4. ॐ३म् दाशरथये विद्महे महादुर्गायै धीमहि ।
   तन्नो राम: प्रचोदयात् ॥

   *OM Dasarathaye Vidmahe Sitavallabhaya Dheemahi, Tanno
   Ramah Prachodayat*

   This is the Gayatri of Rama

5. ॐ३म् देवकीनन्दनाय विद्महे वासुदेवाय धीमहि ।
   तन्न: कृष्ण: प्रचोदयात् ॥

   *OM Devakinandanaya Vidmahe Vasudevaya Dheemahi,
   Tannah Krishnah Prachodayat*

   This is the Gayatri of Krishna

6. ॐ३म् कात्यायन्यै विद्महे कन्याकुमार्यै धीमहि ।
   तन्नो दुर्गा प्रचोदयात् ॥

   *OM Katyayanyai Vidmahe Kanyakumaryai Dheemahi, Tanno
   Durga Prachodayat*

   This is the Gayatri of Durga

7. ॐ३म् महादेव्यै च विद्महे विष्णुपत्न्यै च धीमहि ।
   तन्नो लक्ष्मी: प्रचोदयात् ॥

   *OM Mahadevyai Cha Vidmahe Vishnupatnyai Cha Dheema-
   hi, Tanno Lakshmih Prachodayat*

   This is the Gayatri of Lakshmi

8. ओ३म् वाग्देव्यै च विद्महे कामराजा य धीमहि ।
तन्नो देवी प्रचोदयात् ॥

*OM Vagdevyai Cha Vidmahe Kamarajaya Dheemahi, Tanno
Devi Prachodayat*

This is the Gayatri of Saraswati

9. ओ३म् सर्वसंमोहिन्यै विद्महे विश्वजनन्यै धीमहि ।
तन्न: शक्ति: प्रचोदयात् ॥

*OM Sarvasammohinyai Vidmahe Visvajananyai Dheemahi,
Tannah Shaktih Prachodayat*

This is the Gayatri of Shakti, Cosmic Power

10. ओ३म् गुरुदेवाय विद्महे परब्रह्मणे धीमहि ।
तन्नो गुरु: प्रचोदयात् ॥

*OM Gurudevaya Vidmahe Parabrahmane Dheemahi, Tanno
Guruh Prachodayat*

This is the Gayatri of the Guru

11. ओ३म् भास्कराय विद्महे महाद्युतिकराय धीमहि ।
तन्न आदित्य: प्रचोदयात् ॥

*OM Bhaskaraya Vidmahe Mahadyutikaraya Dheemahi, Tan-
na Adityah Prachodayat*

This is the Gayatri of Surya, the Sun

NIRGUNA MANTRAS

As *saguna* Mantras have form, *nirguna* Mantras are without
form. There are no deities or personalized aspects of God to be
invoked. Rather, one uses the abstract Mantras and vedantic for-
mulas to assert identification with all of Creation. Because people
are of many different temperaments, not all spiritual aspirants are
drawn to a personal deity. Many perceive the universe as diverse
energy patterns, all connected and interrelated, and stemming from
one Source or Primal Cause.

For this type of temperament, the abstract Mantra creates
a vibration in which the meditator identifies with the whole of the
Cosmos. With the repetition of one of these Mantras, the meditator

loses his individual identity and merges with Nature. He avows that he is identical with that homogenous substratum, that energy or power of existence, which underlies and permeates all that exists.

All Mantras are hidden in OM, which is the abstract, highest Mantra of the cosmos. OM is the manifest symbol of the *Sabdabrahman* vibration, or God; but, it must not be equated with the Divine. The universe has come from OM, rests in OM and dissolves in it. AUM, as it is sometimes written, covers the threefold experience of man; *A* represents the physical plane, *U* represents the mental and astral plane, and *M* represents the deep sleep state and everything beyond reach of the intellect. The transcendental sound of OM is heard only by Yogis, not by the ordinary ear.

Letters of the alphabet are emanations from OM, which is the root of all sounds and letters. *A* is the first sound the vocal apparatus can utter, and *M* is the last. In between is the middle range of *U*. The three sounds comprising OM encompass all sound. There is no language, music or poetry outside its range. Not only does all language and thought arise from this word, but also the energy vibrations of the universe itself.

Because of its universality, OM can be used as a Mantra by all who are unable to find a guru. However, its very universality and lack of particular form make it very difficult for a beginner to grasp. The mind must be very strong to be able to concentrate on formless and abstract Mantras such as OM.

Japa meditation on OM has a tremendous influence on the mind. Vibrations set up by this word are extremely powerful. By holding the hands over the ears and intoning it, one can experience its vibrations on a rudimentary physical level. No other sound similarly intoned will have the same vibrational power within the head.

Correctly pronounced, the sound proceeds from the navel, with a deep and harmonious vibration, and gradually manifests itself at the upper part of the nostrils. The larynx and palate are the sounding boards; no part of the tongue or palate is touched. As the *U* is pronounced, the sound rolls from the root of the tongue to the end of the sounding board of the mouth. *M* is the last sound, and is produced by closing the lips. Pronounced merely as spelled, OM will have a certain effect upon the nervous system, and will benefit the psyche. Pronounced correctly, it arouses and transforms every atom in the physical body, setting up new vibrations and awakening dormant physical and mental powers.

Just as the various deities are aspects of the One Supreme, so the various *bija,* or seed, Mantras are aspects of the supreme

Mantra, OM. *Bija* Mantras are seed letters directly derived from the fifty primeval sounds, and are very powerful. Generally a *bija* Mantra consists of a single letter, although some, such as *HREEM,* are compounded. Each has a significant inner mystic meaning, although on the surface the sound itself appears to have no meaning at all. Each element of the universe has its corresponding *bija.* The sounds for ether, air, fire, water and earth are, respectively, HAM, YAM, RAM, VAM and LAM. Every deity also has its own seed syllable. Because of their innate force, *bija* Mantras generally are not given for initiation. *Japa* on them may be practiced by those who are in a pure state, and their use is preceded by intricate rituals.

ABSTRACT MANTRAS

1. सोऽहम्

Soham

I am That I am

The meditator is existence itself. He is without form, without quality, without past, present or future. No bonds or limitations restrict the aspirant who has *Soham* firmly fixed in his mind.

2. अहं ब्रह्मास्मि

Aham Brahma Asmi

I am Brahman

Aham Brahma Asmi is a great Vedantic formula. The meditator asserts himself to be One with the ever-present Brahman. In doing so, he denies confinement to the body and mind, and affirms unity with the Absolute.

3. तत्त्वमसि

Tat Twam Asi

That Thou Art

"That" is the eternal Brahman, and "thou" is the meditator. *Tat Twam Asi,* one of the greatest of the Vedantic statements, identifies the individual as one and the same with Brahman, the Absolute Substratum of Creation.

4. ॐ

OM

There is no translation of OM. It consists of three letters: A, U, and M. It signifies the three periods of time, the three states of consciousness and all of existence. *A* is the waking state, *U* is the dreaming state, and *M* is the deep sleep state. OM contains *nada* and *bindu*. *Nada* is the prolonged vowel sound and *bindu* is the humming sound, made with closed lips, with which the Mantra ends.

BIJA MANTRAS, MYSTIC SEED LETTERS

1. (हौं) HAUM

In this Mantra, *Ha* is Siva and *au* is Sadasiva. The *nada* and *bindu* mean that which dispels sorrow. With this Mantra, Lord Siva should be worshipped.

2. (दुं) DUM

Here *Da* means Durga, and *u* means to protect. *Nada* means Mother of the universe, and *bindu* signifies action (worship or prayer). This is the Mantra of Durga.

3. (क्रीं) KREEM

With this Mantra Kalika should be worshipped. *Ka* is Kali, *ra* is Brahman, and *ee* is Mahamaya. *Nada* is the Mother of the universe, and *bindu* is the dispeller of sorrow.

4. (ह्रीं) HREEM

This is the Mantra of Mahamaya or Bhuvaneshwari. *Ha* means Siva, *ra* is *prakriti, ee* means Mahamaya. *Nada* is the Mother of the universe, and *bindu* is the dispeller of sorrow.

5. (श्रीं) SHREEM

This is the Mantra of Maha Lakshmi. *Sha* is Maha Lakshmi. *Ra* means wealth. *Ee* is satisfaction or contentment. *Nada* is the manifested Brahman, and *bindu* means the dispeller of sorrow.

6. (ऐं) AIM

This is the *bija* Mantra of Saraswati. *Ai* stands for Saraswati, and *bindu* is the dispeller of sorrow.

7. (क्लीं) KLEEM

This is the *Kamabija*. *Ka* means Kamadeva, the lord of desire; it also means Lord Krishna. *La* means Indra, the ruler of Heaven, also lord of the senses. *Ee* means contentment or satisfaction. *Nada* and *bindu* mean that which bring happiness and sorrow.

8. (हूं) HOOM

In this Mantra *Ha* is Siva, and *u* is Bhairava. *Nada* is the Supreme, and *bindu* means dispeller of sorrow. This is the threefold *bija* of Varma.

9. (गं) GAM

This is the Ganesha *bija*. *Ga* means Ganesha, and *bindu* is the dispeller of sorrow.

10. (ग्लौं) GLAUM

This is a Mantra of Ganesha, also. *Ga* means Ganesha, *la* means that which pervades, *au* means luster or brilliance, and *bindu* is the dispeller of sorrow.

11. (क्ष्रौं) KSHRAUM

This is the *bija* of Narasimha, a very fierce half-man half-lion incarnation of Lord Vishnu. *Ksha* is Narasimha, *ra* is Brahma, *au* means with teeth pointing upwards, and *bindu* means dispeller of sorrow.

The science of Mantra is very complex. There are even Mantras for such specific purposes as curing snake bite and chronic diseases, but these are of a lower order. In the modern world, the power of gross sound vibration is just beginning to be utilized in physical therapy, and its potential is being tapped in other fields. The ancient Indian sages had this sophistication thousands of years ago. They have used sound in its gross and subtle states to penetrate the planes of human consciousness and to reach the divine vibration that is the experience of God. Beginning in OM and dissolving in OM, the Mantra comes full cycle.

MEDITATION WITH THE MANTRA

There are various practical aids to progress in *japa* meditation that have been tested for thousands of years and are based on sound psychological and natural principles.

The telling of rosary beads is the form of *japa* most familiar to Western experience. A *japa mala,* similar to the rosary, is often used in Mantra repetition. It helps to foster alertness, acts as a focus for the physical energy and is an aid to rhythmic, continuous recitation. It consists of 108 beads. An additional bead, the *meru,* is slightly larger than the others. It is the signal indicating that with one Mantra recited for each bead, *japa* has been done 108 times, or one *mala.* The fingers should not cross the meru; when it is reached, the beads are reversed in the hand; one continues reciting the Mantra, moving the *mala* in the opposite direction. The thumb and third finger roll the beads; the index finger, which is psychically negative, is never used. The rosary must not be allowed to hang below the navel, and should be wrapped in a clean cloth when not in use.

An appropriate prayer before beginning induces purity of feeling. With eyes closed and the concentration focussed either between the eyebrows on the *ajna chakra* or on the *anahata chakra* of the heart, one should invoke the aid of his chosen deity and guru. The Mantra must be pronounced distinctly and without mistakes, for it and the deity itself are one and the same thing. Repetition must be neither too fast nor too slow, and thought must be given to its meaning. The speed should be increased only when the mind begins to wander. Because the mind will naturally try to drift away after a time, it is necessary to keep alert throughout the practice.

Variety in *japa* is necessary to sustain interest, avoid fatigue and counteract the monotony that can arise from constant repetition of the same syllables. This can be provided by modifying the volume. The Mantra can be repeated aloud for a while, then whispered, and then recited mentally. The mind needs variety or it becomes tired. However, even mechanical repetition that is devoid of feeling has a great purifying effect. Feeling will come later, as the process of purification continues.

Audible repetition is called *vaikhari japa,* while that done by whispering or humming is termed *upamsu japa.* Mental repetition, *manasika japa,* is the most powerful; it requires keener concentration, for the mind tends to shut off after a period of time. The advantage of loud *japa,* which should be used with discretion, is

Japa meditation: the Mantra is repeated once for each bead of the mala.

that it shuts out all worldly sounds and distractions. One should alternate when necessary, particularly when drowsiness sets in.

Unaccustomed to this kind of activity, the beginner at first may find himself giving up too soon, after five or ten minutes of repeating the Mantra. The syllables in this case may sound meaningless — mere syllables and nothing more. By persevering for at least half an hour without interruption, he will give the Mantra time to work itself into his consciousness, and benefits will be felt in a few days.

Meditation on the image of the chosen deity while the Mantra is being repeated adds tremendously to the efficacy of *japa*. Sound and form correspond and reinforce each other. Sound vibrations alone, if made with care and devotion, are capable of producing the form in the consciousness of the aspirant. The process can be greatly facilitated by visualizing the deity in the heart area or the space between the eyebrows. With the visualization, there should be an awareness of the various attributes of the deity. Feel that the Lord is seated within, emanating purity to the heart and mind, and manifesting his presence by the power of the Mantra.

Thus, in meditating on Siva, the physical energy is focussed on rolling the *mala* beads. The image of the deity, with the third eye and the symbolic crescent moon, serpents, trident, drum, etc. occupies the mind on one level. The Mantra *OM Namah Sivaya* is simultaneously being repeated, and on another level is being embedded in the consciousness. Repetition of the Mantra has a cumulative effect, and with continued practice it gains in power. It should be evident that *japa* meditation is far more than a verbal exercise. It is a state of complete absorption.

Concluding prayer and rest are important. When *japa* practice is finished, it is advisable not to plunge immediately into wordly activity. Sitting quietly for about ten minutes, one should reflect on the Lord and feel His presence. As routine duties are commenced, the spiritual vibrations will remain intact. This current should be maintained at all times, no matter what one is engaged in.

If doing manual work, give the hands to work but give the mind to God. Like a woman who continues knitting while talking to her friends, one can sustain mental *japa*. With practice, the manual work will become automatic. When the Mantra can be repeated throughout the day, God-consciousness will permeate one's life.

Mantra writing, *likhita japa*, is another, supplementary form of *japa*. The Mantra should be written daily with a special pen and notebook which have been set aside for this purpose. It should be done for half an hour, during which time complete silence and concentration are observed. If, as one writes, he simultaneously repeats the Mantra mentally, the impression made in the consciousness is intensified. *Likhita japa* may be done in any language and in any script. It greatly helps the aspirant to concentrate and eventually leads to meditation. The practice helps to set up a continuous vibration of divine energy that guides and protects, regardless of what one is doing.

Advanced meditation should not be attempted without the guidance of a guru. *Bija* Mantras and certain mystic Mantras, such as the *Sri Vidya*, should not be repeated by those who are not well acquainted with them and with the Sanskrit language. When improperly repeated, they can actually bring harm to the psychic system. Those who are not qualified, and who do not have access to a guru who has broken the power of these advanced Mantras, should concentrate on their own Mantras.

Deity Mantras are used for *purascharana*, which is concentrated *japa* meditation extended over a long period of time. When performing a *purascharana*, the aspirant sets aside a certain number of hours each day for *japa*. The Mantra is repeated 100,000 times for each syllable of the Mantra. The Mantra is repeated with feelings, and in a particular manner with the right observance, until the fixed number of Mantras have been recited. Slow repetition of the *Maha Mantra* may take as long as three years of finish. The practitioner must observe certain rules and regulations laid down in the scriptures in regard to *purascharana,* and must observe perfect dietary discipline in accordance with those injunctions.

Anushthana is the practice of religious austerity for the sake of obtaining some object or goal, the highest being spiritual. For success, the desire should be spiritual, and it should be kept in view throughout the practice. The rigor of the austerity, which may be of various kinds, depends on the constitution and health of the aspirant.

For *japa anushthana,* a deity Mantra should be selected in accordance with the desired goal. Although his personal deity might be Krishna, if one wanted to compose sublime music, he would repeat the Mantra for Saraswati; if he wished his spiritual obstacles to be removed, he would select a Ganesha Mantra. *Japa* meditation is then performed for a protracted period, with intense concentration of mind and no thought of the external world. This leads to achievement of the desired goal.

There may be other types of *japa* meditation, but the broad theory and techniques do not greatly vary. Approached with faith and devotion, and carried out with perseverance, *japa* is the most direct path to God-Realization.

TIME TO COMPLETE ONE PURASCHARANA TO AWAKEN THE DORMANT POWER IN A MANTRA

MANTRAS	SPEED PER MIN			NO. JAPA DONE IN ONE HOUR			TIME REQUIRED, AT 6 HRS. DAILY, FOR 1 PURASCHARANA					
	Low	Med.	High	Low	Med.	High		Yrs.	Mo.	Day	Hrs.	Mins.
OM	140	250	400	8400	15000	24000	Low	—	—	—	11	54
							Med.	—	—	—	6	40
							High	—	—	—	4	10
Hari Om or Sri Rama	120	200	300	7200	12000	18000	Low	—	—	1	3	47
							Med.	—	—	—	16	40
							High	—	—	—	11	7
Om Namah Sivaya	80	120	150	4800	7200	9000	Low	—	—	17	2	10
							Med.	—	—	11	3	30
							High	—	—	9	1	35
Om Namo Narayanaya	60	80	120	3600	4800	7200	Low	—	1	7	0	15
							Med.	—	—	27	4	45
							High	—	—	18	3	15
Om Namo Bhagavate Vasudevaya	40	60	90	2400	3600	5400	Low	—	2	23	2	0
							Med.	—	1	25	3	30
							High	—	1	7	0	15
Gayatri Mantra	6	8	10	360	480	600	Low	3	0	16	0	45
							Med.	2	5	8	5	30
							High	1	7	15	3	35
Maha Mantra or Hare Rama Mantra	8	10	15	480	600	900	Low	3	0	16	0	45
							Med.	2	5	8	5	30
							High	1	7	17	3	35

Hatha Yoga Meditation — Kundalini

*Kundalini is the cosmic power in individual bodies. It is not
a material force like electricity or magnetism. It is a spiritual
potential, Shakti or cosmic power. In reality it has no form. It is the
coiled-up, sleeping Divine Shakti that lies dormant in all beings.
This mysterious Kundalini lies face.downwards at the mouth
of Sushumna Nadi. When it is awakened, it makes a hissing sound
like a serpent, hence it is also called serpent power. Kundalini
is the goddess of speech and is praised by all. She Herself, when
awakened by the Yogin, achieves for him the illumination.
It is She who gives liberation and knowledge for She is Herself that.
She is also called Saraswati for She is the source of all
knowledge and bliss. She is pure consciousness itself. She is
Brahman. She is Prana Shakti, the Supreme Force. It is by this
Shakti that the world exists. Creation, preservation and
dissolution are in her.*

— Swami Sivananda
Kundalini Yoga

Kundalini Yoga, or Laya Yoga as it is sometimes called, is
the culminating meditative experience of Hatha Yoga. It is for the
advanced student who is practicing under a guru. It requires
thorough knowledge of the psychic body and its structure, as well
as great purification of the physical and psychic bodies. *Kundalini
shakti* is primordial, cosmic power, and cannot be trifled with.
Premature attempts to arouse it without proper preparation can
cause great damage to the aspirant's mental, physical and psychic
balance. The guidance and grace of a guru are absolutely necessary.

In *kundalini* meditation, the divine power that lies dormant
in every human being is aroused and pulled upward through the
chakras, the psychic centers of the body. At the top of the head,
the seat of the highest consciousness, the union of the individual and
Absolute Consciousness takes place. This is expressed symbolically as the union of *Shakti,* or *Kundalini,* with Lord Siva.

KUNDALINI SHAKTI

The equilibrium of the universe is maintained by a polarity of positive and negative, male and female, the static and the dynamic. Whatever exists in the universe, the macrocosm, exists also in man, the microcosm. The masculine passive ground force, Siva, resides in the *sahasrara,* the seventh *chakra,* located in the crown of the head. *Shakti,* the feminine active power, lies coiled at the base of the spine. It is the manifestation of cosmic power in the body and is in a dormant, potential state. Not a material force, it is the pristine psychic and spiritual power that underlies all organic and inorganic matter. Because of its spiral-like upward motion when awakened, it is referred to as serpent power, and is depicted iconographically as a serpent coiled at the base of the spine. The arousal of *kundalini* leads to union with Lord Siva. It is the state of supreme consciousness and spiritual enlightenment.

Hatha Yoga awakens the *kundalini* by disciplining the body; purifying the *nadis,* the astral channels through which flows the *prana;* and controlling the *prana.* Through the physical postures of Hatha Yoga the nervous system is toned, enabling it to withstand the experience of the rising energy. It regulates the flow of *prana* by means of body locks and seals, known as *mudras* and *bandhas. Kriyas,* special cleansing techniques, purify the inner organs of the physical body, and breath control steadies the mind. Vigorous *pranayama, asanas,* and meditation are not enough, however. Mental purification requires selfless service, for seeing and serving the Supreme in all beings is essential for any spiritual progress.

Kundalini and her channel for movement are not to be found in the physical body. Every portion of the physical body has its counterpart in the astral body, and both bodies are interdependent on the material plane. The seven psychic centers, or *chakras,* and the *sushumna nadi,* the passage through which the *kundalini* rises, are in the astral body and correspond to the nerve plexuses and the spinal cord.

According to yogic theory, there are approximately 72,000 *nadis,* astral nerve tubes, the most important of which is the *sushumna,* the astral body's counterpart to the spinal cord. On either side of it are two *nadis* known as *ida* and *pingala,* which correspond to the left and right sympathetic cords in the physical body. *Prana,* vital energy, flows through them. As long as it does so, man is engaged in worldly activities, and is bound by time, space and causation. However, when the *sushumna* operates, he is beyond such limitation.

While Western anatomy recognizes only the gross form a˙⌐ functions, Kundalini Yoga acts on the subtle level. The aspirant, therefore, must have a thorough knowledge of the major *nadis.* The *sushumna nadi* extends from the *muladhara chakra,* the second vertebra of the coccygeal region, to the *Brahmarandhra,* in the crown of the head. The physical spinal cord is made up of gray and white brain matter, and is suspended within the spinal column. Within this cord is a central canal, called in anatomy the *canalis centralis.* The *sushumna,* located within this spinal canal, has several sub-divisions.

THE SPINAL CORD AND THE NADIS

CROSS SECTION OF A VERTEBRA

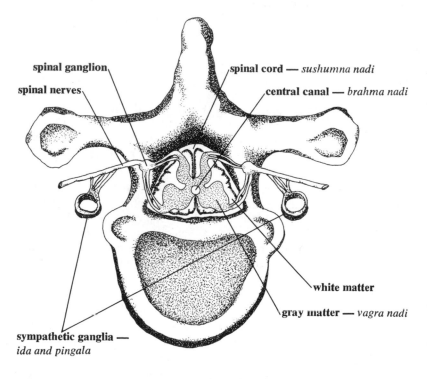

The nadis, indicated in italics, exist in the astral body. They are shown here in relation to their counterparts in the physical body.

Within the fiery red *sushumna* is another *nadi, vajra,* lustrous as the sun, which in turn contains another, the *chitra,* which is pale in color. Inside the *chitra* is a very fine, minute canal known as *Brahma nadi.* When the *kundalini* is awakened, it passes through this canal from the *muladhara chakra* to the *sahasrara.* In this canal exist all of the main *chakras,* each representing a different state of consciousness.

The *chitra nadi* is the most vital part of the body, and is sometimes referred to as the "heavenly way." Within it, at the lower extremity, is the beginning of the *sushumna,* which is called the *Brahma Granthi* or "knot of Brahma." This obstruction is penetrated as the *kundalini* is aroused and passes upward towards the *nadi's* termination point in the cerebellum.

THE CHAKRAS

The six *chakras* are way-stations along the *sushumna,* to the final destination, the *sahasrara chakra.* They are of consciousness, with specific tones of awareness and bliss, as well as storage places for the subtle, vital energy. They have corresponding centers in the spinal cord and nerve plexuses of the gross physical body, with which they are closely related. Vibrations produced in the physical centers by prescribed methods create specific desired effects in the subtle centers. The location of the *chakras* and their corresponding centers in the phyiscal body are:

1. *Muladhara:* at the lower end of the spinal column, corresponding to the sacral plexus.
2. *Swadhisthana:* in the region of the genital organs, corresponding to the prostatic plexus.
3. *Manipura:* at the navel, corresponding to the solar plexus.
4. *Anahata:* at the heart, corresponding to the cardiac plexus.
5. *Vishuddha:* in the throat region, corresponding to the laryngeal plexus.
6. *Ajna:* between the eyebrows, *trikuta,* corresponding to the cavernous plexus.
7. *Sahasrara:* at the crown of the head, corresponding to the pineal gland.

During meditation, each *chakra* is visualized as a lotus with a certain number of petals. The *muladhara, swadhisthana, manipura, anahata, vishuddha* and *ajna chakras* have four, six, ten, twelve, sixteen and two petals respectively, while the *sahasrara* has one thousand. The number of petals is determined by the number and position of the *nadis* that emanate from the *chakra* and give it the appearance of a lotus. Hanging downward when the *kundalini* is dormant, the *nadis* turn upward with its ascendence.

Associated with each petal is one of the fifty sanskrit letters, representing the vibration produced on it by the *kundalini* as it passes through the *chakra*. These sounds exist in latent form, and when manifested as vibrations of the *nadis,* can be felt during concentration. Besides petals and sound vibration, each *chakra* has its own geometric form representing a specific power, as well as its own color, function, element, presiding deity and *bija,* or mystic vibration.

There are various methods of locating the *chakras,* all of which may be approached from the front as well as the back. It may help initially to think of the *muladhara, manipura, anahata,* and *ajna* as localities rather than concentrated points. When attempting to locate the *chakras* from the back, one moves his concentration directly upward along the spinal cord, from *chakra* to *chakra.* If approaching from the front, one moves from the base of the spine up to the navel, the heart, the throat, etc. At all times the consciousness is kept internalized and receptive to experiencing the inner vibrations indicating an energy center. In all exercises, a comfortable meditative posture should be assumed; a straight spine is essential.

The *chakras* may be focussed upon by chanting OM, the all-inclusive universal sound vibration, in different pitches. Fixing the concentration on the *muladhara chakra,* OM is chanted at the lowest pitch. Then moving up the spinal cord to the area of each successive center, the pitch is raised higher each time. The OM sound gradually becomes imperceptible. Another method utilizes the Indian musical scale to locate the psychic centers. There is a definite relationship between the scale and the principle *chakras. Sa* corresponds to the *muladhara, re* to the *swadhisthana, ga* to the *manipura, ma* to the *anahata, pa* to the *vishuddha, da* to the *ajna* and *ni* to the *sahasrara.*

When the *kundalini* is awakened, it does not proceed directly to the *sahasrara,* unless one is an exceptionally pure yogi. It must be moved up from one *chakra* to another, and a great deal of concentration and patience is required. It may drop back and have to be raised again with great effort. Even when the *kundalini* is raised to the *ajna chakra,* it is difficult to keep it there. Only great yogis such as Sri Ramakrishna, Sri Aurobindo and Swami

Sivananda were able to keep it there for any length of time. When the *kundalini* finally rises from the *ajna* to the *sahasrara,* union takes place. But even here it does not remain long. Only after lengthy and continuous practice does the evolved and purified adept experience permanent union and final liberation.

The speed at which the *kundalini* is aroused depends upon the aspirants purity, stage of evolution, dispassion, purification of the psychic nerves and vital sheath, and yearning for liberation. In due time, Nature awakens the power and gives the student knowledge as he is ready. Until he is able to absorb it totally, nothing of deep importance is revealed to him.

There are numerous other exercises, both physical and breathing, to facilitate *chakra* meditation. It cannot be stressed too strongly that this kind of meditation must be done under the guidance of a guru, and then only after many months of purification and preparation. No teacher, however, can give the student the power or the necessary self-discipline.

THE CHAKRAS AND THE IDA, PINGALA AND
SUSHUMNA NADIS

1. *Muladhara*, 2. *Swadhishthana*, 3. *Manipura*, 4. *Anahata*,
5. *Vishuddha*, 6. *Ajna*, 7. *Sahasrara* (Thousand-Petalled Lotus)

MULADHARA CHAKRA

The *muladhara chakra* is located at the base of the spinal column. It has a square mandala representing the earth principle which is yellow in color, and has the *bija* Mantra of *lam.* The four petals which are crimson colored are associated with the sound vibrations of *vam, śam, sham,* and *sam.* These *bijas* begin on the upper right-hand petal and are read in a clockwise direction. Brahma is the presiding deity. Within this *chakra, kundalini* lies dormant. Here also is the *Brahma granthi,* or knot of Brahma, which must be forced open through rigorous *sadhana* and intense purification for the *kundalini* to rise.

Meditation on the *muladhara* confers knowledge of the *kundalini,* as well as the means of awakening it. It bestows breath and mind control, and knowledge of the past, present and future.

SWADHISHTHANA CHAKRA

The *swadhishthana chakra,* situated in the *sushumna* at the genital area, controls the lower abdomen, kidneys, etc. in the physical body. Its element, water, is associated with the white crescent moon, and the *bija* is *vam.* The six vermillion petals are represented by *bam, bham, mam, yam, ram* and *lam.* Vishnu is the presiding deity.

Meditation is fixed on the crescent moon in the *chakra.* It gives control over the water element and confers psychic powers, intuitional knowledge and knowledge of the astral entities. Many impure qualities are annihilated.

MANIPURA CHAKRA

The *manipura chakra* is located in the *sushumna nadi,* at the navel, and corresponds to the solar plexus. The red triangular mandala in its center contains its element, fire. The *bija* Mantra is *ram.* The ten petals which are dark purple like heavy rain clouds, are represented by *dam, dham, nam, tam, tham, dam, dham, nam, pam* and *pham.* The presiding deity is Rudra.

He who concentrates successfully on this chakra has no fear of fire and is free from disease.

ANAHATA CHAKRA

The *anahata chakra* is located in the *sushumna* in the region of the heart. Its element air is located in the smoke colored mandala, shaped like the Star of David, in its center. Its *bija* is *yam*. The twelve deep red petals are represented by *kam, kham, gam, gham, ṅam, cam, cham, jam, jham, ñam, tam* and *tham*. Isha is the presiding deity.

The *anahata* sound, the primal sound of *Sabdabrahman*, is heard at this center. Meditation on the *anahata chakra* bestows pure qualities, cosmic love and various psychic powers.

VISHUDDHA CHAKRA

The *vishuddha chakra* is situated in the *sushumna nadi* at the base of the throat, and corresponds to the laryngeal plexus in the physical body. It also corresponds to the fifth cosmic plane. Within a pure blue circle is its element, ether. The seed *bija* is *ham.* The sixteen smokey purple petals contain the Sanskrit vowels: *am, ām, im, īm, um, ūm, ṛm, ṝm, ḷm, ḹm, em, aim, om, aum, am, ahm.* The presiding deity is Sadasiva.

He who concentrates and ultimately achieves meditation on this *chakra* attains high success. He enjoys complete knowledge of the four *Vedas* and knows the past, present and future.

AJNA CHAKRA

The *ajna chakra,* in the *sushumna,* corresponds to the space between the eyebrows, the *trikuta.* OM is the seed letter for this *chakra* which is the seat of the mind, and is found in the pure white circle within it. On each side are two petals, also pure white, their vibrations represented by the Sanskrit letters *haṃ* and *kshaṃ.* The element is *avyakta,* the primordial cloud of undifferentiated energy and matter. Paramasiva is the presiding deity.

He who meditates successfully on this center destroys the Karma of all past lives, and becomes a liberated soul. Intuitional knowledge is obtained through this *chakra,* the seat of primordial power and soul. It is here that yogis consciously put their *prana* at the time of death. All yogis, particularly *jnanis,* concentrate on this center and OM.

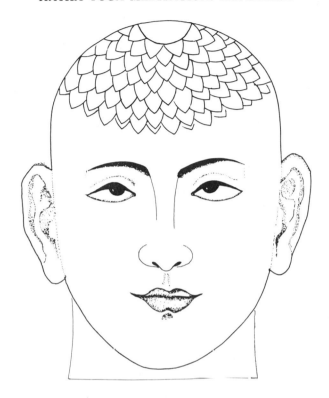

SAHASRARA CHAKRA

The *sahasrara* is a subtle center, above and beyond the other six centers. All others are intimately connected with it. Situated at the crown of the head, it corresponds to the pineal gland of the physical body. It has a thousand petals, on which are repeated the fifty letters of the Sanskrit alphabet. It is the abode of Siva.

The area in the crown of the head that is known as the anterior fontanelle in a new-born child is called *Brahmarandhra,* the "hole of Brahma." At the time of death, when the advanced yogi separates himself from the physical body, it bursts open and the *prana* escapes through it.

When *Kundalini Shakti* is united with Siva at the *sahasrara,* the yogi experiences extreme bliss. He attains the superconscious state and the highest knowledge. He becomes a fully developed *jnani.*

Jnana Yoga Meditation: Vedantic Theory

*A Jnana Yogi sees Atman everywhere through his eye of
wisdom. There is absolutely no personal element in him.
There is no thought of the self. He has not a bit of selfish interest.
The lower self is completely annihilated. He lives for serving all.
He feels the world as his own self. He actually feels that all
is himself only. There is not a single thought or feeling for
a personal little self. He has cosmic vision and cosmic feeling.
Just as the river has joined the ocean, he has joined the ocean of
bliss, knowledge and consciousness. He thinks and feels
and works for others.*

— Swami Sivananda
Vedanta in Daily Life

Jnana Yoga is one of the four main paths of Yoga. *Jnana*
means wisdom, and Jnana Yoga is the intellectual approach to
spiritual evolution or realization. Through inquiry and analysis,
the mind itself is used to examine its own nature. Jnana Yoga is
said to be the most difficult path, not because it is superior to any
other path, but because one must be firmly grounded in each of
the other yogic disciplines before attempting Jnana Yoga. There
must be a strong base of selfless service — serving humanity without
thought of personal gain — and love of God, or deep yearning to
merge with the Absolute. One must also have a strong, healthy
body, control of the vital energies, and control of the mind before
it is possible to actually use the mind as a vehicle to transcend
this world of ignorance. For without these preliminary disciplines,
there will not be the strength or discernment to stay on this path.
It is easy to be confused, tempted, and led astray by the illusion of
the world and the workings of the mind. It is the synthesis of all
Yogas that rounds out the imbalances of life. Without the integration, there is the risk of becoming a dry intellectual from too much
book learning.

Jnana Yoga is a path of evolution toward spiritual realization. It employs and incorporates different methods to achieve this end, but its main tool is Vedanta philosophy. Vedanta is a body of knowledge based on ancient Indian texts. The practice of Jnana Yoga involves inquiry into the nature of the world by putting to use the teachings of Vedanta.

VEDANTA

Vedanta literally means "end of the *Vedas*," for Vedanta is based on the teachings of the *Upanishads,* which form the concluding sections of the *Vedas.* The *Vedas* are the most ancient scriptural texts of India. Their origin is unknown, but it is said that they were given through inspiration to the holy men who sat meditating upon God. There are four *Vedas: Rig, Yejur, Sama,* and *Atharva.*

The *Rig Veda* deals with questions and commentaries on the world and the nature of reality. The *Yejur Veda* lays down all the rituals and sacrifices and the rules for performing them. It is also a discourse on all the Mantras. The *Sama Veda* gives all knowledge on the theory and practice of music and singing. The *Athavar Veda* deals with magic and the black arts. Each of these *Vedas* is divided into four sections: the *Mantra-Samhitas,* which are hymns in praise of God; the *Brahmanas,* or guides for performing sacrifices and pronouncing the Mantras; *Aranyakas,* which are the mystical books that give the philosophical interpretation to the rituals; and the *Upanishads,* which contain the essence or knowledge portion of each of the *Vedas.*

The philosophy of Vedanta is composed of the teachings of all the various *Upanishads* which are still known to man. It is also one of the six major systems of Indian Philosophy. Indian philosophy can be divided into six categories, or schools, each of which was developed by a particular sage, or wise man. He promulgated it to his disciples who then passed it on. These six systems are:

1. *Purva Mimamsa,* founded by Jaimini, prescribes rituals to invoke and placate the gods, and to attain Heaven. *Dharma* and *adharma,* righteous and unrighteous actions, create the world which is based on reward and punishment.
2. *Uttara Mimamsa,* founded by Maharishi Vyasa, is pure, non-dualistic *Advaita Vedanta.* It states that all is Brahman, or unmanifested God, and everything else which appears to exist is only a projection of that Absolute Brahman. It is also the basis of Jnana Yoga.

3. *Sankhya,* by Kapila Rishi, differs from Vedanta in that it is dualistic. That is, it sees a separation between matter, called *Prakriti,* and spirit, called *Purusha.* The material world, *Prakriti,* is seen as the creation and interaction of the three *gunas,* or qualities: *sattwa, rajas* and *tamas* (purity, activity and inertia).

4. *Yoga,* of Pantanjali, is a practical system of concentration and control of the mind, for it is the mind which creates all illusions. It is similar to Vedanta, but suggests that *Purusha* (Brahman), which is untouched by Karma or time, is the cause of creation. Pantajali's *Yoga Sutras,* (see chapters on Raja Yoga) are the essence of Raja Yoga, although *Yoga,* meaning union, actually applies to a broader range of disciplines.

5. *Vaiseshika,* of Kanada Rishi, presents a material or scientific view of the universe. That is, all things are made of basic units called atoms. This has proven to be unsatisfactory for scientists now know that the atom can be broken down indefinitely and the ultimate essence of matter cannot be determined.

6. *Nyaya,* founded by Gautama Rishi, argues that God, or *Ishwara,* is responsible for the creation of the world.

The Vedantic thought of *Uttara Mimamsa* challenges all other systems. It maintains that liberation cannot be attained by ritual, action, duty or charity. Change is the law of this manifest universe. Because of this impermanence, it cannot be real. Brahman alone is real; the world of illusion is unreal, and the individual soul is nothing but Brahman Itself. This Ultimate Reality is beyond the reach of the limited intellect and the knowable world. Renunciation alone, the abandonment of all worldly attachments, can lead to knowledge of the Absolute. This is achieved through a process of negation of all wordly desires, identifications, qualifications and extensions. That which is left after complete abandonment is God.

Vedanta philosophy has a triple basis — in scripture, reason and experience. Although the basic authority is scriptural, this does not mean that Vedanta is a matter of blind, unthinking acceptance. Reasoning is necessary for intellectual understanding of the scriptures. The Vedantin uses logic to distinguish between the real and the unreal and then discards that which is unreal. Intellect can explain only the finite. After exhausting itself through the process of discrimination and negation of all that is unreal, it too must be discarded when it reaches the point where all that is left is the real.

While the path of the Self lies through exhaustive intellectual inquiry and analogy, language is of service only in indicating the nature of the Real. The final Court of Appeal is intuitional experience. Western philosophy tends to ignore direct intuition. It brings the intellect to the brink and abandons it there. Vedanta approaches Self-Realization with the intellect and then pushes on to the final leap, through intuition, to direct experience.

Some religions hold that the universe was created out of nothing, by a fiat of God, and will lapse again into nothingness. It is not possible for something to come out of nothing. A tree, for example, is preceded by invisible energy in the form of a seed. God did not create the universe from nothing. What would be the purpose? Nor did he do so out of love for humanity, for there were no human beings at the time of the Creation. The Law of the Conservation of Matter and the Law of the Conservation of Energy say that neither matter nor energy can be created or destroyed; only its form can be changed.

For all practical purposes, it does not matter whether the world as we know it is real or unreal. If a starving man sees a fruit tree, does he first analyze the tree and count its leaves before plucking the fruit? If a man catches his clothing on fire, will he ask himself, "Hmm, I wonder where this fire came from?" or will he immediately try to extinguish the flames? Time and energy are wasted in useless intellectual speculation and discussion. Concepts lead to no final answer. One's notions of God do not arise from reason. They are preconceptions, mere projections of somebody else's ideas. One group's ideas differ from those of another group, just as individual ideas vary. Vedanta does not try to convert to "isms." It offers a technique for one to experience Ultimate Reality by approaching first through intellectual inquiry and then through direct realization.

Although the questions one runs into during the quest for spiritual fulfillment cannot be appropriately answered through the intellect, nonetheless inquiry, as opposed to discussion or debate, is necessary to lead the true spiritual seeker along the path. If the mind is open and free from prejudice and preconceived ideas, inquiry will eventually lead to direct knowledge.

THE VEILS OF ILLUSION

Brahman, Absolute Consciousness, has neither name nor form. It is infinite, unqualified and undifferentiated. In Raja Yoga, it is called *Purusha*. Just as moonlight is actually reflected sunlight, so also this manifest world, *Maya,* is a reflection of Brahman. Reflected through *Maya,* or *Prakriti* in Raja Yoga, Brahman takes on qualities and is called *Ishwara,* or God.

Maya then is the veiling power of Brahman. It creates the idea of limitation, an illusion that the world is different from Brahman. An empty glass creates the idea of space within defined boundaries, but when it breaks, the illusion disappears. With Self-Realization, the world-illusion disappears and all is experienced directly as the unchanging, unlimited Brahman.

The difference between the individual soul and Brahman is only apparent. The individual soul is Brahman veiled by the illusions of body and mind. As long as man accepts only the manifest world of *Maya,* he is caught in its meshes and bound in Karma. Yet, it is only an apparent binding, for the Self cannot be bound by anything. Like the sky, it is eternally free. It is, however, overlaid with various phenomena, just as the motion picture screen is overlaid with the lights and shadows that play over its surface. Floods, fires, murders, love and death all take place in the shadow play, but they in no way affect the underlying screen.

Like the screen, the "I" is subject to manifold illusions — I am a painter; I am an actor; I am a Catholic; I am a Protestant; etc. These names and forms are only illusions superimposed on the Self and change from lifetime to lifetime and sometimes within a lifetime. They disappear in the light of Self-Realization, just as the shadows vanish from the screen the moment the light is switched on.

Until realization takes place, man is wrapped in *avidya,* which is ignorance or nescience. *Avidya* is the multi-layered veil that lies over knowledge of the Self, which is the only true knowledge. Ignorance is erroneous identification with ones own limiting adjuncts. Unlike the concept of sin, ignorance does not imply guilt, but rather a condition in which knowledge is yet to be acquired. The *Panchadasi,* an ancient Indian text, asserts, "Man's present miseries and sufferings, his pains and limited pleasures, births and deaths, are all due to his erroneous identification with the five sheaths and three bodies. (The three bodies are the physical body, the astral body and the causal body, while the five sheaths are the food sheath, the vital sheath, the emotional sheath, the intellectual sheath and the bliss sheath. They are described in detail in *The Complete Illustrated Book of Yoga).*

When one says, "I am Mr. California Muscle Beach; look at my body", he is identifying with the physical food sheath. Its qualities are existence, birth, growth, decay and death. He identifies with the vital sheath when he is concerned with hunger, thirst, heat, cold and other such sensations. The mental sheath deals with thinking, emotions, doubt, exhilaration, depression, etc. When one boasts of intellectual achievements, it is identification with the intellectual sheath. Such associations constitute true ignorance. When one identifies with the blissful sheath there is an attachment to striving for realization of the Self. Even this must ultimately be transcended. Attachment to the food sheath will bring only pain, for muscular accomplishments will wane. So it is with them all. Only by throwing off bondage to these shadows can one be free. Vedanta is an intellectual method of disassociating from all the sheaths.

One person may identify with one of these limiting sheaths more than another. For instance, if the intellectual sheath predominates, one might assume the role of a philosopher. Identifying with that role, a momentum would be created that translates everything into intellectual terms of experience, thus setting up obstacles to balanced integration as a human being and to finding true identity with the Divine. Thus in addition to being misplaced attachment, *avidya* is also causal ignorance, that which creates binding karmic actions. It is the root of all actions and reactions.

Attachment to the various sheaths also affects relationships with others. One who dwells predominantly on the emotional plane has difficulty communicating with another who associates with the intellectual sheath. Depending on which sheath prevails, people are attracted to various gurus. A true guru, however, is unattached to any body or sheath. His only identification is with I AM.

In essence all is Brahman. However, Nature, as the reflection of Brahman, manifests in the individual soul as *avidya* or a veil of ignorance. As it is only a reflection, the material world, emotions and intellect, are all illusion. This illusion is called *Maya.* To be more exact then, *avidya* is the state of being trapped in *Maya.* This ignorance is always present until Unity is realized. As long as one experiences diversity, there will also be the experience of fear. In regarding others as different from himself and from Brahman, man becomes prey to various fears of what might happen to him in his separateness.

Avidya, manifesting through illusion or *Maya,* has neither beginning nor cause. As the projection of Brahman, *Maya,* which is the manifest world, cannot exist independently. It is both real and unreal — real to mankind, unreal in the light of Brahman. The magician who pulls a rabbit out of a hat or saws a woman in half creates such an illusion. He does not really cause a rabbit to materialize inside an empty hat nor does he bisect a woman and then put her together, yet the *illusion* exists for the audience which sits and watches. Thus the trick is both real and unreal. This universe is real because man participates in the illusion, but when he reaches Self-Realization, its reality dissolves. In the same way, a dream is real at the time that it occurs but is recognized as unreal upon awakening. Its unreality lies in its impermanence.

The beginning of a dream cannot be fathomed. Its subtle roots lie in the unknown reaches of the past. Even the beginning of the actual experience of dreaming is unknown to the dreamer. Suppose that one were to go to sleep at 11:00, begin dreaming of a Hawaiian vacation at 11:30, and wake up at 12:00, thus ending the dream. While asleep, can anyone know what time his dream begins? It has an infinite past, just as it has an infinite future while it is being dreamed. After awakening, however, one knows that it must have taken place between 11:00 and 12:00. In the waking state, the dreamer knows that the dream had not an infinite past, infinite future, nor reality.

The dream of *Maya* does not begin with one's birth. It weaves through many lifetimes and has an infinite past. Although archaeologists and anthropologists keep pushing back their theories on the dates of man's origin, his past is infinite. In the highest state of consciousness on the path of man's spiritual evolution, there is neither past nor future; time and space are transcended. Such concepts are recognized to be illusory. There is only one eternal now.

There is no real difference between the dream of sleep and the dream of *Maya*. When we identify with the body and mind, they seem real enough; but on reaching the fourth, or highest state of evolution, *turiya,* one realizes that they are not real. Just as darkness disappears in the light of the sun, the illusion of space and time vanish in the light of realization. As long as *Maya* exists as the projection of Brahman, man will be subject to its illusion. While the dream action is taking place, it is impossible to remove the illusion by any action within the dream. One must step outside the dream to see clearly. Likewise, man must learn to step outside of *Maya*. All of man's sufferings stem from identification with the shadow of *Maya*.

It takes light only an instant to remove darkness. Darkness, however, can never remove light. Though ignorance enshrouds man, it can never bring darkness to the Self which remains untouched. Man is eternally the pure Self. Space is always space whether occupied by air, water, earth or any other form of dense matter. It can never be removed, negated or destroyed. So, too, the Self remains the same in all conditions.

True knowledge refers only to the Immortal Self, untouched by causal ignorance. Vedanta uses the analytical method to break the attachment to the five sheaths. By following this method, a highly advanced student will eventually experience the feeling of separation from the sheaths. When the pale of ignorance is thus lifted, he will realize his true identity.

Throughout life, one is conditioned to think of himself in terms of qualifications. The question "Who are you?" may elicit such response as, "I am Fred", "I am the sales manager", or "I am a black man". There is a lifelong process of brainwashing going on in which people think of themselves as rich or poor, tall or short, Prime Minister or bricklayer. They go on endlessly with this charade, becoming more and more limited in their ideas of themselves.

How does one realize identity with the Immortal Self which existed before he was born and will exist after the death of the body? The authority for such knowledge is the scriptures as revealed through the sages and passed on through the instrumentality of a teacher. The classic Vedantic analogy for enlightenment of the deluded human condition is that of "The Snake and the Rope".

A man is walking along a poorly lighted path at dusk when he sees what appears to be a snake and he becomes frightened. When a light is produced, he sees with relief that it is only a rope. The illusion of a snake has disappeared and no further convincing is needed. The moment the Self is realized, ignorance, ego and limiting adjuncts disappear. You know who you are. Illusion disappears in the light of Reality. Nothing can stop a man from eventually reaching this goal. It is his very birthright.

WHO IS THIS "I"?

In all of Vedanta nowhere is it stated that the Self is an object which is to be obtained. One can obtain an external object, but the Self is not an external object. More to the point, how can one obtain what he already has? One Vedantic path to Self-Realization is that of negation — "Neti, Neti", meaning "not this, not that". Everything that can be known is experienced through the senses and the mind, and therefore cannot be the attributeless Brahman. After negation of the sheaths, what is left IS. Just as the idea of a snake is negated from the coiled rope when the light is brought, the non-Self also is negated from the Self which is eternally existing.

That which one must strive hardest to control is the *aham-kara,* or ego. The ego is that quality of the mind which considers itself to be separate from others. It is the ego that creates the illusion that people are entities separate from the rest of reality. This illusion separates one from the Self. Because of its proximity to the Self, the ego appears to be conscious. Hence, the two ideas "I" and "mine" are fabricated causing a false perception of the Self. Identification with the false self causes the ego to emerge. The world when seen as separate from the individual becomes an adversary and an object of exploitation, rather than a harmonious whole. Then various objects are needed to satisfy the ego's voracious appetite.

The Self is the Indweller, and body and mind are its reflections, like the sun reflected in a mirror. A mirror has no inherent light. Reflected light, however, has certain qualities. It can illumine a dark object, blind the eyes and be mistaken for the real sun.

The ego experience is the reflected experience of the Self. If it reflects through the blissful sheath, one is a holy man. If it reflects through the intellectual sheath, one is an Einstein. Reflected in all five sheaths, the ego will manifest strongest in the higher ones. With meditation, these higher sheaths become more developed and tranquility and joy are experienced.

The reflection of a face in a mirror is different from the face itself. It imitates the real face and partakes of the mirror's qualities. It depends on the mirror for its very existence. The real face is not subject to this dependency and therefore differs from the reflection. Similarly the reflection of the Self in the ego is different than the real Self. The individual ego depends on limiting qualities, *upadhis,* but the real Self depends on nothing.

In the case of the reflected face, it is not real, for it is not always there in the mirror. At the same time, it is not totally unreal, as it can sometimes be seen. It is also used at times, such as when combing the hair. By extension, the existence of the ego cannot be denied. Yet by analysis, we know that reflected things are only temporary.

The mirror has an existence independent of the face. The intellect, however, which is the reflecting medium of the pure Self, does not exist independently of and apart from the Self. Therefore, the distinction between pure Self and its reflection is only apparent.

The reflection of the Self in the ego is the individual soul experiencing and acting in this universe. It is sometimes said that the individual soul is a real entity with its own properties, like the shadow of a tree that refreshes those who come into it on a hot day. However, the shadow does not have an existence of its own, for it is merely the result of the leaves blocking the sun's light and heat. Therefore, it is said that the shadow is only the ever-changing result of the sun and the tree's leaves. Pure Self remains unacting, untouched and unchanging. It does not participate in the experiences of existence, birth, death and non-discrimination. A Self-Realized person knows that death and birth are false experiences.

Knowledge of the appearance and disappearance of the mental modifications or changes of the mind rests on the existence of the Self as witness, and that it alone exists after the negation of everything else. If one accepts the idea that the Self is reflected in the individual soul, then it is possible for the intellect to know itself to be Brahman. The intellect, like the body and senses, is not conscious. The knowledge I AM BRAHMAN can be possible only through the agency of reflection.

Ignorance leads us to regard ourselves as individuals suffering transmigratory existence; we are born again and again, and we will die again and again. This idea results from identification with the body, and is only a reflection. Transmigratory existence cannot be predicated on the Self, which is actionless, nor can it be predicated of the ego, which has no real existence. Those who maintain that the Self is the experiencer of transmigratory existence, and is therefore subject to change, mistake the ego to be the Self.

We have all looked into the distorting mirrors of a carnival. Each mirror reflects differently, although we ourselves remain the same. Wars occur because people look into the mirror and cannot agree upon the image. The Self is neither good nor bad, but the *upadhis,* or limiting adjuncts, create the problems of pain, suffering, birth and death. The wheel of birth and death reflects in different egos, and the continuously differing reflections create endless problems.

ADHYAROPA

In reality, the world as we know it was never created. This world is superimposed on Brahman. Understanding of Vedanta is impossible without understanding the principle of superimposition, *adhyaropa. Adhyaropa* means superimposing the idea of the world with all its qualities and pairs of opposites upon the one attributeless Cosmic Existence.

The classic example of superimposition, "The Snake and the Rope," has already been cited. As another example, suppose someone were to visit a friend and discover that he is out but will be returning in half an hour. The person waits outside the house for about half an hour, when he then sees someone approaching. Although it is actually a stranger whom he has never met, he mistakes him for his friend. This is called positive superimposition. On the other hand, assume that the person approaching really is the friend but he is thought to be somebody else. This is called negative superimposition. In both cases, a certain false attribute is superimposed upon the original friend.

Adhyaropa is illusion resulting from ignorance of the real object. It vanishes with the realization that the apparent snake was, in fact, a rope. The snake was not there in the past, is not there in the present, and will not be there in the future. The snake exists only in the imagination. Once enlightenment takes place, the same mistake will not be made again. In the same way, all that one sees as diverse objects and conditions in this world is really Brahman. It was Brahman, alone, in the past, and will remain so in the future.

Dream is a vivid example of superimposition on reality. Mind and the manifest world have power, however, to create illusions far more pervasive and lasting than dreams that occur in sleep. Everyday life is full of illusory transactions. For instance, in getting a bank loan to pay off a mortgage, all sorts of papers are signed by various people. The bank manager lends money that does not exchange hands and is not even seen. It is only a record on a piece of paper somewhere in the bank. The entire transaction is pieces of paper; a paper dream. But at the same time, it seems very real.

One is continually getting in this type of situation. The ordinary man gets completely caught up in it. The Vedantin, or *jnani,* on the other hand, keeps his awareness of the world as illusion and remains unattached as he performs his duties. Jnana Yoga teaches that even though one is dreaming, one can intellectually dissociate from the "world dream" and associate with the Self.

Vedanta leads to the detachment necessary for successful meditation. When there is no detachment, worldly objects and thoughts — the play of *Maya* — intrude in meditation and the aspirant identifies with them rather than with the Self or God. Accepting the world of appearance, he hungers for diverse objects, feels pleasure and pain, undergoes sufferings and tribulations, and is subject to likes and dislikes. But to a *jnani* there is no world at all; he resides in the Self.

Awareness of unity and identity with Brahman may seem hopelessly unattainable, for we are conditioned to think of ourselves as unique individuals. No man stands alone. We are all the body of Brahman. One part of the body is not regarded as different, or better, or more useful than another part. The brain cells are not treated better than the bladder cells. There are trillions of cells in the body, but they are not differentiated. Even though they are actually independent and can function independently in the laboratory test tube, we regard the body as one. In the light of the Supreme Brahman, the whole universe is one body. Individuals are like cells. We think that we are different from the body of Brahman, however, and we cling to the idea of our little independent identities.

The organs of knowledge and action enable man to discern the diverse objects of the world. But when reality is cognized, the world no longer appears real. Brahman, the Self, alone is everywhere. You may dislike your body or anything outside of yourself, but it is impossible to dislike the Self. When everything is seen as the Self, who can be hated? One becomes the embodiment of pure cosmic Love.

Man has been made in the image of God. This does not mean that God has eyes, nose, liver, freckles, pain, death and ignorance. This is man's image, not God's. God is what remains after all such qualifications have been negated. There is a natural limit to the play of loving the body and enjoying the physical world. Real love begins when people are seen, not as individuals, but as the beholder's own Self.

NYAYAS

Because its abstract truths cannot be easily understood by the finite intellect, the philosophy of Vedanta is best taught through practical illustrations. Its main purport is that Brahman alone is real, the whole world of appearance is unreal, and the individual soul is nothing but Brahman Itself. This truth is taught by the following classical analogies, or *nyayas*.

Rajjusarpa Nyaya (Snake and Rope) At night, a man treads upon a rope and mistakes it for a snake. When a light is brought, he sees his error and his fears vanish. This illustrates how qualities of the world are superimposed on Brahman until Realization is reached.

Mrigatrishna Nyaya (Mirage in the Desert) A mirage gives the appearance of water and lures the wanderer to his destruction. Just so, the pleasures of this world appear to be real and lure the *jiva* the individual soul away from the spiritual path. Ultimately, however, the attachment to pleasure brings pain.

Shuktirajata Nyaya (Man and the Post) At dusk, a post is seen in the distance and it is imagined to be a man. Like the "Snake" illustration, this is another example of superimposition. The unreal is superimposed upon the real.

Kanakakundala Nyaya (Gold and Ornament) Although ornaments are of diverse forms, they are gold in essence. Likewise, there are various kinds of pots — big, small, round, narrow — but basically, all of them are only clay. This *nyaya* illustrates that the names and forms of the world are in essence Brahman alone; Brahman appears in all shapes and forms.

Samudrataranga Nyaya (Ocean and Waves) There are countless waves in the ocean, and each can be perceived separately. But all are water, inseparable from the ocean. In reality, they are identical with it. Brahman and the individual souls are the same body.

Sphatikavarna Nyaya (Crystal and Color) Crystal is pure and color-less. Yet, when it is placed near a colored object, it will reflect that color. Brahman is attributeless, but the limiting adjuncts and the reflection of the three qualities of nature, or *gunas,* make it appear to have qualities.

Padmapatra Nyaya (Lotus Leaf) When it rains on the lotus, the drops will gently roll off the leaves and fall to the ground without wetting the leaf. So also, Brahman is the untainted substratum of the world. It is like the movie screen — unaffected by the play of light and shadow upon it.

Vatagandha Nyaya (Wind and Color) Wind carries whatever scent is exposed to it, whether good or bad, but itself is unaffected by it. Although Brahman puts on various names and forms, it is unattached.

Oornabhi Nyaya (Spider and Thread) The spider brings forth its web from its own body, and later reabsorbs it. The thread is nothing but the body of the spider and is one with it. Even so, this world is projected from Brahman, withdrawn into Brahman, and is always one with Brahman.

Surya Bimba Nyaya (Reflection of the Sun) The sun may be reflected in ponds, rivers and puddles, yet there is only one sun. Despite the many reflections of Brahman, there is but one Reality. It appears as many in the form of *Maya.*

Ghatasasha Nyaya (Pot and Space) Space, ether, is unaffected by the walls of a pot which appear to separate the space into "inside" and "outside." But when the pot is broken, what was "inside" and what was "outside" are seen to be the same and have undergone no change at all. The *Atman* may seem limited by the mind and body, but it is one with the Supreme.

Dagdhapata Nyaya (Burned Cloth) If a cloth is burned, its form will remain intact until touched, when it will crumble to ashes. In the same way, the *jnani's* ego is burned in the fire of wisdom; only his body remains.

Arundhati Nyaya (Star) If it is difficult to find a certain star in the heavens, the teacher may point to stars which are brighter and easier to locate. From these, one is guided to look at the star he seeks. Thus the aspirant is first shown Karma Yoga, Bhakti Yoga, Hatha Yoga, etc. These lead him to Self-Realization.

Bija Vriksha Nyaya (Seed and Tree) The seed is the cause of the tree, yet the tree is the cause of the seed. It cannot be said which came first. This illustrates that each statement has a counter-statement, and the world is bound up in relativity.

Markata Kishora Nyaya (Monkey and Baby) A baby monkey will cling to its mother, by its own strength, while she travels about the trees. Even so, an aspirant of Jnana Yoga struggles for himself to attain wisdom. In contrast, the Bhakti Yogi is helpless in his surrender to the Lord, like a kitten dependent upon its mother to pick it up.

Ashma Loshta Nyaya (Stone and Mud) Mud is hard compared to cotton, but soft compared to stone. There is no quality in things by themselves. Qualities exist by virtue of their relativity.

Kakadanta Nyaya (Crow and Teeth) Looking for happiness in this world is like looking for the teeth of a crow, or the son of a barren woman. It is meaningless to question the contradictions and mysteries of existence, for in reality, there is no creation at all.

Dandapoopa Nyaya (Stick and Cakes) In India, cakes, that is, pastry-like breads, are often tied to a stick and carried to the market place. It is said that when many cakes are tied to a stick and the stick disappears, the cakes are missing also. That is to say, that all the doubts and delusions of this world disappear when the world disappears and Self-Realization occurs.

Kshaurikaputra Nyaya (Barber and Son) When asked by the king to find the most beautiful boy in the kingdom, the barber searched in vain until he thought of his own son, who, in reality, was the embodient of ugliness. This illustrates the blinding quality of attachment. Everyone is shut up within his own limited experience.

Visha Krimi Nyaya (Poison and Worms) Worms thrive in poison that would kill a man. One man's cake is another man's poison. This illustrates that good and bad are relative. Sensual pleasures are poison for evolved beings.

Kakataliya Nyaya (Crow and Palm Tree) A crow sat on a palm tree and was killed by a falling coconut. Is the death of the crow attributed to the coconut, or to his being in that place at that time? We each experience the world independently. Experience of this world that is common to all is accidental and has no meaning. Reality is the experience of the undifferentiated Self.

A child might see the sun reflected in a dozen pots of water, and think that he sees a dozen different suns. The reflected suns will have certain qualities, but they are not comparable to the real sun which is many times brighter and more powerful. When the water in the pots dries up, the illusions are gone but the sun still remains.

The Self, like the sun, is reflected in all. The quality of the reflection depends on the purity of the reflecting surface. It is only limited by ignorance, *avidya* of the mind. A person whose reflection is obscured by ignorance might be called a sinner, and one whose reflection is bright could be called a saint. But a Jnana Yogi never forgets that there is no difference between a saint and a sinner, for both are the same unlimited Self.

Jnana Yoga Meditation: Vedantic Practice

Vedanta must enter your bones, nerves, cells and interior chambers of your heart. I do not believe in lip Vedanta. This is pure hypocrisy. Even a little of real practical Vedanta will elevate a man quickly and make him immortal and fearless. I believe in practical Vedanta. I believe in solid spiritual practice. I believe in thorough overhauling of worldly nature and worldliness of all sorts. We should become absolutely fearless. That is the sign of life in Atma. No more words. No more talk. No more arguments, heated debates or discussions. No more study. No more wandering. Live in OM. Live in truth. Enter the silence. There is peace. Peace is silence.

— Swami Sivananda
Sadhana

There are various Vedantic methods for realizing the Self. All are based on the removal of limiting ideas, or *upadhis*, in regard to oneself and the universe. Just as a container creates the illusion that the space inside it is separate and smaller, so the mind creates its own walls, and hence, the illusion of separation from the Self. Removal of the limiting adjuncts is the very core of Vedantic meditation regardless of the mode used. In the practice of Jnana Yoga, one does not merely sit for meditation at a specific time, but one also applies the meditative process throughout the day. In this way, even though participating in the world, the Jnana Yogi is untouched by it.

NETI NETI: NOT THIS, NOT THIS

Neti Neti, meaning "Not this, not this", is the method of Vedantic analysis by negation. It is the keynote of Vedantic inquiry. It is a means of approach. By finding out what a particular subject is not like, one can move towards an understanding of what it is like. Through this process of negation, one can approach an under-

113

standing of real happiness by realizing that it does not lie in wealth, power, fame or any other object of worldly pursuit. Through negation of everything that can be known via the senses, one exhausts the mental modifications and finds the answer within. Ultimately, direct experience is necessary, for it is not a matter of intellectual understanding. When the intellectual resources have been completely drained, the goal is 99.99% reached. The 100% mark is direct intuitive realization.

A man is not his house nor is he his job, for these are subject to change, but the man remains the same. It is useless to identify with clothing or hairstyle, yet all are subject to this form of illusion from time to time. The Self, which is one's essential nature, is neither body nor senses; the body and senses are mere external qualities of the Self. The *Jnani* negates identification with all things of this world which are not *Atman*. He negates the mind by saying, "I am not these desires", "I am not these fears", "I am not this personality", until eventually, all things within worldly experience are negated. Finally, worldly experiences are transcended for all has been negated and nothing remains but the Self.

In this kind of meditation, union with the Absolute is achieved by denial of body, mind, name, form, intellect, senses and all limiting adjuncts. The true "I" remains, which is *Sat-Chit-Ananda,* or Absolute Existence-Knowledge-Bliss. Meditate with full concentration, bringing the mind back when it wanders to externals. They are not the *Atman* or Self. Eventually the mind will become steady and will rest in thoughless, motionless state of pure Bliss.

SAKSHI BHAV: WITNESS STATE

The *Sakshi Bhav* method is the witnessing approach. One observes the play of life as though he were watching a movie but, again, does not identify with it. Whatever situations the aspirant experiences, his reaction is, "I am not involved in this; I am only watching it happen". It entails introspection and close awareness of the mental waves. The mind does not want to be watched and will soon slow down its activities, but it does not give up without struggle. In many ways it will deceive and persuade one to stop watching it. It is such a powerful force that it is capable of dragging the attention wherever it goes, unless extreme vigilance is practiced. Many, many times it will divert the attention from its focus. One must observe this with patience, then firmly return to the witness state, taking care not to fight the mind but only to gently guide it. With the repetition of *OM sakshi aham* (I am witness of all my actions), and continual disassociation from those actions, the individual ego eventually vanishes.

ABHEDA BODHA VAKYA: ELIMINATING NAME AND FORM

This method recognizes that every sentient being and insentient object in the universe has five components — name, form, existence, knowledge and bliss. All things, whether animal, vegetable, or mineral, have these attributes, but it is the names and forms that seem to differentiate them and set one thing apart from another. Name and form are impermanent and illusory, while existence, knowledge and bliss are permanent. Matter is the visible manifestation of spirit, and inseparable from it, but through the meditative technique of *Abheda Bhoda Vakya,* name and form are discarded. Only man has the vehicle to realize that what remains is Existence-Knowledge-Bliss, or *Sat-Chit-Anada,* the eternal "I" which continues through many changes of name and form.

When parts of the body are damaged, such as eyes, heart, kidneys, liver and blood, they may be replaced with spare parts from other beings. What then becomes of the body's identity? What becomes of the individual's identity? The consciousness of "I" remains constant and cannot be taken from anything animate or inanimate. A tree may be destroyed to become a plank, or gold may become a ring, but only the name and form have changed. By identifying with the underlying, attributeless essence of all objects of the universe, the final stage of meditation is reached.

LAYA CHINTANA: ABSORPTION

The *Laya Chintana* method is one of involution or absorption. In this system, effect is absorbed into cause. Each cause is the effect of its preceding cause, so this process continues progressively. There are three avenues of this approach. First, one concentrates on merging into the understanding, *buddhi,* which is then merged into the unmanifest universe, *avyaktam,* that state where the three qualities of nature *(sattwa, rajas, tamas)* are in equilibrium. Finally *avyaktam* is merged into the Supreme Imperishable Brahman. In the second approach, the elements of the world merge with each other, starting with the grossest and proceeding to the subtlest. This is the reverse of the process by which the earth was formed, where a mass of swirling gasses gradually cooled and condensed to a solid planet. The focus is on manifestation of the five traditional elements: earth, water, fire, air and ether. Earth is merged into its cause, water; water is merged into its cause, fire; air, which is the cause of fire, absorbs the fire and, in turn, is absorbed into ether. The ether is absorbed into the unmanifest, *avyaktam,* and that finally merges with Brahman. In the third path, the microcosm merges with the macrocosm. The individual merges with the universe; in other words, the *jiva,* soul, merges with Brahman. Thus all external attributes are gradually merged into their Source.

There are no qualities in the universe that are not in the human body. An atom is a complete replica of the solar system, with electrons encircling a nucleus just as planets revolve around the sun. The atom is a microcosm and everything that is happening in the microcosm of the human body is also occurring in the earth and in the universe. Individual cosmic creation and destruction are taking place all of the time. Instead of identifying with the individual self, which is only a tiny fraction of the universal scheme, one can find his larger identity by merging with the Cosmos itself. It is matter in its most subtle state. Before the sun and earth came into existence, they were gas molecules, and before evolving into the molecular state, they existed in the etheric or energy state.

The water molecule is composed of the atoms of hydrogen and oxygen. When atoms were smashed in the cyclotron, it was discovered that this was not the end of matter. Regardless to what extent scientists subdivide atoms, they continue to find smaller and smaller particles. If the earth and sun were suddenly blown to pieces, the matter would revert to ether. Ultimately it would return to the Supreme Mind, compared to which ether itself is gross. Mind is the last reduction of matter to its original source, Brahman. As such, it is the source of ether, which evolves into air or gas, and then condenses into fire, water and earth. It can evolve no further than that. Gross matter is thus the last stage of Cosmic Mind's evolution. On this gross level, mind becomes physical nature.

In its most dense manifestation, as gross matter, mind exhibits the least amount of consciousness. It is too far away from its Source to express itself. Take for instance a rock. It contains the potential for infinite energy and power, but unless put to intelligent use, it remains inanimate. The further matter moves from its Source towards gross evolution, the more limited is its effect.

A close look at these elements which we take for granted leaves one in awe of the guiding Cosmic Intelligence. Water, for instance, is made up of two hydrogen atoms and one oxygen atom. When hydrogen by itself comes into contact with fire, it reacts with an explosion. Oxygen reacts with fire to make it burn more fiercely. Yet in combination, as water, they will quench fire and cool the body. What is the source of this intricate engineering? Only an intelligent power is capable of such creation.

All life is interconnected. Animals breathe in oxygen, the by-product of plants, and exhale carbon dioxide. In their bodies the oxygen combines with glucose to produce energy for the various bodily functions. Plants take in carbon dioxide and release oxygen into the air which is then used by animals. They take nutrients from the soil and use the sunlight for photosynthesis. Man eats the plants for nourishment and when he dies, his body is returned to earth where it becomes food for the plants. This is but one small example of the complicated and interdependent relationships that exist among all things. It hardly seems possible that such a world could have been created by an accident of nature.

Relationships like this exist throughout the cosmos. Consider the size of the universe. It is impossible that these miracles occur only on earth. How many suns with planets can there be in our galaxy, and how many galaxies can there be? How large is this universe? Its size cannot be imagined, nor can the number of planets capable of supporting life be counted.

There are physical laws which cause the planets to rotate and to revolve around the sun in certain, precise ways. These same laws cause whole solar systems, indeed even galaxies, to hurtle through space at tremendous speeds — all in perfect coordination. These laws cannot have accidentally come about without an originating cause. Only a guiding intelligence could be responsible.

PANCHIKARANA: DOCTRINE OF QUINTUPLICATION

Allied to *Laya Chintana,* which is meditation by thinking rather than stilling the thought waves, is the Doctrine of Quintuplication. It further develops the concept of absorption of the gross into the more etheric by breaking down the components of the body and its functions into the five basic elements called *tanmatras.* When it is seen that these are not Brahman, they may be either absorbed into each other as in *Laya Chintana* or discarded by negation as in *Neti Neti.* In either case, one arrives at the Self, which is beyond them all. To this end, the Doctrine of Quintuplication is applied.

According to this ancient theory, owing to ignorance one

identifies with the physical body which is made up of five basic, pure elements: *akasha,* ether; *vayu,* air; *agni,* fire; *apas,* water; and *prithivi,* earth. These undergo permutations and combine with each other in definite proportions. This is called quintuplication. Thus it is said that wherever there is hardness in the body, it is due to the portion of earth; wherever there is fluidity, it is due to the portion of water. Body warmth is due to the portion of fire, and movement, to air. The quality of space found in the body is attributed to the ether. These differentiations are also the basis of *ayurvedic* medicine.

The three most gross elements, earth, water and fire, can be easily experienced by the five senses. Although air cannot be seen, it can be sensed indirectly through smell and hearing, and directly through touch. Ether has two meanings, one of which denotes the sky. When used as an element, however, it signifies primordial energy, or the primordial cloud.

In the process of Creation, primordial energy came first, then matter on a subtle level, and then the world as we know it now. Behind it all is *Shakti,* the cosmic energy. It is also known as *Maya,* that power which is both veiling and projecting, for it veils the knowledge of Brahman and projects the illusion of this universe. Drawing energy from the Source, *Shakti* forms the various elements, resting only after reaching the grossest form.

In their subtle or pure form, the five basic elements combine in definite proportions to form gross elements. It is these gross elements upon which the existence of the earth depends. While this traditional Vedantic view may not seem to correspond exactly with modern science, by following the essence of the thought behind it, one gains insight into the intricate relationship between matter and spirit. According to the Doctrine of Quintuplication, each gross element is made up of one half of its corresponding pure element and one eighth of each of the four other subtle elements. An exam-

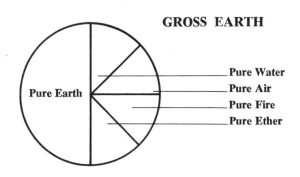

GROSS EARTH

Pure Earth

Pure Water
Pure Air
Pure Fire
Pure Ether

ple of this can be seen clearly in the chart for gross earth in which the earth is composed of one half subtle earth and one eighth each of subtle ether, subtle air, subtle water and subtle fire.

It can be seen that each element, when quintuplicated, is not pure, but contains a portion of each of the other elements. Each quintuplicated element produces a special effect according to its predominance. Each contains qualities of the others, and has a particular function in nature and in man.

Further, each of these elements has five properties. These properties are based upon the interaction of the subtle elements within the gross elements, and total twenty-five in number.

QUINTUPLICATED ELEMENTS

GROSS ELEMENTS	SUBTLE ELEMENTS				
	1/8 Ether	1/8 Air	1/8 Fire	1/8 Water	1/8 Earth
ETHER	Grief	Desire	Anger	Delusion	Fear
AIR	Running	Bending	Walking	Expansion	Contraction
FIRE	Hunger	Thirst	Laziness	Sleep	Luster
EARTH	Semen	Blood	Saliva	Urine	Sweat
WATER	Bone	Flesh	Skin	Arteries	Hair

In order to better understand this portion of the theory, let us examine the properties associated with quintuplicated ether. The five properties of ether are grief, desire, anger, delusion and fear, which are all generated in the ether which belongs to the space of the heart. Grief is the chief part of ether for with grieving the body feels empty like space. Desire is fleeting like the wind, therefore it belongs to that part of air found in ether. When anger arises, the body becomes hot. Anger belongs to that part of fire found in quintuplicated ether. Delusion is as pervasive as water and belongs to that portion of water found in ether. Finally, when we are frozen with fear, the body becomes inanimate and statue-like; thus, fear belongs to the earth principle. The remaining twenty properties can be understood in a similar manner.

Although the emotions are actually attributes of the astral body, they are treated as if they belonged to the physical body for this is where their influences are directly perceptible. Because the emotions belong to the ether portion of the quintuplicated elements, they cannot be the Self. They are negated and identification with them is not possible. "I am not these emotions. I am not this body. I am not these actions. I am the Self." The Jnana Yogi abandons the idea of I-ness and my-ness and identifies with the imperishable *Atman,* which is entirely different from the five elements. He is the knower, seer and witness of all these products.

The physical body is reduced to nothing as it is analyzed and all temporary qualities are removed. It is merely a product of the five elements and their twenty-five combinations. Modern scientists and doctors only understand the gross attributes of the body. The five elements and twenty-five properties are mere limiting adjuncts. When the body is stripped of them, that which remains is the Self.

Jnana Yoga teaches the aspirant not to identify with these quintuplicated elements that make up the five sheaths. The body is a fictitious play of illusion and ignorance *(Maya* and *avidya).* Attachment to it is bondage. By negating the ideas of possessiveness and attachment to its illusory qualities, one can achieve emancipation.

MAHAVAKYAS or THE GREAT PROCLAMATIONS

Where there is true knowledge, knowledge of the immortal Self, there is no trace of causal ignorance. The scriptures, the *Vedas* and the *Upanishads* exist to impart knowledge to humanity. Scriptural declarations can be grouped under three heads: injunctions, prohibitions, and proclamations of the highest truth.

The first two, injunctions and prohibitions, give the aspirant a glimpse of the Truth and raise him to the proper level of understanding and receptivity. They are similar to the *yamas* and *niyamas* of Raja Yoga or the Ten Commandments in that they give basic spiritual instruction. The third, the proclamations, is a set of four Upanishadic statements which express the highest truth of the identity between the individual soul and the supreme Soul. They are only for those who have purified their minds and are capable of sublime understanding. They are known as the *Mahavakyas.* Understanding them enables the individual soul to identify with the Supreme Soul. There are four *Mahavakyas,* one contained in each of the four *Vedas.* They are:

1. *PRAJNANAM BRAHMA* (Consciousness is Brahman) — The nature of Brahman is existence, or absolute knowledge, or cosmic consciousness.
2. *AHAM BRAHMA ASMI* (I am Brahman) — This is the idea on which the aspirant fixes his mind during meditation. Identifica-

tion is with the Supreme, not with limiting adjuncts.
3. *TAT TWAM ASI* (That Thou Art) — *Tat* represents Brahman, *Twam* is the individual, and *Asi* is union. This is the *Mahavakya* through which the teacher instructs the spiritual aspirant.
4. *AYAM ATMA BRAHMAN* (This Self is Brahman) — This expresses the inner intuitive experience of the meditator.

Of these four declarations, *TAT TWAM ASI* is the most important. The guru initiates the disciple into the knowledge of Brahman through this declaration, for it is the one that gives rise to the other three. The disciple reflects and meditates on it, and eventually experiences *samadhi,* or superconscious state. He is then able to give expression to the other three statements.

The words *Tat Twam Asi* must be dissected carefully, for they are pregnant with meaning. They can be repeated to different people and interpreted in different ways depending of the person's evolution. When right understanding is reached, the aspirant is better able to disown all actions, reactions and attributes. He can lead a worry-free life.

To begin with, one must have a basic understanding of the relationships of the Absolute, the world and the individual. Brahman, the unmanifest Absolute, projects Itself as *Prakriti,* the world as we know it. *Prakriti* is made up of the three qualities of nature: purity, activity, and inertia *(sattwa, rajas* and *tamas).* In turn, it manifests into two aspects as *Maya,* the phenomenal world, and *avidya,* identification with the individual self.

In the phenomenal world, Brahman reflects through *sattwa,* purity, as *Maya,* and it is called *Ishwara. Ishwara is* a name meaning God with qualities, God with attributes. *Ishwara* has full control over the world, and can appear as Jesus, Rama, Siva, and the Holy Mother. *Ishwara* appears as any aspect of divinity to which one relates in a personal sense. In its other projection, *Prakriti's* natural purity is adulterated and overbalanced by the qualities of action and inertia *(rajas* and *tamas).* These produce the impure state of ignorance, *avidya.* Brahman reflecting through it results in individual souls who are colored by the same ignorance.

As both are reflections of the same unqualified Brahman, there is no basic difference between *Ishwara* and the individual soul, or *jiva.* However, the clarity of the reflection differs. When a clean mirror and a dirty mirror are placed in the sun, more light reflects from the clean mirror. The amount of Divine Reflection that a being projects depends upon his degree of purity.

The only real distinction is that *Ishwara* has full control over *Maya,* while the individual is caught in the web of *Maya.* Just as a spider weaves a web for itself, Brahman has projected the world. The spider can move anywhere within the web and is not affected by the threads of its own creation. When a fly gets caught in it however, it becomes entangled. We are like flies caught in the web of *Maya.*

Like the spider, *Ishwara* can move in his own creation on any level and in any manifestation. He can be incarnated on any plane and can withdraw the incarnation. As Vishnu, Rama and other *avatars, Ishwara's* manifestations remain unaffected by *Maya.* In such stories as the *Ramayana* in which Rama is shown as experiencing emotions, God has had human traits and responses superimposed upon Him. He is not really subject to human emotions, however. Just as the spider must follow its own threads, Rama cannot interfere with the karmic laws of his own creation. The game must be played out.

To sum up, when Brahman reflects through *Maya* the reflected consciousness is called *Ishwara* and it controls the universe. Reflected through *avidya,* the consciousness is the individual soul. No matter what the name, Brahman is One, just as milk is milk whether produced by a French, German or Indian cow. The brand name and the container are irrelevant. *Maya* is the container inside of which is only one *Ishwara.* The reason one is unable to feel THOU ART THAT is because his reflection is tarnished by the veil of ignorance.

When Christ said, "I and my father are One," He was in effect saying, "Aham Brahma Asmi," "I am Brahman." Moses had the same revelation with the burning bush: *"Jahweh* — I am that I am." "I and my Father are One" could be added to the *Mahavakyas.* Jesus was a highly developed Jnana Yogi, but he was crucified because his contemporaries could not understand his statements. If He were to appear today, He would still be crucified. People look for a Messiah who fits their own preconceptions. They are not interested in proclamations of truth.

Avidya, ignorance, is the cause of conflict. Why do Protestants and Catholics fight in Ireland? They are not fighting for God, because God already exists. Why do Hindus and Muslims fight? Ignorance is responsible for all misunderstanding and dissention. Only true spiritual aspirants can transcend it by long, hard discipline and practice.

Because of ignorance, the common man could not understand when Christ said, "The Truth shall make you free". Jesus was a highly advanced *Adwaita Vedantin,* however He used Bhakti Yoga (i.e. the Path of Devotion) to encourage worship of the Father, and a little Raja Yoga in the form of *yamas* and *niyamas.* He could not take them beyond that even though He had the highest knowledge. Vedanta was never meant for the masses. When Jesus said, "I and my Father are One," He meant *Aham Brahma Asmi* — I am Brahman — eliminating body, name and external qualifications. The disciples assumed that these words applied only to Christ and not to themselves. Jesus did not find a single person who actually understood his meaning.

BHAGATYAGA LAKSHANA

The *Bhagatyaga Lakshana* method of Jnana Yoga explains the proclamation *TAT TWAM ASI,* That Thou Art. In Vedanta, the word *Tat* represents unqualified Brahman and *Twam,* the individual soul; *Asi* represents union. Meditation on these words is a process of dehypnotization. One negates all of the qualifications and attributes that limit the individual soul which is then realized as Brahman.

To explain in more detail, the meaning of a word or phrase can be approached in three ways:

1. *Vachyartha* — Primary meaning, conveyed directly by the word
2. *Lakshyartha* — Implied meaning
3. *Vyangyartha* — Suggested meaning, hinted at by the words associations.

A word and its meaning are linked by a *vritti,* mind wave. When the word "fire" is pronounced the corresponding mind wave is energized and there is visualization of the concept. The reverse also takes place. When one sees a fire, the mental image gives rise to the corresponding verbal utterance, "Fire." This relationship between word and meaning can be simple or complex. It is simple when it generates the word's primary meaning. "The sun is hot," is an example of *Vachyartha,* for "hot" is directly related to "sun." If a child is asked to draw a leaf, he copies it from nature, but an artist will draw it indirectly. Similarly, *Lakshyartha* is based on an indirect relationship between word and meaning. In the statement, "It is hot today", the implied meaning is that the sun is hot. Indirect relationships between word and meaning fall into three categories: *Jahallakshana, Ajahallakshana* and *Jahadajahallakshana.*

When the direct meaning of a word is dispensed with and only the implied meaning is taken into account, it is called *Jahallakshana*. The statement, "The house is on the river" does not mean that there is a house on the surface of the river, but on the bank of the river. The direct meaning of a flowing river is discarded and the implied meaning "on the bank" is substituted. Although the river and its bank are quite different things, one being water and the other earth, there is a spatial proximity which creates a relationship. The implied meaning is based on the direct meaning, which is then discarded.

In the *Ajahallakshana* category, both the direct and implied meanings are operative. Imagine a man is at a horse show and asks, "Which horse is jumping?" He might receive the reply, "The white is jumping". A color cannot jump, but in this case, the direct meaning "white" refers to the implied meaning "horse", both of which are relevant to the sentence. The whole is understood to mean, "The white horse is jumping".

Jahadajahallakshana, the third category, is also known as *Bhagatyaga Lakshana*. Here a portion of the direct meaning is retained and a portion is discarded. Assume that ten years ago a certain Dr. Smith lived in New York City and was last seen by a friend at the opera. Now imagine that this same friend sees him, ten years later, as a derelict on Skid Row in San Francisco. He exclaims, "This is that same Dr. Smith". There is a certain discrepancy in this statement for the word "this" refers to the Dr. Smith that is seen here and now, associated with the idea of a derelict in rags in San Francisco. But the word "that" refers to the Dr. Smith known before. It is associated with the idea of a successful professional man, dressed in a tuxedo and separated in time and space by ten years and three thousand miles.

Certain elements are contradictory and must be eliminated. A successful doctor is not an unemployed derelict. San Francisco is not New York and Skid Row is not the Metropolitan Opera House. Also, the period of ten years cannot be equated with the time at which the statement was made.

In the statement, "This is that same Dr. Smith" only a portion of the direct meaning of "this" and "that" is retained. The contradictory factors of time, space and external appearances are eliminated while Dr. Smith himself, the person, remains. It is only the idea of a Dr. Smith free of impermanent qualities which is noncontradictory. Only after the mind has gone through this complicated process — which it does in a flash — can "this Dr. Smith" be identified with "that Dr. Smith". After the opposing associations of name and form have been set aside, THIS IS THAT remains. Dr. Smith, the person common to both, stands as the implied meaning.

Tat Twam Asi can be understood only in light of this kind of reasoning. "That Thou Art" does not refer to the direct meaning of the body. It asserts that each individual soul is in reality the Supreme Absolute. Such impermanent qualities as body, color, sex and religion are eliminated. Although we may now be in the garb of human beings, before being incarnated here in earth, each existed in the Brahmic state. *Tat,* That, refers to pure consciousness or Brahman; *Twam,* Thou, refers to reflected consciousness in ignorance, or the individual soul; *Asi,* Art, proclaims their unity, which alone exists, for all are projections of Brahman.

Thus, *avidya,* leads the individual soul, *jiva,* to identify with his intellect, emotions and physical body, creating activity, suffering and pain. The *upadhis* give the appearance of individualization and separation, but there is only one Brahman. In identifying with the various sheaths of the individual being, we fail to realize our true nature. An Olympic champion identifies with the physical sheath; a politician with the vital sheath; someone in love, with the emotional sheath; a college professor, with the intellectual sheath. One who is happy and pure all the time identifies with the bliss sheath. Who is closest to Self-Realization? None of them for they are all prisoners; they are all at a distance. Even goodness is binding, for the bliss sheath is an *upadhi* as are all the others. Chains may be made of gold or of iron, nonetheless they are chains.

Once Indra, king of the Gods, and Virochana, king of the demons, approached Prajapati, the Creator, to learn knowledge of the Self. After thirty-two years of rigorous discipleship, they were told to look at themselves in a looking glass and report what they saw. After doing so, they replied, "We see ourselves as we are." Prajapati then asked them to put on their best clothes and to look again. On hearing the same reply, he told them, "That is the immortal Self."

Virochana, satisfied, preached to his followers that the body alone is to be worshipped. Indra, however, was unconvinced that the body is the Self. After a second period of thirty-two years' discipleship he decided that the dreaming self is the true Self. Still dissatisfied however, he underwent an austerity program of one hundred and one years, and learned that the real Self is above all individualistic implications.

Like Virochana, most people misunderstand the body to be the Self. They cannot understand TAT TWAM ASI, because they lack the patience to consider deeply the significance of the words. Words are double-edged weapons. If misunderstood, they will be detrimental to one's progress; properly understood, they can carry one across the abyss of ignorance. The significance of TAT TWAM ASI can be grasped only after long, detailed and careful consideration. Then it will be apparent that if man was made in God's image, it does not mean that God resembles a human being. Rather, one must look into man and realize the God nature enshrined therein.

Bhakti Yoga Meditation

True religion does not consist in ritualistic observances, baths and pilgrimages, but in loving all. Cosmic love is all-embracing and all-inclusive. In the presence of pure love all distinctions and differences as well as all hatred, jealousy and egoism are dispelled just as darkness is dispelled by the penetrating rays of the morning sun. There is no religion higher than love. There is no knowledge higher than love. There is no treasure higher than love because love is truth, love is God.

— Swami Sivananda
Practical Lessons In Yoga

Bhakti Yoga is the path of devotion. While Jnana Yoga appeals to the intellectual, and Raja Yoga to the rational and scientific mind, Bhakti Yoga comes naturally to those who are predominantly emotional in temperament. Stemming from the innate and unselfish drive toward Unity, it is the most direct way to God-Realization. It is the approach of pure love, which is poured upon the chosen deity, or aspect of God. The path of Bhakti Yoga is essentially the same as that of the Christian tradition. Through placing all his concentration on God, the devotee endeavors to increase his remembrance of and communion with the Lord. With faith, prayer and self-surrender he attains direct perception of his Ideal. When merging takes place and Oneness alone remains, the goal is reached.

CONVERTING THE EMOTIONS

Emotions have no place in other paths of Yoga, and, because they are bound up with attachment, they are rigorously uprooted. However, the Bhakti converts the emotions into unconditional love for God, which is neither binding nor selfish. The emotions, when channeled properly, can be used to attain liberation.

127

The practice of Bhakti Yoga transmutes the lower emotions into devotion. Emotion is weakness, and must not be equated with divine love, which manifests as peace and joy. The lower emotions are not suppressed, however, but are utilized and sublimated. Without emotion there is no love, and without love one cannot approach that infinite Love that is God. Through the higher emotions the devotee reaches out to the Divine. His practice is carried out by both formal worship and by seeing the Lord in all names and forms at all times. With purification the receptive heart receives the continual flow of divine love.

The barrier between the individual soul and the Supreme Soul is the ego, the ever present enemy. It manifests as a feeling of separateness. Bhakti does away with this feeling of separation, for in the ecstasy of pure love and devotion, the consciousness of the individual self is lost. With the surrender of the ego, the individual becomes an instrument in the hands of God. This state is beautifully symbolized by the image of Krishna playing the flute. Just as the flute is a hollow instrument through which the breath of God moves, so the individual must empty himself of all egoism, to enable the Lord to act fully through him. He takes neither credit nor blame for his actions, for God does the action. The devotee thinks of nothing but God. The Lord is his constant thought wave, and fills every mental space. He is the consummation of everything; hence everything is to be worshipped.

God is experienced by each individual in his own way. This idea is strikingly illustrated in the *Srimad Bhagavatam,* in which Krishna assumes as many forms of himself as there are cowherd women, his disciples, and manifests to shower love on each individually. Their yearning for him lies in their knowledge that he is the Lord, and their fulfillment is the fulfillment of divine love. While immersed in the bliss of dancing with him, they experience *samprajnata samadhi,* in which there is still awareness of duality. This gives way to *asamprajnata samadhi,* the highest superconscious state, when they become one with him. However, Krishna separated himself from them when their egoism made them feel that they had ensnared and could control him. A true spiritual master treats his devotees in the same way, relating to each individually, but withdrawing temporarily when pride and egoism infect the disciple.

Control of the mind and annihilation of the ego are the essence of all yogic disciplines, including Bhakti Yoga. Even on this essentially emotional path, the intellect must not be neglected.

If it is disregarded, Bhakti Yoga can degenerate into fanaticism. If, on the other hand, it is transcended, the devotes experiences *para-bhakti,* the highest state of supreme devotional ecstasy.

Ashrams and solitude are not necessary for the Bhakti Yogi. The mental attitude alone is important. This attitude of devotion is also necessary for progress on the paths of Yoga. Even the intellectual approach of Jnana Yoga needs the element of *bhakti* for success in attaining God's grace.

Those who turn to Bhakti Yoga are moved by one of four general motivations. Distress can be a powerful factor. When all else has failed, there is no recourse left but to turn to God. How many soldiers in battle and people burdered by extreme sorrow have found God as their final refuge? Curiosity is another impetus. Looking beyond the external trappings of worship, the mind seeks to understand what lies behind the symbolism, words and rituals, and pushes on to the other shore. A third motive is desire for gain, whether it be of love, knowledge or wealth, etc. God is petitioned as the benevolent father who will grant favors if approached with faith and devotion. The highest *bhakti* is selfless. The motivation is the simple desire to love and serve God. Only with this attitude will the ego disappear. One cannot attain liberation until all desires, including spiritual desire itself, have been burned.

The Bhakti Yogi makes use of gross forms and rituals as aids to self-surrender. Altars, statues, pictures, etc., are not in themselves objects of worship. Like the Christian cross, which stands for Jesus, they are all symbols. The omnipresent Lord is as present in the image as anywhere else. The image is merely used as a focal point for worship of God.

FORMS OF DEVOTION

Indian tradition recognizes nine forms of worship in the practice of Bhakti Yoga. From the simple to the more difficult, they are:

1. *Sravanam* — Listening to stories of the Lord's *lila,* or play. Book knowledge is not sufficient. The stories must be imparted by inspired teachers and wise men.
2. *Kirtanam* — Singing of God's glories. Christian hymns also fall into this category.
3. *Smaranam* — Remembrance of His name and presence, in mental attitude and unceasing prayer.
4. *Padasevanam* — Service at the Lord's feet. The world is seen

as God's feet; and in serving humanity one mentally is offering worship to His feet.

5. *Archanam* — Worship of God through such rituals as puja. One offers himself to the Lord, thus breaking the ego.
6. *Vandanam* — Prostration to the Lord, with full awareness of His presence in all names and forms. This develops humility.
7. *Dasyam* — Cultivation of the feeling of being a servant of God.
8. *Sakhyam* — Cultivation of feeling friendship toward the Lord, thus establishing a personal relationship.
9. *Atmanivedanam* — Complete surrender of self. This is the equivalent of *asamprajnata samadhi,* the seedless state in which there is complete acceptance and surrender, and no duality.

Practice of the lower stages, such as listening to stories, is relatively easy. It keeps the mind centered on the Almighty, creating positive thought waves and a receptive mind. Even those who are intellectually oriented derive benefit from the stories and chanting, if they will open their hearts as well as their minds. When the devotee has been prepared by the earlier stages of worship, he can attempt the more difficult higher stages.

In any case, the *bhava,* or devotional feeling, of the devotee is of extreme importance. Accommodating the various temperaments of people, there are five different ways of relating to God:

1. *Shanta* — This pure feeling of peace is devoid of desire, ignorance and emotion. Its presence is not externally apparent. This is the devotional attitude of the Jnana Yogi.
2. *Dasya* — The devotee regards himself as the servant of God, whom he sees in everything but himself. He sees himself as inferior to the rest of humanity. Humbly placing himself in God's hands, he takes delight in service to all. Hanuman, the monkey chieftain of the *Ramayana,* who dedicated his life to the service of Rama, exemplifies this relationship.
3. *Sakhya* — God is regarded as a spiritual friend, to whom one can turn for advice, comfort and companionship. One becomes unable to live without His company. Arjuna's relationship with Krishna, as set forth in the *Bhagavad Gita,* is of this nature.
4. *Vatsalya* — The relationship is that. of parent and child, with God being viewed as a Divine Child. It is exemplified by Yashoda's relationship with the baby Krishna.

5. *Mathurya* — This is the feeling of the lover toward the beloved. It is pure love, untinged by lust, and is difficult to develop. Encompassing a pure desire to touch and embrace His physical and astral form, this method is encountered frequently in the poetry and writings of the Sufi and Christian mystics. In Yoga it is symbolized by the union of Siva and Shakti in the *sahasrara chakra* at the crown of the head. This is the highest type of devotional feeling.

There is one more *bhava,* which remains outside the pale of normal relationships. It is not deliberately cultivated as a path to God, nor is it easy to maintain. This is the feeling of extreme hatred toward God. When one is in constant remembrance of Him, even with hatred, the mind becomes one-pointed and fixed. Through this concentration one is redeemed, for evil always falls before goodness. Various demons of Hindu mythology, such as Kamsa and Ravana, achieved salvation in this manner.

According to classical tradition, the human being experiences fourteen different states of consciousness: physical, astral, mental, supramental, superconscious, unconscious, subconscious, dream, supracosmic, dual, multiple, *virat* (God as Cosmos), divine and absolute. The practice of Bhakti Yoga can lead the aspirant through any or all of them. The devotee is particularly subject to visions, lights in the forehead and other manifestations of psychic phenomena. These experiences can be frightening, particularly the loss of physical consciousness, which may feel like dying. However, the aspirant must not be faint-hearted, nor should he cling to these experiences, which will appear and reappear for brief periods at the beginning of serious spiritual progress. With persistent and regular practice, one goes beyond these phenomena to meditation, peace and bliss. One must struggle to reach meditation, and struggle even harder to reach *samadhi,* the superconscious state.

In all religions Truth becomes diluted by and for the masses. It becomes an external object to be sought after, rather than an inner state of consciousness, which is its true nature. The essential attitude to be taken in any religion is one of taking refuge, of confession, prayer, and ultimate surrender to a higher power. It is this inner state of consciousness that Bhakti Yoga nurtures. Without its presence, all other paths of Yoga and any true spiritual progress will fall short of the mark.

Raja Yoga Sutras: Theory

*There is something beyond the mind. That is the Self,
Consciousness. Psychoanalysis should be combined with Raja Yoga.
We must not only have a thorough knowledge of the Western
science of psychology, but combine it with Raja Yoga and
spirituality also. Psychologists should have a perfect knowledge of
Patanjali's Raja Yoga. They will be better able to understand the
workings of the mind. Then, they will be able to do more service
to the world.*

— Swami Sivananda
Conquest of the Mind

Raja Yoga, the royal path of mind control, is the most comprehensive and scientific approach to God-Realization. The pre-
cepts and doctrines of this ancient science were first compiled and
explained by Patanjali Maharishi, the greatest psychologist of all
time. Never has man's mind been so completely analyzed. Never
has a process for eliminating human woes and frailties been so
succinctly presented. The methods of Raja Yoga are profoundly
timeless. Though of ancient origin, they are still the most useful
technique available to modern man beset by the tremendous
stresses and strains of competitive society. The eight limbs of Raja
Yoga have been described in the chapter "Concentration: Practice."
They may be practiced by anyone regardless of religious or philosophical persuasion.

Raja Yoga, as a system for probing the mind, is not one to
be practiced by one person on another. It is a method of self-
inquiry that takes the individual through personal changes, step by
step. Its essence was written down by Patanjali about 2000 years
ago. He wrote in a simple and lyrical style, so that the *sutras,* or
aphorisms, could be easily understood and committed to memory.
The philosophy is contained in four chapters. The first chapter
deals with the general theory of Yoga, how the mind functions,
and the various levels of *samadhi,* the superconscious state.

CHAPTER ONE: THE ROAD TO SAMADHI

1. अथ योगानुशासनम् ।

Atha yoganusasanam

Now Yoga is explained.

The word *Yoga* means union. It refers to the process of uniting the individual with the Universal Soul. It brings about that state of mind which is unruffled and calm in all situations.

2. योगश्चित्तवृत्तिनिरोधः ।

Yogas chitta-vrtti-nirodhah

Yoga is restraining the activities of the mind.

The mind is neither visible nor tangible. It exists not in the physical body, as does the brain, but in the astral body. Its magnitude cannot be measured, for it carries all feelings, ideas and impressions from this life and all previous lives, as well as intuitive knowledge of what is to come. It is the mind, and nothing else, that must be corralled and controlled in order to achieve the true peace of Union.

The Sanskrit word *chitta* translates as mind-stuff, or mental substance. It is, in a sense, the ground floor of the mind. In Vedanta philosophy, it is referred to as *antahkarana,* which means inner instrument. The *antahkarana* contains four main elements. The *manas,* mind, engages in thinking, doubting and willing. The *buddhi* is the intellect, and it performs the functions of discriminating and making decisions. That portion of the mind which is self-arrogating and sees itself as separate from the Source is the *ahamkara,* ego. Finally, there is the subconscious, which serves as a storehouse of past experiences and memory; this is also called the *chitta.*

As can be seen, the word *chitta* has several meanings. While in Vedanta philosophy it refers specifically to the subconscious, Patanjali uses *chitta* in a broader sense: it refers to that underlying substratum, the very foundation that makes up one's mental apparatus. The *chitta* may manifest in one of five forms, at any given time. These are: 1) *kshipta,* scattering; 2) *mudha,* darkening, dull; 3) *vikshipta,* gathering, centering; 4) *ekagrata,* one-pointed, concentrated; 5) *niruddha,* absolute suspension of activity.

The *kshipta,* scattering, form is activity, and tends to be experienced as pleasure or pain. The mind acts to justify its desires, and does not care about consequences. It thinks of a frankfurter, and must have one. When warned of the poisons it contains, the reaction is to cover the frankfurter with more mustard and eat it anyway. In the *mudha* state of mind, the tendency is to see and cause suffering, and to negate happiness. The *vikshipta* form functions when the mind struggles to draw itself to its center. The rays of the mind are normally scattered, going in every direction. Here there is the conscious effort to gather and focus them. When the mind is in *ekagrata* state, it is one-pointed, which finally leads to the ultimate state, *niruddha,* where there is suspension of activity, and *samadhi,* the experience of supreme bliss.

The *chitta* is thus the background of the mind. It is like a lake on which rise and fall waves, which are comparable to the thoughts. These thought waves are called *vrittis.* A *vritti* is a "mental whirlpool," or mental modification; it is the difference between action and the absence of action in the mind. In the average person there are thousands of *vrittis* arising each minute in the mind. It is impossible for the conscious mind to keep track of the minute and intricate changes through which the mind is travelling every second. It is no surprise, therefore, that it takes many years of observation of one's own mind to understand its workings.

The Self is the witness of all that is perceived, but it neither acts nor reacts, for all action and reaction take place in the mind, appearing as *vrittis.* Thought, the most powerful force in the universe, initiates all action. Activity carried out on the physical plane is only a mirror of the inner workings of the mind. That which is assumed to be reality, the physical environment in which each person lives, is only a projection of the mind. In truth, when the many mental modifications, *vrittis,* are restrained, one is no longer affected by the comings and goings of the world, and the Self shines forth in undisturbed purity.

3. तदा द्रष्टुः स्वरूपेऽवस्थानम् ।

Tada drastuh svarupe 'vasthanam

At that time (when the thought waves are stilled), the perceiver rests in his own true nature.

That state of pure consciousness is achieved when the mind is no longer modified by the activities of thought waves. When the waves of a lake are stilled, one can see the bottom clearly. Likewise, when the *vrittis* of the mind subside, one's essential nature becomes evident. When the mind's agitation stops, the world no longer exists for the meditator, for he is in union with the Self.

4. वृत्तिसारूप्यमितरत्र ।

Vrtti-sarupyam itaratra

When the mind is not concentrated, the perceiver identifies with its modifications.

When thought waves arise, there is the immediate tendency to identify with them. One thought wave spawns a host of others. If one's neighbor has a swimming pool that is two inches larger, the *vritti* arises that "I must have a larger pool". If not caught in its formation, this thought repeats itself, followed by others of a related nature. One follows in the wake of the previous, each giving more and more power to the overall attitude. If, out of covetousness, one buys his neighbor's pool and house, there will be more taxes to pay in addition to two swimming pools and two houses to be cleaned. This may entail hiring help, which further entails supervision. If the second house is rented out, perhaps the tenant will damage either it or the pool. To get away from the headache of it all, one goes for a vacation. The swimming pool is exchanged for one in Hawaii, and the bed and television, for those in the hotel room. One sits in the hotel lobby instead of his own living room, worrying about whether or not the neighbor is remembering to let the dog out each day, and how things at the office are going.

What is the real difference between the hotel lobby and one's own living room? There is none, for the mind is a slave to its preoccupations, identifying with the same problems wherever it is. One *vritti* gives rise to countless others, all in search of happiness. But in fact, it is only foolishness, for the very rising of the thoughts themselves destroys the peace that the mind craves. It is only when these thoughts are stilled in concentration that identification with agitation and desire are eliminated.

5. वृत्तय: पञ्चतय्य: क्लिष्टाक्लिष्टा: ।

Vrttayah pancatayyah klistaklistah

There are five types of thought waves, some of which are painful and some of which are not.

Learning may be both enjoyable and painful for the student. He wants knowledge, and yet he wants to escape. The mind plays a tug of war. The painful thoughts are eliminated when the internal conflict ceases through concentration of the mind. Meditation is predicated on a gathered state of mind. If this could be maintained at all times, one would be continually resting in happiness.

6. प्रमाणविपर्ययविकल्पनिद्रास्मृतयः ।

Pramana-viparyaya-vikalpa-nidra-smrtayah

The five kinds of thought waves are correct knowledge, erroneous understanding, verbal delusion, sleep and memory.

Correct knowledge brings painless experience. It is the only kind of mental modification that is beneficial.

7. प्रत्यक्षानुमानागमाः प्रमाणानि ।

Pratyaksanumanagamah pramanani

Direct perception, inference and competent testimony are proofs of correct knowledge.

Correct knowledge, that is, knowledge based on fact, can be proved in any of three ways, but none of the proofs may contradict any other. The first is direct perception, in which the knowledge is experienced directly through the senses. This is acceptable only if the senses are pure and not deluded, and if one perception of the experience does not differ from another. The second proof, inference, is based on reasoning. There may be no physical perception of the truth, but it is arrived at through logic and past experience.

The third proof, competent testimony, is knowledge given by a person of unimpeachable character. He has had direct experience himself; his words do not contradict the scriptures; his motives are pure and the knowledge he gives is of benefit to mankind; and his experience must be such that it agrees with men of wisdom. The Truth is One. All proofs of correct knowledge arrive at the same conclusions.

8. विपर्ययो मिथ्याज्ञानमतद्रूपप्रतिष्ठम् ।

Viparyayo mithya-jnanam atad-rupa-pratistham

Erroneous understanding is a false conception of an idea or object whose real nature does not conform to that concept.

The second type of *vritti*, erroneous understanding, may also be based on a perception of an external object, but in this case the mental image does not correspond to the reality of that object. This may be caused by faulty perceptions, incorrect analysis of perceptions or distortion of perceptions by the ego. It is like the mirage in the desert but is very common in daily life. Very often judgement is passed on a person or situation when there is no relationship between reality and the mental impression.

9. शब्दज्ञानानुपाती वस्तुशून्यो विकल्पः ।

Sabda-jnananupati-vastu-sunyo vikalpah

Verbal delusion is caused by the identification with words that have no basis in reality.

Verbal delusion is the mental impression created by reactions to words that are not founded on fact. If one man calls another a fool, it is only a verbalization, a vibration in the air. But what a thundering thought wave it creates. One simple, unreal word wreaks havoc, throwing the physical and emotional bodies into chaos, destroying all happiness and peace.

One is not a fool because he is called a fool. If a person were called a donkey, he would not grow long ears and a tail. Yet, it is not unusual for people to react in anger to such statements and, in the process, actually give validity to them. The mind attributes meaning and nuances to words, giving them a false reality. Such reactions to meaningless vibrations is the cause of countless human troubles.

Overreaction to words and jumping to conclusions are weaknesses of the mind. The *vrittis,* thought waves, must be restrained not only during meditation but at all times. One must be particularly wary of praise, for this too is verbal delusion, and the ego is ever ready to pounce on any opportunity to see itself as better or different from others. Not everyone is going to feel the same way as one who bestows a compliment. Inevitably the pendulum swings in the other direction, and criticism will be heard sooner or later. But happiness should not rest on praise or abuse, for in all conditions, the only reality is the Self which is beyond qualities and beyond change.

The Catholics and Protestants quarrel in Ireland; Jews and Arabs fight in the Middle East. In all parts of the world there are those who see themselves as different from others, rather than as one. Unable to control their thought waves, they are swayed by words that instigate action, which invariably leads to reaction. A strong mind will not be affected in this way. The weaker a person is, the less restraint he has over verbal delusion. Examine yourself the next time that you are angry or miserable. Reason it out, and note the modifications of the mind. Gaining freedom from verbal delusion is essential for progress in meditation as well as for strengthening the mind.

A great Hindu holy man was once insulted in front of his disciples by a non-believer who spat upon his face several times. Not one muscle twitched, nor did his calm facial expression change, because he did not identify with his physical sheath. His mind was centered in God. Can you imagine the strength of that mind? Swami Sivananda prostrated before the man who tried to kill him, and Jesus forgave those who crucified him. No matter what was done to them, they responded with one thought, that of pure love. A true master will not react in anger, for to him insult and praise are the same.

Restraint of thought waves does not mean suppression. Suppression dams up violent emotions. For various reasons, people suffer abuse, suppressing anger or pain by smiling and carrying a stiff upper lip. The restrained thought waves must be given an outlet. They must be sublimated and channelled into such uplifting activities as Mantra repetition, exercise, singing and meditation on opposite, positive thoughts. Exchange love for anger and joy for sorrow.

10. अभावप्रत्ययालम्बना वृत्तिर्निद्रा ।

Abhava-pratyayalambana vrttir nidra

That mental modification which encompasses an absence of any content in the mind is called sleep.

During the deep sleep state the mind is blank. There is an experience of voidness in which the mind is attending to no thoughts. Some people may even experience this void state of mind with eyes open. But this *vritti* must not be mistaken for the superconscious state in which there is full concentration, awareness and realization of the Self.

11. अनुभूतविषयासंप्रमोषः स्मृतिः ।

Anubhuta-visayasampramosah smrtih

Memory is the retention of past experiences.

Memory, or *smriti,* exists when the impressions received by the mind do not slip away permanently and can be recalled to consciousness. If one knowingly performs an action, it will be recorded in the mind. If there is no awareness of an action or event, it cannot be retained. Memory can arise out of the three previous *vrittis* — erroneous understanding, verbal delusion and sleep. Past impressions exist in the mind from thousands of years of life, but these are latent and are only considered memory when they surface to the conscious awareness.

12. अभ्यासवैराग्याभ्यां तन्निरोधः ।

Abhyasa-vairagyabhyam tan-nirodhah

Their control (of chitta vrittis) is brought about by practice and non-attachment.

The different forms of mental modifications which bring about pain can be controlled in two ways. The first is *abhyasa*, which is practice or repetition. A change in character occurs only through formation of new habits. The second way is through non-attachment, or eliminating emotional reactions to situations and individuals. Non-attachment does not mean that there should not be love or compassion, but rather that emotional thought waves are ignored. The *vrittis* may arise, but they are observed in a disinterested fashion, then put aside.

13. तत्र स्थितौ यत्नोऽभ्यासः ।

Tatra sthitau yatno 'bhyasah

Abhyasa is the continuous effort towards firmly establishing the restraint of thought waves.

In order to free the mind from the various thought-forms, it is necessary to practice with regularity over an extended period of time. There are a great many means by which this practice is carried out. While the eight limbs of Raja Yoga are given here, there are many other forms of practice that lead to the same goal of Supreme Bliss, including the other forms of Yoga explained in this book.

14. स तु दीर्घकालनैरन्तर्यसत्कारासेवितो दृढभूमिः ।

Sa tu dirgha-kala-nairantarya-satkarasevito drdha-bhumih

Practice becomes firmly grounded on being continued over a long period of time without interruption and with sincere devotion.

If there are interruptions in the practice of stilling the mind, or if the effort is not continued over many many years, the results will only be temporary, and all progress will fade. Practice must be constant. It must also be done with an attitude of earnestness.

Only when there is true desire to reach the Goal is success assured.

15. दृष्टानुश्रविकविषयवितृष्णस्य वशीकारसंज्ञा वैराग्यम् ।

Drstanusravika-visaya-vitrsnasya vasikara samjna vairagyam

Vairagya, or non-attachment, is that state of consciousness in which the cravings for objects both seen and unseen is controlled through mastery of the will.

Non-attachment is a state of mind. It is indifference to objects of the world. It involves being unaffected by the pull of likes and dislikes. Whenever the mind acquires a taste for a particular sensation of pleasure, it becomes attached to it. The mind recalls the experience and desires repetition of it. It is this craving that creates pain. The state of *vairagya* does not necessarily mean the cessation of life in society; it involves separating oneself from the binding emotions of that life.

Renunciation is a great aid to the attainment of *vairagya*. By giving up objects of the senses, the mind is quickly stilled. But it is best to remember that non-attachment is not synonymous with not having. One can own nothing and yet be full of desires. If a person is fond of cherry ice cream, binding his hands and taping his mouth will not keep his mind from dwelling on this treat.

The basis of *vairagya* is the internal realization of the worthlessness of the external world. Objects and desires then automatically fall away. But renunciation does not mean running away from society, duties, and responsibilities, as is sometimes assumed. It means carrying on with one's duties in a dispassionate, unattached way.

16. तत् परं पुरुषख्यातेर्गुणवैतृष्ण्यम् ।

Tat param purusa-khyater gunavaitrsnyam

The highest state of non-attachment stems from awareness of Purusha; it renounces even the three qualities of Nature.

True *vairagya* is identification with *Purusha* alone. *Purusha* is the Self, also referred to as Brahman in Jnana Yoga. It is unmanifest and without qualities. It is that all-pervading Supreme Being that exists in the soul of every person. It is to be distinguished from *Prakriti,* which is causal matter, the Lord manifested, appearing as the various aspects of the world. *Prakriti* has *gunas,* qualities, and these are *tamas,* inertia or lethargy; *rajas,* or passion and activity; and *sattwa,* purity.

In extreme non-attachment, there is no identification with the limiting adjuncts, which define the individual. Even these three qualities are renounced when the source of all knowledge is understood to be the Self. One who claims to be a saint is attached to his quality of purity and goodness. If he regards himself as a sinner, he is identifying with the quality of spiritual lethargy that caused bad action. On the spiritual path, *tamas* is gradually replaced by *rajas;* that is, good actions replace inactivity. One is further balanced by taking on *sattwic,* or pure, qualities. Then purity itself is ultimately transcended when one rests in the Self, for *Purusha* is limitless and thus beyond even the three qualities of *Prakriti.*

17. वितर्कविचारानन्दास्मितानुगमात् संप्रज्ञातः ।

Vitarka-vicaranandasmitanugamat samprajnatah

Samprajnata samadhi (samadhi with consciousness) is accompanied by reasoning, discrimination, bliss, and an awareness of individuality.

Samadhi, the superconscious state, is of two types. The first, *samprajnata,* means "with seed", and is the state where there is full concentration and the experience of bliss, but duality still exists. Here there remains awareness of the object of meditation as separate from the individual who is meditating. The second type, *asamprajnata samadhi,* is said to be "seedless". It is the highest state of consciousness, in which there is no duality and the meditator is completely merged with *Purusha.*

Through *samprajnata samadhi* come all the powers of controlling the elements and, hence, nature. Knowledge alone is power, and when one has knowledge of something, he gains power over it. For example, one who meditates on the stars may lose track of all else, but as long as *vrittis* remain, there is still duality. In this concentrated state, even though there is no merging, knowledge of the stars is gained, and hence the powers of an astrologer. To control any element or its modification, one must concentrate on it, and with meditation comes power.

Those beings called angels or *devas* are entities who, through their good actions and meditations, have attained a place, or plane, where they can enjoy and use their powers. Many think this is the ultimate goal, but it is not. There is still duality, a sense of individuality. No matter how pure the ego is, as long as it exists, it must be transcended in order for the knower, knowledge and known to become One. *Samprajnata samadhi* is not an end in itself but is a state attained along the path. There are four kinds:

1. *Savitarka:* Meditation on elements in time and space.
2. *Nirvitarka:* Meditation on elements outside of time and space.
3. *Sananda:* Meditation on the mind, accompanied by bliss.
4. *Sasmita:* Identification with the unqualified ego.

When the mind fixes on a gross external element or object and meditates on it, it is called *savitarka* meditation. *Vitarka* means question; *savitarka,* with question. Because it has no reality, all matter is questionable and open to examination, and the faculty of reason is applied. This mode of meditation scrutinizes the elements and the universe that they may yield up their secrets and powers to the meditator.

In their search to find out about matter, scientists employ this method. They concentrate on an element and experiment to discover its nature. Thus they have learned how to split the atom and utilize its energy for constructive or destructive purposes; modern man can now push a button and explode a hydrogen bomb.

Knowledge of something not only gives control over it, but over those who have no knowledge of it. One buys a certain brand of toothpaste in preference to another out of ignorance; the advertisers know human weaknesses. They claim that one brand has more sex appeal than another, and thus play on the weaknesses of the mind. Everybody manipulates power in this way. Politicians concentrate their energies on outwitting each other and the public. They come up with such mantras as "Law and order" and "Peace with honor", and bombard the public with their energy in order to control the mass mind. Even some yogis and swamis use such simple, silly tricks and devices as tiger skins, turbans and beards to capture one's imagination and hence the mind. If the mind can be tricked, it can be controlled.

Gaining power over an element is not a miracle; it is only knowing its secret. Laboratory experimentation is, in effect, scientific meditation. When the scientist discovers what has caused a certain mysterious disease, he will then have a basis for cure. He is trying to discover the secrets of nature, in order to manipulate and control its energy. A sage knows directly how to tap this energy. By concentrating on one element and excluding all others, he gains direct knowledge. This is *savitarka* meditation. Its goal is the acquisition of powers, but one can never go beyond that.

When meditation is on the same gross elements, but they are isolated from time and physical space, and considered as being in the original state, it is called *nirvitarka,* without question. This is the mode of approach practiced in Kundalini Yoga. It is the type of *samadhi* that is reached through meditation on more subtle energy forces, *chakras,* visualizations, and symbols. In meditating on the *chakras,* or psychic centers, and their corresponding elements, no questions are being asked. The centers and elements involved in this subtle state are directly visualized. As they do not exist in the material world, they are outside of time and space. The object of meditation is thus a part of the meditative process itself. Questioning and experimentation are not involved, nor are meaning and powers being sought. Only discrimination is applied in order to remain focussed on the chosen image or sound. Control over the elements and the attainment of power come as fringe benefits. They are not the goal.

Samanu pranayama, the process by which the astral tubes are cleansed, is another example of *nirvitarka* meditation. It is a breathing exercise accompanied by simultaneous concentration on the psychic centers, their corresponding elements, and repetition of the element's primal sound energy. One takes the element out of time and space and directly uses their vibrational energy to purify the subtle astral channels. In repeating the seed sound *RAM,* one is not dealing with actual burning fire but with its subtle energy.

By controlling the subtle elements one can perform miracles in the eyes of ordinary people, but one is not necessarily progressing on the spiritual path. The mind, though concentrated, is fixed on unreal and limited objects, not on the Self. Meditation on the elements can only bring powers. It cannot bring liberation. Like a battery running down or a diminishing bank account, the powers run out, and their exhibition is limited. The higher the powers, the more voltage is used up. When they disappear, one must start at the bottom of the spiritual ladder again in the next lifetime.

There is no liberation in the acquisition of powers. They lead only to enjoyment of this life and to the reinforcement of the need for that enjoyment. In the end they bring intensified suffering. Even if one gained sufficient powers to become king of heaven, he could not stay there indefinitely. Power, like beauty, cannot be held forever.

The third kind of *samprajnata samadhi* is *sananda.* The elements, whether in or out of time and space, have all been progressively merged in the mind. As its own object of meditation, the mind rests in a state of bliss. One may not want to proceed further, for the ecstasy is supreme. But this is only a taste of the ultimate bliss, for there is still identification with the fruits of meditation. A duality exists in the very enjoyment of the blissful state.

When one offers flowers to the statue of the guru, the devotee is offering one gross element to another. There is awareness of both as concrete physical entities, but neither is important. What matters is the concentration of the mind, which is fixed on an external object. This is *savitarka*. Whether one worships a living guru or a statue makes no difference. Both are external and secondary to the devotional state of mind, which remains the same.

Meditation on the guru internally, seeing him not in time and space but in oneself, takes more concentration. If one puts him in the heart and mentally offers a flower, it is *nirvitarka*. Neither the body nor an outside object is brought into play. The mind alone acts in devotion with the mental offering of a flower.

In *sananda* the flower is forgotten, and association is with the guru as God. He is not seen as separate from the meditator; the previous apparent separation is now recognized as being a product of the mind. When the idea of separation is withdrawn and the thought wave stilled, the mental and emotional sheath is being transcended. The meditator experiences the supremely blissful awareness that the divinity worshipped is no different from himself.

In the last stage, *sasmita,* the mind itself is still the object of meditation, which deepens until only the awareness of the individual in his most purified form, the unqualified ego, remains. Unqualified egoism is identification with the Self, while qualified egoism is identification wth a limiting adjunct or false quality. The latter gives rise to such statements as "I am a liberated woman" or "I am a lawyer". If really liberated, the only thing left is I AM. In *sasmita samadhi* the food, vital, and mental sheaths have faded out. The intellectual sheath, the purest ego state, remains predominant. Conscious only of his own pure ego and God, the aspirant still experiences duality.

Although it is possible at this point to merge in nature, the final goal is not yet reached. One still feels distinct from the Self. If he should die while in this stage of consciousness, there is no merging with the Absolute. He becomes a highly evolved angel, still subject to Karma and subtle ego. Like Swami Sivananda, he will be reborn as a sage, and will need only a word to speed him to God-Realization.

The aforementioned stages are all phases of *samprajnata, samadhi* with seed. Their differences are those of degree, in progression of concentration and in disassociation from the gross ego. As the gross ego falls away, the psychic centers and elements dominate the consciousness. The elements, from dense to subtle, are then merged into the mind, which becomes its own object of meditation. On reaching the pure state of ego, one is unaware of physical, astral or blissful experience. Consciousness resides in the individual in his purest form, which remains separate from the object of meditation, just as the sun's reflection is separate from the sun.

This is a very difficult time for the spiritual seeker. He has reached a stage of development in which spiritual powers are thrown in his lap. Nature will hold him back as long as there is even a little ego. One is tested by the acquisition of powers, supramental experiences, obstacles and pressures. Do not be beguilled by external powers. Whether they are desired or not, they come naturally as the yogi advances along the path. Then people inevitably come to seek advice and counsel. This is a testing period for the ego. Credit should not be expected for the performance of duty. This level is reached only after a long evolution of several lifetimes. It is necessary to push on to the unqualified experience of the *asamprajnata* state, in which there is no dualism.

18. विरामप्रत्ययाभ्यासपूर्वः संस्कारशेषोऽन्यः ।

Virama-pratyayabhyasa-purvah samskara-seso 'nyah

Asamprajnata samadhi (seedless state) is reached when all mental activity ceases and only unmanifested impressions remain in the mind.

Asamprajnata or seedless *samadhi,* is most clearly grasped if there is an understanding of the seven *bhumikas,* the stages of consciousness which lead to Self-Realization. These are:

1. *Subhecha,* longing for truth. One realizes his state of ignorance, and sincerely wishes to acquire spiritual knowledge.
2. *Vicharana,* right inquiry. One is convinced of the worthlessness of the world, and searches sincerely and deeply for the Truth.
3. *Tanumanasa,* fading of the mind. The mind loses its taste for objects of the world and becomes intensely immersed in knowledge of the Soul. This corresponds to the latter states of *savitarka* and *nirvitarka.*
4. *Sattwapatti,* purity of mind. All mental modifications are reduced

to identification with the Self. This corresponds to *sananda* and *sasmita.*

5. *Asamsakti,* detached state. The meditator is unaffected by anything in the world, due to his knowledge of the Self.

6. *Padarthabhanava,* knowledge of truth. Karma is almost completed and external things do not appear to exist.

7. *Turiya,* the state of liberation. The yogi sees God everywhere. He does not perform action, for this state is of short duration while the body and sheaths are completely burned.

Asamprajnata samadhi begins with the fifth stage of consciousness, and is characterized by an absence of thought waves. When the thought waves are active, they manifest as *samskaras,* or impressions in the mind. They can also exist in a passive state. When one meditates in *samprajnata,* which corresponds to the third and fourth stages of consciousness, the waves are stilled but not absent. Lurking deep in the subconscious, they will eventually emerge as desires. They are like seeds placed in a jar. Although temporarily dormant, they retain the potential for future germination.

For this reason a person in the fourth stage will never achieve liberation while in that stage. He is also in danger of toppling from whatever heights he has reached. No matter how high one goes, the possibility of slipping always lies in wait. The fourth stage is like a spiritual mountain peak, and one cannot perch eternally on top of it. Until Nature and conscious concentration are transcended, and seedless *asamprajnata samadhi* is reached, there is the danger of falling.

It takes great strength and control to achieve the superconscious state. Without adequate preparation it is easy to be overpowered by lethargy. One can be deceived into thinking that it is *samadhi,* just as a little backache is sometimes mistaken for the awakening of the *kundalini.* A person in sleep and one who is experiencing superconsciousness appear to be in the same state, for energy at its lowest level resembles energy at its highest. When the blades of an electric fan are revolving with great velocity, they appear not to be moving at all.

Extremes are very much alike. Darkness cannot be seen, and neither can extreme light. In extreme lethargy there are no activities or desires. A person who is sleeping does not want to eat, make money or go to parties. Desires are absent. It is the same with *asamprajnata samadhi,* although this state is the height of awareness. One wants neither sensual nor sexual experience. The only

difference is that in deep sleep there are still seeds in the jar, and
the next morning they will sprout as desires.

When the mind is empty and the thought waves and impressions are completely gone, it is the seedless *asamprajnata* state. No
seeds are left to manifest in the form of desires or tendencies.

Tendencies have the power to create. Who made one person
male and another female? One's own thought impressions are responsible. The soul is neither male nor female. When the mind
begins acting and wants to behave like a woman, it creates a suitable body for those tendencies. As long as there are thought impressions and tendencies, there will be more reincarnation. The
tendency of the ego itself must be broken down, for it, too, is illusion. *Maya* projects qualities onto the individual, and he thinks
that he is tall, fat, man, woman, talented or dull. When all such
ideas, good as well as evil, have been overcome, the soul stands
alone.

Asamprajnata samadhi is that state of merging with the Absolute, which is beyond knowledge. Any objective experience is
knowledge. If one sees Krishna, it is objective knowledge. However,
if one knows that he *is* Krishna, that is beyond knowledge. Then
there is no more seed, and nothing can touch him.

19. भवप्रत्ययो विदेहप्रकृतिलयानाम्

Bhava-pratyayo videha-prakrtilayanam

*(Asamprajnata samadhi may be attained) by birth (in those
who have previously achieved) bodilessness or a merging
with Prakriti.*

The highest state of *samadhi* is not achieved in one lifetime.
It takes many incarnations to make the innumerable fine adjustments necessary for God-Realization. Many who do reach *asamprajnata samadhi* have done the major part of their work in previous
lives and return only to attain the final goal. Some have already
reached the level of a *deva,* an advanced spiritual being not living
in a physical form. Or they may have progressed as far as merging
with *Prakriti,* when meditation on the elements of nature has been
perfected. In either case, merging with the Self is all that remains
to be achieved.

20. श्रद्धावीर्यस्मृतिसमाधिप्रज्ञापूर्वक इतरेषाम् ।

Sraddha-virya-smrti-samadhi-prajnapurvaka itaresam

For others, asamprajnata samadhi is attained through faith, energy, recollection and keen awareness.

For others, the highest state is reached through sincere life-long appplication, as well as through past life efforts. Faith is the firm conviction that the truth exists and that it can and will be attained. With this basic positive attitude, failure is impossible. Energy, or will, is the drive that carries one along the path, bouncing back after failures and maintaining courage through difficult times. Recollection is past spiritual *samskaras* rising to the surface of the mind and reinforcing the seeker's journey to his Goal. Keen awareness is focussed application of the mind, the intense intellectual input that is necessary for merging with the Supreme.

21. तीव्रसंवेगानामासन्नः ।

Tivra-samveganam asannah

Liberation comes quickly when the desire for it is intense.

The stronger the desire for liberation from the bondage of this world, the sooner will that goal be reached.

22. मृदुमध्याधिमात्रत्वात् ततोऽपि विशेषः ।

Mrdu-madhyadhimatratvat tato 'pi visesah

Desire for liberation can be mild; moderate or intense.

The intensity of desire for liberation will reflect the effort that is put into achieving it, as well as the fruit — the success of one's endeavors towards God-Realization.

23. ईश्वरप्रणिधानाद्वा ।

Isvara-pranidhanad va

(Success is swift for those who are) devoted to Ishwara (God).

While *Purusha* (Brahman or the Self) is the abstract view of the Lord in his purest absolute form, *Ishwara* is God as seen with attributes such as love, kindness, mercy, omniscience and so forth. Because the human mind is too limited to focus on abstractions, most people focus on his manifested form, *Ishwara*. In Western tradition, He is usually referred to as God, or Jehovah. In the Indian tradition, He is related to in various forms, such as Vishnu, the Preserver; Rama, the Righteous; and Durga, the Divine Mother. These various deities are not different gods, but *Ishwara*, the one God, who is so omnipotent that he is able to manifest in as many forms as are needed by individuals of different temperment to help each focus on the Supreme.

Thus *samadhi* comes most quickly to those who place themselves in consciousness of God however they may see him. That is, they have devotion, dedication and self-surrender to his will.

24. क्लेशकर्मविपाकाशयैरपरामृष्टः पुरुषविशेष ईश्वरः ।

Klesa-karma-vipakasayair aparamrstah purusa-visesa Isvarah

Ishwara is that particular center of Divine Consciousness that is untouched by misery, Karma, or desires.

Ishwara is the immortal Self, or *Purusha,* with form. He is perceived as a being, and yet He is totally untouched by the ignorance of unhappiness, the law of cause and effect, and cravings. For Him, the opposites of the phenomenal world, such as pleasure and pain, do not exist.

25. तत्र निरतिशयं सर्वज्ञबीजम् ।

Tatra niratisayam Sarvajna-bijam

In Him lies the seed of omniscience.

God, or *Ishwara,* is not just all-knowing, but is knowledge itself. In uniting with Him, the highest knowledge is obtained. This does not refer to intellectual knowledge only, but also knowledge of the entire universe through the eye of wisdom and intuition.

26. स पूर्वेषामपि गुरुः कालेनानवच्छेदात् ।

Sa purvesam api guruh kalenana-vacchedat

Unlimited by time, He is the Teacher of all other teachers, from the most ancient of times.

The highest teacher is the Self, *Purusha.* All ancient sages, such as Jesus and Buddha, realized the Self. While they may have had earthly teachers, the Source of their vast knowledge was not of this plane. Living in a superconscious state, they had direct access to the Truth, that knowledge which is absolute.

27. तस्य वाचकः प्रणवः ।

Tasya vacakah pranavah

He manifests in the word OM.

OM (AUM), the sacred word of the Hindus, is one of the oldest known words. Over 5000 years ago, and probably much earlier in ancient Sumer, OM was known and used as a secret word by Sumerian mystics and priests.

When the Indo-Aryan tribes wandered east from Sumer to Northern India, they carried the precious and sacred word OM with them. In the oldest known Indian scriptures, OM has always had a place of prominence. Nearly all Mantras and hymns begin and end with OM. OM is also used alone as a Mantra and is considered to be the most powerful one.

There are countless stories still circulating in India telling that if a person can pronounce the word OM with the right vibration and proper concentration, he can attain all *siddhis,* that is power to perform all kinds of miracles, such as healing people, producing rain, or walking over water.

Some contemporary Indian authorities on the subject have also a rational explanation for the miraculous power of OM. For instance, Swami Sivananda, who was a practicing medical doctor before he became a yogi, explains that the vibrations produced in nasal cavities by the continuous chanting of OM stimulate the activity of the hypophysis and gladula pinealis by a direct massage-like action. Since those organs have great importance in the psychological and physiological functions of man, it may explain part of the mystery behind OM.

It is impossible to describe the absolute meaning of OM, as it is said that only the enlightened can understand it completely. Its vibration is synonymous with union with the Divine. Its meaning is Supreme Reality itself. It is the same as *Sat-Chit-Ananda,* or Existence-Knowledge-Bliss Absolute.

All vibration, and hence all language, falls within the range of OM. Word and thought, name and form, cannot be separated, for word is thought manifested through the vocal cords. Every thought has its corresponding word of some kind, as well as weight, power, form and energy. OM contains within itself all language, all thought. It is the Primal Vibration and Divine Power.

28. तज्जपस्तदर्थभावनम् ।

Tajjapas tad-artha-bhavanam

Constant repetition of OM and meditation on its meaning (leads to samadhi).

Focussing on the abstract is more difficult than focussing on concrete images of the Lord. However, because repetition of OM produces thought waves which correspond to those of the Supreme, it is a direct path to *samadhi*.

Swami Sivananda would always emphasize the power and glory of OM. In *Bliss Divine,* his greatest compilation of spiritual essays, he writes, "Live in OM. Meditate on OM. Inhale and exhale OM. Rest peacefully in OM. Take shelter in OM."

29. ततः प्रत्यक्चेतनाधिगमोऽप्यन्तरायाभावश्च ।

Tatah pratyak-cetanadhigamo 'py antaraya-bhavas ca

From (the repetition of OM) is gained enlightening introspection and elimination of all obstacles.

Through meditation on OM, the highest of Mantras, Self-Realization is possible. This is because the vibration of OM removes hindrances on the path and leads to realization of the Self which exists within every individual.

30. व्याधिस्त्यानसंशयप्रमादालस्याविरतिभ्रान्तिदर्शनालब्धभूमि
कत्वानवस्थितत्वानि चित्तविक्षेपास्तेऽन्तरायाः ।

Vyadhi-styana-samsaya-pramadalasya-virati-bhranti-
darsanalabdhabhumi-katvanavasthitatvani citta-viksepas te
'ntarayah

The obstacles to Realization are disease, mental torpor, doubt, indifference, laziness, craving for pleasure, delusion, inability to practice and maintain concentration, and restlessness of mind due to distractions.

If the body is not healthy, cosmic consciousness cannot be reached. The practice of *asanas* and *pranayama* wards off disease and helps to maintain alertness. Doubt and the various mental obstacles can be dispelled by the spiritual experiences that come through meditation. Especially when progress seems to be at a standstill, it is essential to plod on doggedly with the practice. Yoga, like any other kind of learning, is never a straight ascent; there are ups and downs and plateaus. Bear this in mind, do not become discouraged, and be aware that all seekers encounter these same obstacles. They should be regarded as challenges which induce growth opportunities to develop strength. With regularity in practice, the mind eventually rights itself.

31. दुःखदौर्मनस्याङ्गमेजयत्वश्वासप्रश्वासा विक्षेपसहभुवः ।

Duhkha-daurmanasyangamejayatva-svasa-prasvasa
viksepa-sahabhuvah

*Mental pain, depression, physical nervousness, and irregular
breathing are the symptoms of a distracted state of mind.*

These are outward manifestations of an internal state of
being. They are the result of the above mentioned obstacles to
meditation. They are also a way of life for many thousands who
never undertake spiritual disciplines such as meditation and Yoga.
But they can be thoroughly remedied by repetition of OM, surrender to the Lord, and regularity in practice. Even during periods
when one's original enthusiasm wains, continuing in the daily
schedule of spiritual practice strengthens the will and builds positive spiritual habits, or *samskaras.* In due time, each test is passed
and meditation is approached with renewed vigor.

32. तत्प्रतिषेधार्थमेकतत्त्वाभ्यासः ।

Tat-pratisedhartham eka-tattvabhyasah

*In order to remove these obstacles, one should meditate on
one aspect of Truth.*

The seeker should choose one of the many forms of meditation in order to carry out his practice, focussing his mind on one
specific object of concentration or embodiment of perfection. If
he jumps from one object to another, steadiness of mind can never
be developed. Not only must concentration be focussed on one
object alone during any given sitting, but it should be the same
object from year to year. This is the only way to gather the rays
of the mind and to perfect one-pointedness.

33. मैत्रीकरुणामुदितोपेक्षाणां सुखदुःखपुण्यापुण्यविषयाणां भावनातश्चित्त
प्रसादनम् ।

Maitri-karuna-muditopeksanam sukha-duhkha-punyapunya-
visayanam bhavanatas citta-prasadanam

*The mind becomes clear through the cultivation of friend-
liness, kindness, contentment, and indifference towards happiness, vice and virtue.*

Taming of the mind requires the development of good will
and universal love toward all. Any kind of negative feeling or iden-

tification with the dualities of good and bad destroys peace of mind.

34. प्रच्छर्देनविधारणाभ्यां वा प्राणस्य ।

Pracchardana-vidharanabhyam va pranasya

It is also achieved by the expulsion and retention of the breath.

This is a reference to the practice of *pranayama* as a method of purification. Regulation of the breath gives control over the thought waves, for control of breath is directly related to control of mind. There are many *pranayama* exercises, each of which has a special effect on the autonomic nervous system and the psyche.

35. विषयवती वा प्रवृत्तिरुत्पन्ना मनसः स्थितिनिबन्धनी ।

Visayavati va pravrttir utpanna manasah sthiti-nibandhani

Steadiness of the mind is easily established when the higher senses come into operation.

Concentration on the higher objects of sensation, such as the *anahata,* or internal sounds, quiets the mind.

36. विशोका वा ज्योतिष्मती ।

Visoka va jyotismati

Or (by concentration on the internal) state of luminescence which is beyond sorrow.

Patanjali is here giving a series of methods that can be utilized for control of the *vrittis,* thought waves. One of the possible objects of meditation is a visualized light, either in the heart or the space between the eyebrows.

37. वीतरागविषयं वा चित्तम् ।

Vita-raga-visayam va cittam

Or by fixing the mind on one who has transcended human passions and attachments.

Another highly regarded object of meditation is a saint or sage who has attained liberation. A picture of an inspiring soul, such as Swami Sivananda, Buddha or Jesus, may be kept on the altar or other place of meditation. He may be focussed on either visually or mentally.

38. स्वप्ननिद्राज्ञानालम्बनं वा ।

Svapna-nidra-jnanalambanam va

Or (by meditating upon) knowledge gained in dreams or deep sleep.

Many times the Truth is revealed by the superconscious during sleep. Usually this information is forgotten, and is only utilized by the subconscious. But if that knowledge is meditated upon consciously, great progress can be made upon the path.

39. यथाभिमतध्यानाद्वा ।

Yathabhimata-dhyanad va

Or by meditation on what is agreeable.

Patanjali has given only a few of the many techniques for meditation. An aspirant should choose one that suits his temperament, and stick to that method until reaching liberation.

40. परमाणुपरममहत्त्वान्तोऽस्य वशीकारः ।

Paramanu-parama-mahattvanto 'sya vasikarah

(Thus a yogi's) mastery extends from the smallest atom to infinity.

That is, a yogi, when perfected, has no limitations. He is master of the universe, in all its forms.

41. क्षीणवृत्तेरभिजातस्येव   मणेर्ग्रहीतृग्रहणग्राह्येषु तत्स्थतदञ्जनता समापत्तिः ।

Ksina-vrtter abhijatasyeva maner grahitr-grahana-grahyesu tatstha-tadanjanata samapattih

For the person who has controlled the vrittis through meditation, there is a merging of the perceiver, perceived, and perception, just as a crystal assumes the color of the background.

When the mind waves are controlled, there is complete union between the subject, object, and the relationship between the two. A crystal has no color of its own, yet when placed on a colored background, it assumes and reflects that same color. The pure mind, abandoning its own form, assumes the form of whatever subject it meditates on.

42. तत्र शब्दार्थज्ञानविकल्पैः संकीर्णा सवितर्का ।

Tatra sabdartha-jnana-vikalpaih samkirna savitarka

Savitarka samadhi is that state in which the mind alternates between knowledge based on words, true knowledge, and knowledge based on sense perception or reasoning.

Savitarka samadhi is known as *samadhi* with reasoning. This is the lowest level of *samadhi* in which there is perfected concentration, but the meditator is focussing on natural elements and using his intellectual faculties. The purity of the various levels of knowledge is yet to be clarified.

43. स्मृतिपरिशुद्धौ स्वरूपशून्येवार्थमात्रनिर्भासा निर्वितर्का ।

Smrti-parisuddhau svarupa-sunyevartha-matra-nirbhasa nirvitarka

Nirvitarka samadhi is that state in which the memory is clarified and the mind, devoid of subjectivity, reflects true knowledge.

Nirvitarka samadhi is *samadhi* that is beyond reason. It is meditation on an abstract object such as the *chakras,* or symbols. The mixing of the sources of knowledge ends. In *savitarka samadhi* there is some confusion between the element of reason and lower forms of knowledge. In *nirvitarka samadhi,* the element of reason, or intellectual argumentation, fades. In both cases there is a blissful experience, yet there is full awareness of subject and object.

44. एतयैव सविचारा निर्विचारा च सूक्ष्मविषया व्याख्याता ।

Etayaiva savicara nirvicara ca suksmavisaya vyakhyata

By this (what is stated in the previous two sutras), samadhi with inquiry, samadhi without inquiry, and that which is still more subtle is explained.

Here Patanjali is distinguishing the various types of *samprajnata samadhi*. They include forms which may or may not involve inquiry, the mental process of reflection. Or they may include levels which involve meditation on more and more subtle objects.

45. सूक्ष्मविषयत्वं चालिङ्गपर्यवसानम् ।

Suksma-visayatvam calinga-paryavasanam

The state of samadhi concerned with subtle objects extends as far as the unmanifested state.

This is a way of saying that the degree of subtlety in objects of meditation is limitless — it extends as far as the unmanifest state itself. Yet, they remain objects separate from the meditator, and hence there is still duality.

46. ता एव सबीज: समाधि: ।

Ta eva sabijah samadhih

These all constitute meditation with "seed."

All forms of *samadhi* that are arrived at through meditation on an external object remain *sabija,* "with seed", meditation. No matter what the degree of subtlety, the meditator is still within the realm of *Prakriti,* where there is subject-object relationship.

47. निर्विचारवैशारद्येऽध्यात्मप्रसाद: ।

Nirvicara-vaisaradye 'dhyatma-prasadah

On attaining the utmost purity in samadhi without inquiry, Illumination dawns.

Only when the meditator achieves that state of *samadhi* in which there is no longer the process of inquiry, and has purified himself, does Realization dawn. The states of *Samadhi* through which he passes before that final goal are very rewarding and blissful, and many powers manifest in those states. But the seeker must see even these rewarding experiences as obstacles for they, too, though the most rewarding, must be transcended in order to merge with the Self.

48. ऋतम्भरा तत्र प्रज्ञा ।

Rtambhara tatra prajna

The knowledge that is attained in this state is Absolute Truth.

All duality, all relativity vanishes. Intuitive cognition supersedes all other forms of knowledge.

49. श्रुतानुमानप्रज्ञाभ्यामन्यविषया विशेषार्थत्वात् ।

Srutanumana-prajnabhyam anya-visaya visesarthatvat

*Knowledge gained from inference and testimony is not equal
to that obtained in higher states of consciousness, because it
is confined to a particular object.*

This refers back to the seventh *sutra,* which defines correct
knowledge. Even if knowledge is gained through intellectual process
or through the statement of a great sage, it is limited, and this is
inferior to direct experience itself. In this case, the direct experience
is the intuitive limitless knowledge of *Purusha,* or the Self.

50. तज्जः संस्कारोऽन्यसंस्कारप्रतिबन्धी ।

Taj-jah samskaro 'nya-samskara-pratibandhi

*The result (of that knowledge) is that its samskaras replace
all others.*

Direct knowledge of the Lord obscures all other forms of
knowledge, and in its light past *samskaras* and impressions fade.

51. तस्यापि निरोधे सर्वनिरोधान्निर्बीजः समाधिः ।

Tasyapi nirodhe sarva-nirodhan nirbijah samadhih

*When even this is restrained, the "seedless" state of samadhi
is entered.*

This is the climax of the evolution of *sadhana,* spiritual practice. When the last seeds of Karma are burnt, and even the *vritti*
of direct cognition of the Lord is restrained, then *samadhi* is of the
seedless type. This is the last phase of *asamprajnata samadhi.* The
meditator, having spent many lifetimes perfecting himself, no longer
has need of a physical form, and shortly enters *Mahasamadhi,* in
which he merges with God.

Raja Yoga Sutras: Practice

Chalk out a program of life. Draw your spiritual routine.
Stick to it sytematically and regularly. Apply yourself diligently.
Waste not even a single precious minute. Life is short. Time is
fleeting. That "tomorrow" will never come. Now or never. Stand up
with the firm resolve: "I will become a Yogi in this very birth, this
very moment." Do rigid, constant Yoga sadhana or abhyasa. *If you*
are really very sincere in your practice, and if your mind is filled
with vairagya *or dispassion and keen longing for Liberation, you*
will reach the goal of perfection within six years. There is no doubt
about this.

— Swami Sivananda
Sure Ways for Success in Life
and God-Realization

Although Patanjali Maharishi is the author and compiler of
the *Raja Yoga Sutras,* it is said in the *Yajnavalkya Smriti* that Hiranyagarbha was the original teacher of Yoga. Hiranyagarbha is the
Cosmic Mind, or Cosmic Intelligence, also called Brahman. He is
the sum-total of all the subtle bodies, the highest created being
through whom the Supreme Being projects the physical universe.
Patanjali, as a realized sage whose intuitive abilities were developed
to the highest degree, received the knowledge of Yoga directly, and
wrote it down for the benefit of all mankind.

While the first chapter of the *Sutras* explains the functions of
the mind and the various levels of *samadhi,* the following chapters
are more concerned with the specific practices that lead to that
superconscious state. Patanjali covers all phases of Yoga from the
very basics to levels of practice that are beyond the comprehension
of all but liberated saints and sages. The last two chapters in particular deal with the vast realm that is experienced after attaining *sa-*
madhi. While reading through them, it is best to bear in mind that
realization of the Self is attained only after many lifetimes of striving for that goal. And, as emphasized in the last pages of the pre-

158

vious chapter, even the attainment of powers and the experience of bliss during meditation are but stepping stones along the path. These are mere distractions when seen in light of the ultimate end, merging with the Divine.

CHAPTER TWO: YOGA SADHANA

Patanjali's second chapter sets forth the practice of Yoga, or *sadhana*. It discusses Kriya Yoga, which is purification through discipline, study, and self-surrender. It enumerates the five main afflictions, or causes for human suffering, and the methods for eliminating them. Finally, it discusses the first five limbs of Raja Yoga — *yama, niyama, asana, pranayama,* and *pratyahara* — the foundations for meditation.

1. तप:स्वाध्यायेश्वरप्रणिधानानि क्रियायोग: ।

Tapah-svadhyayesvara-pranidhanani kriya-yogah

Austerity, self-study, and surrender to God constitute Kriya Yoga.

Austerity does not mean physical abuse or severe rigors. It refers to strict control of the senses in order to conserve energy for higher pursuits. Austerity in this sense means fasting occasionally, rising early to meditate instead of sleeping late, and reducing certain physical comforts for the sake of greater control of mind. Study of the scriptures and other spiritual works keeps the mind flowing in the desired direction. In surrendering to God's will one also surrenders the fruit of work performed. This leads to Karma Yoga, the path of selfless service, in which one regards oneself as the instrument of God, and serves humanity with no thought of either credit or blame.

2. समाधिभावनार्थ: क्लेशतनूकरणार्थश्च ।

Samadhi-bhavanarthah klesa-tanukaranarthas ca

It alleviates afflictions and brings about samadhi.

By following the three practices of Kriya Yoga mentioned above, the student eliminates the source of his woes and eventually reaches the superconscious state.

3. अविद्यास्मितारागद्वेषाभिनिवेशाः क्लेशाः ।

Avidyasmita-raga-dvesabhinivesah klesah

Ignorance, egoism, attraction and aversion, and fear of death are the afflictions which cause suffering.

Ignorance, *avidya,* is the lack of awareness of Reality. It is identification with the temporal world rather than with the imperishable *Atman,* or Self. Egoism is the "I-ness" and "my-ness" which create the illusion that one person is different from another, bringing about conflict. *Raga-dvesha* translates as "likes/dislikes"; when a person is swayed by feelings of attraction and aversion, he is identifying with the material world and setting himself up for the pain of loss and disappointment. Fear of death, or clinging to life, is binding and stifling. Many who have been pronounced dead and were later revived have reported the experience of death as indescribably beautiful and peaceful. None can say when death will come. Fear of death is useless imagination, a waste of energy, and creates waves of pain which exist only in the mind.

4. अविद्या क्षेत्रमुत्तरेषां प्रसुप्ततनुविच्छिन्नोदाराणाम् ।

Avidya ksetram uttaresam prasupta-tanu-vicchinnodaranam

Ignorance is the cause of (the above-mentioned afflictions) which follow it, whether they be latent, weak, suppressed or aggravated.

The suffering which comes from egoism, attraction and repulsion, and fear of death all stem from *avidya,* ignorance, regardless of the degree to which they manifest. As the root of the other obstacles, ignorance of the true nature of the Self is identification with the body and mind. When *avidya* is replaced by Enlightenment, all other causes of pain automatically disappear.

5. अनित्याशुचिदुःखानात्मसु नित्यशुचिसुखात्मख्यातिरविद्या ।

Anityasuci-duhkhanatmasu nitya-suci-sukhatmakhyatir avidya

Ignorance mistakes the perishable, impure, painful, and non-Self for the eternal, pure, good, and Self.

When in a state of ignorance, man mistakes what is mundane for what is Supreme. He cannot differentiate between that which will bring pain — the mind and body — and that which will bring immortality.

6. दृग्दर्शनशक्त्योरेकात्मतेवास्मिता ।

Drg-darsana-saktyor ekatmatevasmita

Egoism is the identification of the Seer with the instrument of seeing.

The instrument of seeing in this case refers not only to the eyes but also to all the senses. Egoism is manifest when the individual cannot distinguish his Self from his senses and mind. He sees himself as separate from the rest of mankind, reacting to others with a sense of competition rather than cooperation.

7. सुखानुशयी रागः ।

Sukhanusayi ragah

Attraction is that which dwells on pleasure.

Most think of attraction and pleasure as positive things, but when associated with objects of the material world they inevitably bring pain. Nothing in the physical world is permanent; hence the constant fear of loss and loss itself keep those seeking pleasure in an unhappy state. This is why the yogi learns to cultivate a dislike for worldly pleasures. He is never disappointed or unhappy. The result, ironically, is that by not seeking pleasure he is always happy.

8. दुःखानुशयी द्वेषः ।

Duhkhanusayi dvesah

Aversion is that which attempts to avoid pain.

Just as attraction brings pain, so does aversion. The mental attitude of aversion is a negative one, and often makes a neutral situation appear as if it were one to be avoided. It is not possible to avoid all distasteful circumstances. When there is *raga-dvesha,* or likes and dislikes, a person cannot be happy. He is dwelling on illusory pairs-of-opposites rather than learning to be content in all situations and surrendering to the Lord's plan for his growth.

9. स्वरसवाही विदुषोऽपि तथा रूढोऽभिनिवेशः ।

Svarasavahi viduso 'pi tatha rudho 'bhinivesah

Fear of death is the continuous desire to live which is rooted even in the minds of the wise.

The fear of death is the fear of loss of identity, of letting go of the ego. Even when all else is given up, there is still the clinging to life. It is only when a sage reaches the very last stage of *asamprajnata samadhi* that he cares for nothing but merging with the Lord; and when this level is reached he remains in the body for only a few days.

10. ते प्रतिप्रसवहेयाः सूक्ष्माः ।

Te pratiprasava-heyah suksmah

Their subtle forms (of the pain-bearing afflictions) can be avoided by reabsorbing them into their cause.

When these various afflictions are a minor distraction to the aspirant they can be merged back into their cause by substituting the opposite mental modifications. For example, if egotistical thoughts arise, they can be combatted by focussing on the brotherhood of all mankind. If feelings of attraction or avoidance enter the mind, then contentment or acceptance can be substituted.

11. ध्यानहेयास्तद्वृत्तयः ।

Dhyana-heyas tad-vrttayah

Their active forms can be avoided through meditation.

If the afflictions are overt and a great distraction to the mind, they can be alleviated through regular meditation.

12. क्लेशमूलः कर्माशयो दृष्टादृष्टजन्मवेदनीयः ।

Klesa-mulah karmasayo drstadrsta-janma-vedaniyah

Karma, whether worked out in this or future lives, has its roots in the pain-bearing afflictions.

The law of Karma states that every action brings about an equal and opposite reaction. Whatever is done to others will return to the doer in some form or another. Most people are continually creating new karmic situations. This is due to ignorance and its accompanying afflictions. Before final emancipation, all Karmic debts must be worked out, whether one decides to do so in the present life or leaves this work for later lifetimes.

13. सति मूले तद्विपाको जात्यायुर्भोगाः ।

Sati mule tad-vipako jaty-ayur-bhogah

As long as the root remains, the Karma must be fulfilled, resulting in various social situations, lifespans and experiences.

Each must reap what he sows. Various life experiences are due to the Karmic situations that each has earned for himself by his thoughts, words and deeds.

14. ते ह्लादपरितापफलाः पुण्यापुण्यहेतुत्वात् ।

Te hlada-paritapa-phalah punyapunya-hetutvat

They have pleasure or pain as their fruit, according ho whether their cause is virtue or vice.

Understanding this, the yogi strives to do only good actions and to accept peacefully the ill that comes his way so that all his seeds of Karma are burned and no new ones are sown.

15. परिणामतापसंस्कारदुःखैर्गुणवृत्तिविरोधाच्च दुःखमेव सर्वं विवेकिनः ।

Parinama-tapa-samskara-duhkhair guna-vrtti-virodhac ca duhkham eva sarvam vivekinah

To those who are discriminating, every action brings pain due to the anticipation of loss, new desires, or conflicts arising out of the interaction between the mind and the three qualities of nature.

The wise man realizes that no happiness is to be found in the material world, for pain eventually arises from all actions. Where there is lack of discrimination, happiness is accompanied by the fear of its loss; and since change is a law of nature, loss is inevitable. When not concerned with loss, the mind is often conjuring up new ideas, and there is no happiness until those are satisfied, which is, again, immediately followed by fear of loss. The uncentered mind is never at rest for it is ever caught in the play of the qualities of nature — purity, activity and lethargy. Peace can only be found beyond the phenomenal world.

16. हेयं दुःखमनागतम् ।

Heyam duhkham anagatam

The misery that has not yet manifested should be avoided.

Karma has been worked out, is being worked out, or is waiting to be worked out by one's actions. Karma that has already been incurred cannot be changed, but its misery can be avoided by positive thinking. Future pain can be avoided by carefully attending to present actions.

17. द्रष्टृदृश्ययोः संयोगो हेयहेतुः ।

Drastr-drsyayoh samyogo heya-hetuh

The cause of future Karma is the identification of the experiencer with the object that is being experienced.

When a person is identifying with this illusory world, the ego predominates, and he acts without wisdom, incurring new Karma for himself.

18. प्रकाशक्रियास्थितिशीलं भूतेन्द्रियात्मकं भोगापवर्गार्थं दृश्यम् ।

Prakasa-kriya-sthiti-silam bhutendriyat-makam bhogapavargartham drsyam

The universe, which is experienced through the interaction between the elements and the perceptions of the sense organs, is composed of sattwa, rajas, and tamas, and exists solely for the purpose of (man's) experience and liberation.

As has been explained, *Purusha* is absolute and without qualities. However, man sees not the Divine, but *Prakriti,* or nature, and its three *gunas,* or qualities. These are *sattwa,* purity; *rajas,* activity; and *tamas,* inertia. Through his senses he perceives and interprets nature and its elements. In life after life he gains experience in the realm of *Prakriti* until he finally realizes that the qualities are nothing but his interpretation of Reality, and that in Truth, he is one with all. The purpose of life is to work through this physical plane, using its conditions to clear away Karma. Through constant purification and balancing of the mind, *sattwa, rajas* and *tamas* are brought into equilibrium, and man returns to the Source that is beyond the manifest world.

19. विशेषाविशेषलिङ्गमात्रालिङ्गानि गुणपर्वाणि ।

Visesavisesa-lingamatralingani guna-parvani

The states of the three gunas are gross, fine, manifest and unmanifest.

The three qualities pervade all of nature, whether in the

elements of the earth or in the subtler matters of mind and spirit.

20. द्रष्टा दृशिमात्रः शुद्धोऽपि प्रत्ययानुपश्यः ।

Drasta drsimatrah suddho 'pi pratyaya-nupasyah

The Seer is pure consciousness only, and though pure, he appears to see through the mind.

The Seer is the Self, or *Purusha.* It is untainted, pure, and without qualifications, but is reflected through the intellect of individual consciousnesses and is colored by *sattwa, rajas,* and *tamas.* It is veiled, appearing to have attributes, but in fact, it is Absolute Consciousness itself.

21. तदर्थ एव दृश्यस्यात्मा ।

Tad-artha eva drsyasyatma

The very existence of the seen is for the Seer.

The seen, *Prakriti,* exists for and is subordinate to the Seer, or Self. Its sole purpose is to provide experience for the growth and Self-Realization of man.

22. कृतार्थं प्रति नष्टमप्यनष्टं तदन्यसाधारणत्वात् ।

Krtartham prati nastam apy anastam tad-anya-sadharanatvat

Even though it (Prakriti) becomes non-existent for him who has fulfilled its purpose, it continues to exist for others for it is common to all.

To one who has attained liberation, *Prakriti* ceases to exist, and its purpose has been carried out. But Nature, the phenomenal world, remains a common experience for those who have yet to realize the Self; it continues to exist for them.

23. स्वस्वामिशक्त्योः स्वरूपोपलब्धिहेतुः संयोगः ।

Sva-svami-saktyoh svarupopalabdhi-hetuh samyogah

The purpose of the union of Purusha and Prakriti is that the former gains awareness of his true nature and realizes the powers latent in him and in Prakriti.

Here Patanjali answers the very basic question as to why the soul must pass through the trials of worldly existence at all. *Purusha* here refers to the Soul which, though universal, has its individual manifestations. The Soul incarnates in order to experience *Prakriti,* to learn its lessons, and to comprehend and actualize its natural powers.

24. तस्य हेतुरविद्या ।

Tasya hetur avidya

The cause (of this union) is avidya.

The Soul, by its very nature, is eternal, omniscient and free. But it forgets its divinity through *avidya,* ignorance, and desires objects of the senses. So it must enter *Prakriti,* incarnating on earth to relearn that all in the material world is temporary and wrought with pain. This lesson is learned in time, depending on the desire for liberation, and the Soul returns to its Source.

25. तदभावात् संयोगाभावो हानं तद् दृशे: कैवल्यम् ।

Tad-abhavat samyogabhavo hanam tad drseh kaivalyam

With the elimination of avidya comes the disappearance of the association of Purusha and Prakriti, and the Seer is liberated.

Ignorance is the reason for *Purusha* or Soul to associate itself with *Prakriti.* When ignorance is replaced by Illumination there no longer is need for the individual soul to exist in the material world, and it is liberated from the trials of earthly life.

26. विवेकख्यातिरविप्लवा हानोपाय: ।

Viveka-khyatir aviplava hanopayah

The means of destroying avidya is unbroken discrimination.

The word *viveka* is translated as discriminative cognition, awareness of the distinction between the Self and the non-Self, and awareness of Reality. So the remedy for ignorance is the constant unwavering awareness that the individual is but Brahman itself. This can only be achieved through many years of conditioning the mind to turn to divine thoughts each time worldly thoughts enter. This is the purpose of meditation and other forms of *sadhana.*

27. तस्य सप्तधा प्रान्तभूमि: प्रज्ञा ।

Tasya saptadha pranta-bhumih prajna

Enlightenment is reached through seven steps.

Patanjali begins his explanation of the eight limbs of Raja Yoga. There are seven limbs before the aspirant reaches *samadhi.*

28. योगाङ्गानुष्ठानादशुद्धिक्षये ज्ञानदीप्तिरा विवेकख्यातेः ।

Yoganganusthanad asuddhi-ksaye jnana-diptir a viveka-khyateh

By practicing the various steps of Yoga, impurities are destroyed and spiritual illumination arises, which develops into awareness of Reality.

The theoretical aspects of Yoga having been dealt with, Patanjali now points out that following the practical steps is necessary.

29. यमनियमासनप्राणायामप्रत्याहारधारणाध्यानसमाध्योऽष्टावङ्गानि ।

Yama-niyama-asana-pranayama-pratyahara-dharana-dhyana-samadhayo 'stav angani

Yama, niyama, asana, pranayama, pratyahara, dharana, dhyana and samadhi are the eight limbs.

Raja Yoga is sometimes called *Ashtanga Yoga,* or the Yoga of eight limbs. They translate, in the order given above, as self-restraints, observances, postures, regulation of breath, withdrawal of the mind from sense objects, concentration, meditation and the superconscious state.

30. अहिंसासत्यास्तेयब्रह्मचर्यापरिग्रहा यमाः ।

Ahimsa-satyasteya-brahmacarya-aparigraha yamah

The yamas consist of non-injury, truthfulness, non-stealing, continence, and non-acquisitiveness.

The *yamas,* or abstentions, make up the most basic of all spiritual practices. They are the injunctions common to every religion. These forms of self-restraint purify the individual and eliminate all of one's negative influences on others and the environment.

Violence to others, whether in thought, word or deed, must be avoided. Non-injury means more than refraining from inflicting physical pain. Mental pain can be far more devastating. When one is established in complete harmlessness, even wild animals will approach in peace.

The function of truth is to maintain harmony through trust.

It is better to be silent than to tell a truth that will cause pain or that springs from a wrong motive. A truthful person has power, for what he says comes to pass, and his word becomes law.

Brahmacharya, sexual abstinence, is necessary for rapid progress on the spiritual path. When sexual energy is under control, 99% of one's spiritual life is under control. This is very difficult, for, next to breathing, it is the body's strongest impulse. Be humble, pray for strength, and be regular in discipline, which will flatten out the sexual thought waves. With continence comes spiritual power. Ten months of control brings tremendous energy, and the chaste mind develops enormous will power.

It is wise not to acquire possessions, for they often have strings attached, and tend to make the owner dependent. A person who has possessions is a prisoner of those objects, and must expend energy and time caring for them. The man who owns and desires nothing is absolutely free. Possessions satisfy the body, encouraging identification with it, and tend to muddy the mind.

31. जातिदेशकालसमयानवच्छिन्नाः सार्वभौमा महाव्रतम् ।

Jati-desa-kala-samayanavacchinnah sarvabhauma
maha-vratam

These (abstentions) are not limited by social structure, location, time or circumstances, and they constitute the great (universal) vow.

These abstentions are universal, and are meant to be practiced at all times, regardless of the situation. Any inconvenience or pain that accrues as a result of their practice should be accepted as the result of karmic obligation.

32. शौचसंतोषतपःस्वाध्यायेश्वरप्रणिधानानि नियमाः ।

Sauca-samtosa-tapah-svadhyayesvara-pranidhanani niyamah

The niyamas consist of cleanliness, contentment, austerity, self-study and self-surrender.

The *niyamas* are observances which cultivate positive qualities. They involve purification, stilling the mind, self-discipline, inquiry into the nature of the Self, and surrendering the personal will, or ego, for the Supreme Will.

Aside from cleanliness, one should cultivate indifference toward the body. Cleanliness means internal as well as external purification. A proper diet based on vegetarianism and natural foods, specialized yogic cleansing techniques, and the Yoga exercises keep the body internally pure and free from obstructions. Cleanliness also extends to the mind. Only when it is purified of all dross can it be a pure mirror for the reflection of the Self.

Laughter comes from stimulation, but a smile comes from inner peacefulness. Satisfied with itself, the mind needs nothing else for its contentment, which grows in proportion to awareness of the inner Self. The mind should not be affected by external objects. They may be possessed, but with detachment. Do not let them possess the mind.

Austerity means curtailing the insatiable demands of the senses. Drink water instead of coffee, practice silence instead of talking, control greed by eating bland food, and counteract sleep by getting up early. When the mind learns that its demands for pleasure will not be met through the senses, it stops its useless wandering and turns inward. Control of the senses clears the way for such powers as telepathy and clairvoyance.

Study of spiritual works and the scriptures helps to keep a person on the right path. Books alone, however, can only take one so far, and can lead to intellectual pride. Surrender to the will of God is necessary, for ultimately everything depends upon His grace.

33. वितर्कबाधने प्रतिपक्षभावनम् ।

Vitarka-badhane-pratipaksa-bhavanam

When negative or harmful thoughts disturb the mind, they can be overcome by constant pondering over their opposites.

The yogi is ever alert, always watching his mind. When he sees useless thought waves arising, he immediately replaces them with positive thoughts, thus creating new mental habits that are conducive to spiritual growth.

34. वितर्का हिंसादयः कृतकारितानुमोदिता लोभक्रोधमोहपूर्वका मृदुमध्याधिमात्रा दुःखाज्ञानानन्तफला इति प्रतिपक्षभावनम् ।

Vitarka himsadayah krta-karitanumodita lobha-krodha-moha-purvaka mrdu-madhyadhimatra duhkhajnanananta-phala iti pratipaksa-bhavanam

Negative thoughts and emotions, such as violence, whether committed, abetted, or caused through greed, anger or delusion, and whether present in mild, medium or great intensity, result in endless pain and ignorance. Thus there is the neces-

sity for pondering over the opposites.

All thoughts, emotions and actions that are in opposition to the basic tenets of the *yamas* and *niyamas* bring about the Karma of further pain and ignorance. This is true whether the action is actually carried out, remains in thought form, or is incited in others. Whatever the cause, whatever the degree of involvement, Karma is still incurred. This is why it is necessary to substitute positive and sublime thoughts the moment negative ones are caught arising in the mind.

35. अहिंसाप्रतिष्ठायां तत्संनिधौ वैरत्यागः ।

Ahimsa-pratisthayam tat-samnidhau vaira-tyagah

When non-violence is firmly established, hostility vanishes in the yogi's presence.

One who is firmly rooted in non-violence radiates this conviction to others. He is so powerful that not even violent thoughts can exist in his presence.

36. सत्यप्रतिष्ठायां क्रियाफलाश्रयत्वम् ।

Satya-pratisthayam kriya-phalasrayatvam

When truth is firmly established, the yogi attains the result of action without acting.

The words of a person who has practiced truth to the highest degree will manifest, for the words of such a person reflect the Truth of *Atman*.

37. अस्तेयप्रतिष्ठायां सर्वरत्नोपस्थानम् ।

Asteya-pratisthayam sarva-ratnopasthanam

When non-stealing becomes firmly established, all wealth comes to the yogi.

The more a yogi flees from material objects, the more they seem to come to him. The purpose of this natural law is two-fold. The first is so that he may be tested and confirmed in his renunciation. The second is so that he, as a wise person, may appropriately dispense the wealth to benefit mankind.

38. ब्रह्मचर्यप्रतिष्ठायां वीर्यलाभः ।

Brahmacarya-pratisthayam virya-labhah

When brahmacharya, or sexual continence, is firmly established, vibrant vitality is gained.

When sexual energy is sublimated and preserved it is converted into *ojas*, or spiritual energy. This *ojas* is such a radiant force that it uplifts all who come into contact with the *brahmachari*.

39. अपरिग्रहस्थैर्ये जन्मकथंतासंबोध: ।

Aparigraha-sthairye janma-kathamta-sambodhah

When non-acquisitiveness is established, an understanding of the purpose of birth is gained.

When the yogi no longer desires to have possessions he frees himself from the material world. This gives him a perspective of the purpose of his birth, both in this life and in past ones. He gains comprehension of the law of Karma and understands what lessons remain to be learned before attaining Realization.

40. शौचात् स्वाङ्गजुगुप्सा परैरसंसर्ग: ।

Saucat svanga-jugupsa parair asamsargah

From purification comes disgust for one's own body and a disinclination to come into physical contact with others.

Cleanliness, both internal and external, and mental purification help to turn the mind towards the Divine. Through purification one sees quite clearly that beauty is only skin deep and that real beauty exists in the spirit only. When the body is kept immaculately clean, it becomes more easily apparent that it is but an instrument for carrying out the work of advancing toward God-Realization.

41. सत्त्वशुद्धिसौमनस्यैकाग्र्येन्द्रियजयात्मदर्शनयोग्यत्वानि च ।

Sattvasuddhi-saumanasyaikagryendriya-jayatma-darsana-yogyatvani ca

From purification also come clarity of mind, cheerfulness, one-pointedness, control of the senses, and fitness, for realization of the Self.

From internal and external cleansing come all of the above, that is, a prevailing sense of *sattwa*, the quality of purity and light.

42. संतोषादनुत्तमः सुखलाभः ।

Samtosad anuttamah sukha-labhah

From contentment comes supreme happiness.

Man is ever searching for happiness in external objects, but it can only be attained when the mind is satisfied with what has been alloted and is no longer looking. When the mind is stilled and contented, happiness is automatic.

43. कायेन्द्रियसिद्धिरशुद्धिक्षयात् तपसः ।

Kayendriya-siddhir asuddhi-ksayat tapasah

The destruction of impurities through austerities brings about powers to the body and senses.

When austerities, self-imposed disciplines, are practiced, great will is developed, and the abilities of the physical body and senses are extended beyond what is considered normal.

44. स्वाध्यायादिष्टदेवतासंप्रयोगः ।

Svadhyayad ista-devata-samprayogah

Through study that leads to knowledge of the Self comes union with the desired ishta devata.

Intense self-inquiry and study lead one to communion with his personal deity, or *ishta devata*. However a person conceives of God, that is how he encounters Him. This *sutra* also alludes to the use of Mantra. Constant repetition of the name of Deity will bring His grace.

45. समाधिसिद्धिरीश्वरप्रणिधानात् ।

Samadhi-siddhir Isvara-pranidhanat

From surrender to Ishwara comes the accomplishment of attaining samadhi.

Only by surrendering one's will, one's ego, one's life, to God is the superconscious state attained.

46. स्थिरसुखमासनम् ।

Sthira-sukham asanam

Asanas should be steady and comfortable.

Having thoroughly explained the *yamas* and *niyamas*, Patanjali now moves on to the next limb of Raja Yoga, the *asanas*, or postures. This is the whole subdivision of Raja Yoga known as Hatha Yoga, which works directly with the *prana* and *kundalini*, the more subtle energy currents of the body. Hatha Yoga postures, always done in a specific order, massage the endocrine glands and release energy blockages in the system so that a meditative state is brought about physically rather than through sitting and watching the mind. Hatha Yoga is best practiced in conjunction with meditation for the *asanas* are a vital aid, but not the end, on the path to *samadhi*.

It is said that the *asana* should be steady and comfortable. Whether the posture is a simple cross-legged meditation position or part of a set of Hatha Yoga exercises, it is important that the practitioner not be strained. He should be able to relax in the position — yet hold it perfectly still for a given amount of time. Fidgeting and loss of concentration only waste energy. Just as in meditation, the mind and body must remain one-pointed.

47. प्रयत्नशैथिल्यानन्तसमापत्तिभ्याम् ।

Prayatna-saithilyananta-samapattibhyam

Posture is mastered by releasing tension and meditation on the Unlimited.

There should be no strain, but only a firm and relaxed maintaining of the position. Then with the mind focussed on the Infinite, one's limitations are more easily extended, and the *asana* is mastered.

48. ततो द्वन्द्वानभिघातः ।

Tato dvandvanabhighatah

From that (mastery of asana), no assaults come from the pairs of opposites.

When *asanas* are mastered, the yogi is not touched by the play of duality. His will and concentration are developed to such an extent that heat and cold, pleasure and pain, good and bad, and all other worldly influences do not touch him.

49. तस्मिन् सति श्वासप्रश्वासयोर्गतिविच्छेदः प्राणायामः ।

Tasmin sati svasa-prasvasayor gati-vicchedah pranayamah

The next step is pranayama, which is the control of the inhalation and exhalation of breath.

The fourth limb of Raja Yoga is *pranayama,* which includes specific breathing exercises for heating and cooling the body, raising its energy levels, or relaxation.

Prana, the vital energy, may be obtained from food and water, but the primary source is the air that is breathed. Control of it is directly linked with control of the mind. Because of its power, the techniques should be practiced under the guidance of a teacher. The awakening of the *kundalini* as a means of Self-Realization depends on control over the breath, and hence the *prana.*

50. बाह्याभ्यन्तरस्तम्भवृत्तिर्देशकालसंख्याभिः परिदृष्टो दीर्घसूक्ष्मः ।

Bahyabhyantara-stambha-vrttir desakala-samkhyabhih
paridrsto dirghasuksmah

Pranayama is inhalation, exhalation or retention of breath; it is regulated by place, time and number, and (becomes progressively) prolonged and subtle.

Here all the variations in *pranayama* are given, each yielding a different result. With practice, each breath and retention is prolonged and made more silent, and the yogi develops more control and concentration.

51. बाह्याभ्यन्तरविषयाक्षेपी चतुर्थः ।

Bahyabhyantara-visayaksepi caturthah

The fourth type (of pranayama) goes beyond the sphere of inhalation and exhalation.

Beyond inhalation, exhalation and retention is the fourth type of *pranayama,* which involves actually directing the subtle prana, rather than the breath itself. When this is achieved, the flow of external breathing stops, and the yogi is able to move his *prana* in such a way as to awaken the great psychic force of *kundalini.*

52. ततः क्षीयते प्रकाशावरणम् ।

Tatah ksiyate prakasavaranam

That unveils the light.

The fourth type of *pranayama*, that which activates the *kundalini*, brings Illumination. It clears the mind so that the Inner Light can shine.

53. धारणासु च योग्यता मनसः ।

Dharanasu ca yogyata manasah

And makes the mind fit for dharana (concentration).

Pranayama is the link between the physical and mental disciplines. While the action is physical, the effect is to make the mind calm, lucid and steady.

54. स्वविषयासंप्रयोगे चित्तस्वरूपानुकार इवेन्द्रियाणां प्रत्याहारः ।

Sva-visayasamprayoge citta-svarupanukara ivendriyanam pratyaharah

Pratyahara is the imitation of the mind by the senses, which comes by withdrawing the senses from their objects.

In meditation the mind is withdrawn from external stimulation so that it can be at peace. *Pratyahara,* the fifth limb of Yoga, involves the same thing with the senses. Whatever objects are agitating to the senses are simply eliminated from sensory contact. The eyes do not watch a stimulating film. The ears are not given an opportunity to hear music that raises feelings of discontent. The tongue is given no opportunity to taste food that is detrimental. In this way the mind is much less likely to take on thought forms which are detrimental since the sense organs are withdrawn from the objects that cause the unwanted *vrittis* to arise. A good portion of the more difficult aspects of discipline can be dealt with in this way, and the mind is more easily stilled.

55. ततः परमा वश्यतेन्द्रियाणाम् ।

Tatah parama vasyatendriyanam

From that comes the highest mastery over the senses.

The senses are man's connection to the physical plane. When it is decided that it is time to transcend the distractions of the world, the most difficult undertaking is mastery of the senses. Through perfection of *pratyahara* the greatest obstacles to Enlightenment are overcome.

CHAPTER THREE: DIVINE MANIFESTATIONS OF POWER

Chapter Three of the *Raja Yoga Sutras* elucidates the last three limbs of Raja Yoga, *dharana, dhyana* and *samadhi.* These three highest levels of meditation practiced together are called *samyama,* which is also explained in detail. Patanjali also describes many of the *siddhis,* or powers, that are attained through the protracted practice of meditation.

1. देशबन्धश्चित्तस्य धारणा ।

Desa-bandhas cittasya dharana

Dharana is fixing the mind on one object.

The object of *dharana,* concentration, may be external or it may be an internal plexus. It may also be a Mantra. If there is difficulty in keeping the mind within a limited area of focus in the early stages of practice, one may keep it moving within a broader circumscribed area in which everything relates to the object. Then, the area of focus is narrowed as greater control is gained. When the mind can be limited to one point, it is concentrated.

2. तत्र प्रत्ययैकतानता ध्यानम् ।

Tatra pratyayaikatanata dhyanam

An unbroken flow of perception between the mind and objects is dhyana, meditation.

In meditation the mind is not distracted but holds steadily to the object of concentration. No other thoughts enter the mind.

3. तदेवार्थमात्रनिर्भासं स्वरूपशून्यमिव समाधिः ।

Tad evarthamatra-nirbhasam svarupa-sunyam iva samadhih

When consciousness of subject and object disappears and only the meaning remains, it is called samadhi.

Samadhi is a merging of the mind into the essence of the object of meditation. Nothing exists but that pure awareness.

4. त्रयमेकत्र संयमः ।

Trayam ekatra samyamah

(The practice of) these three together is samyama.

When concentration, meditation and *samadhi* flow in an unbroken sequence on one object, the process is called *samyama*. This flow cannot be forced. Any such attempt means that thought waves are being summoned to control thought waves, which is self-defeating, for the aim is to still all thought waves. The ability to practice *samyama* comes from years of pratice and purification.

5. तज्जयात् प्रज्ञालोक: ।

Taj-jayat prajnalokah

By mastering it (samyama) comes the light of direct knowledge.

When *samyama* is mastered, higher consciousness is attained. All intuitive knowledge becomes available.

6. तस्य भूमिषु विनियोग: ।

Tasya bhumisu viniyogah

Its (of samyama) application (should be) in stages.

Even though a person must be highly evolved in order to be able to achieve *samyama,* a caution is still given here that progress should be gradual. *Samyama* is very powerful, and its application requires great wisdom.

7. त्रयमन्तरङ्गं पूर्वेभ्य: ।

Trayam antarangam purvebhyah

These three are more internal than the preceding ones.

Dharana, dhyana and *samadhi* are internal; they are practices of the mind. This is in contrast to the first five limbs of Raja Yoga which work through the physical system.

8. तदपि बहिरङ्गं निर्बीजस्य ।

Tad api bahir-angam nirbijasya

But even these are external (compared) to the "seedless" state.

In *nirbija samadhi,* mentioned in the last *sutra* of the first chapter, there is absolutely nothing remaining but union with the Lord. So, it is said that *samyama* is but an externalization in relation to that ultimate state.

9. व्युत्थाननिरोधसंस्कारयोरभिभवप्रादुर्भावौ निरोधक्षणचित्तान्वयो
निरोधपरिणामः ।

Vyutthana-nirodha-samskarayor abhibhava-pradurbhavau
nirodha-ksanacittanvayo nirodha-parinamah

*Through the constant replacement of disturbing thought
waves by ones of control, the mind is transformed and gains
mastery of itself.*

Reaching the superconscious state is a matter of practice. If
useless thoughts are eliminated the moment they appear, they are
gradually weeded out.

10. तस्य प्रशान्तवाहिता संस्कारात् ।

Tasya prasanta-vahita samskarat

Its flow becomes undisturbed through repetition.

Mastery of control of the mind comes through creating new
habits. When the *samskaras* of restraint are reinforced often enough,
the mind becomes tranquil.

11. सर्वार्थतैकाग्रतयोः क्षयोदयौ चित्तस्य समाधिपरिणामः ।

Sarvarthataikagratayoh ksayodayau cittasya samadhi-
parinamah

*The transformation (leading to the ability to enter) samadhi
comes gradually through the elimination of distractions and
the rise of one-pointedness.*

Both control of the mind, as described in *sutra* 9, and
entering *samadhi* are gradual transformations. This is being emphasized because of the inherent responsibility involved in entering
the higher levels of consciousness.

12. ततः पुनः शान्तोदितौ तुल्यप्रत्ययौ चित्तस्यैकाग्रतापरिणामः

Tatah punah santoditau tulya-pratyayau cittasyaikagrata-
parinamah

*One-pointedness of the mind occurs when the contents of
the mind that rise and fall at two different moments are
exactly the same.*

Vrittis are called thought waves, for they are rising and

falling moment by moment. In normal thinking, there are literally thousands of different waves within just a few minutes. As one *vritti* falls, another rises — one after another in succession, for the mind can only entertain one thought at a time. One-pointedness occurs when the *vritti* that is falling and the *vritti* that is arising both carry the same though.

13. एतेन भूतेन्द्रियेषु धर्मलक्षणावस्थापरिणामा व्याख्याताः ।

Etena bhutendriyesu dharma-laksana-vastha-parinama
vyakhyatah

By this (what has been said in the previous sutras) changes in the form, time, and condition of the elements and sense organs are explained.

The preceding *sutras* have dealt with the gradual gaining control of the mind. By mastering the mind, its relation to the elements and the sense organs changes. These changes are explained in the following series of aphorisms.

14. शान्तोदिताव्यपदेश्यधर्मानुपाती धर्मी ।

Santoditavyapadesya-dharmanupati dharmi

There is a substratum that remains consistent through all changes, past, present and future.

All things, whether of the physical world or etheric, have an underlying essence. While they may go through change, as water becomes ice or steam, they still retain their basic Reality.

15. क्रमान्यत्वं परिणामान्यत्वे हेतुः ।

Kramanyatvam parinamanyatve hetuh

The cause of various transformations is the different natural laws.

Whether change is brought about in the normal course of events, or it is due to the will of the yogi, it still proceeds from natural laws. Science is just beginning to discover and work with the many forces beyond gross physical perception that have been utilized by yogis for many thousands of years.

16. परिणामत्रयसंयमादतीतानागतज्ञानम् ।

Parinama-traya-samyamad atitanagata-jnanam

By performing samyama on the three kinds of changes (form, time and condition) comes knowledge of the past and future.

Beginning with this *sutra,* the remaining aphorisms in the third chapter deal with the various *siddhis.* While the word *siddhi* is usually taken to mean power, it actually refers to the accomplishments of an advanced yogi. It is of paramount importance that the student understand that yogic powers are not, and should not, be considered a goal in themselves. They are the by-product of the struggle toward God-Realization. Those who strive for the powers alone are bound to the ego and eventually suffer because of this lack of purification. There is often a fascination on the part of the beginning student with yogic powers, but this is replaced in time with the understanding that power corrupts, and that these inevitable accomplishments are but distractions and temptations to the sincere yogi.

On the other hand, it is best that it be clearly understood that these *siddhis* do exist. It takes a most highly advanced spiritual person to perform them, yet one who is so near God-Realization knows that he is wasting spiritual energy and abusing the powers by displaying them to the idly curious. These abilities are due to natural laws, as mentioned in the fifteenth *sutra,* although science has only begun to investigate them. In the past, science has dealt mostly with laws of the physical plane. Yogic *siddhis* work directly with the more subtle and powerful aspects of Nature. Research is now beginning in the West, although the Soviet Union and other Eastern European countries have done extensive work in recent years.

In this particular *sutra,* it is explained that knowledge of the past and future are achieved by practicing *samyama* on form, or physical properties; on time, or changing characteristics; and on condition, or the temporary state in which an object exists at any given time. Sometimes this *sutra* is interpreted to mean that one may gain knowledge not of the past and future, but of the *nature* of past and future. In other words, all things must change, and this knowledge is a fundamental attainment, for it brings acceptance and contentment.

17. शब्दार्थप्रत्ययानामितरेतराध्यासात् संकरस्तत्प्रविभागसंयमात् सर्वभूतरुतज्ञानम् ।

Sabdartha-pratyayanam itaretaradhyasat samkaras tatpravibhaga-samyamat sarva-bhuta-ruta-jnanam

*Sound, meaning and corresponding ideas are usually con-
fused together in the mind; but when samyama is performed
on the sound, their meaning and ideas are resolved, and
comprehension is gained of the sounds of all living beings.*

This is most easily understood through the use of Mantra,
in which constant meditation on the Lord's name brings realization
of His qualities and even the experience of His presence. Generally, however, the *sutra* refers to any word of any language, and
even to the sounds of animals.

18. संस्कारसाक्षात्करणात् पूर्वजातिज्ञानम् ।

Samskara-saksatkaranat puvra-jatijnanam

*By perceiving samskaras comes knowledge of the previous
birth.*

When *samyama* is performed on the *samskaras,* or habitual
impressions of one's mind, knowledge of past births comes. This
is because the Karma that must be worked out in this life depends
on the impressions carried over from past lives that were not dealt
with at the time.

19. प्रत्ययस्य परचित्तज्ञानम् ।

Pratyayasya para-citta-jnanam

*(By performing samyama on) another's mind, its mental
images are known.*

20. न च तत् सालम्बनं तस्याविषयीभूतत्वात् ।

Na ca tat salambanam tasyavisayi-bhutatvat

*But other mental factors which are not the subject of
samyama cannot be known.*

21. कायरूपसंयमात् तद्ग्राह्यशक्तिस्तम्भे चक्षुःप्रकाशासंप्रयोगेऽन्तर्धानम् ।

Kaya-rupa-samyamat tad-grahya-sakti-stambhe caksuh-
prakasasamprayoge 'ntardhanam

*Samyama performed on one's physical body suspends the
ability of another to see it; the reflected light (from the*

*body) does not come into contact with another's eyes, hence
the power of invisibility.*

22. एतेन शब्दाद्यन्तर्धानमुक्तम् ।

Etena sabdady antardhanam uktam

*From this can also be explained the disappearance of sound
and other physical phenomena.*

23. सोपक्रमं निरुपक्रमं च कर्म तत्संयमादपरान्तज्ञानमरिष्टेभ्यो वा ।

Sopakramam nirupakramam ca karma tat-samymad aparanta-
jnanam aristebhyo va

*Karma may be either dormant or active; by performing
samyama on both, and through omens, the yogi may know
the time of death.*

24. मैत्र्यादिषु बलानि ।

Maitry-adisu balani

*(By performing samyama) on friendliness (mercy, love etc.),
their strengths are gained.*

25. बलेषु हस्तिबलादीनि ।

Balesu hasti-baladini

*(By performing samyama) on strengths (of various animals)
comes the power of an elephant (or any other species).*

26. प्रवृत्त्यालोकन्यासात् सूक्ष्मव्यवहितविप्रकृष्टज्ञानम् ।

Pravrtty-aloka-nyasat suksma-vyavahita-viprakrsta-jnanam

*(By performing samyama) on light comes intuitive knowledge
of that which is subtle, hidden or distant.*

27. भुवनज्ञानं सूर्ये संयमात् ।

Bhuvana-jnanam surye samyamat

*By performing samyama on the sun comes knowledge of the
world.*

28. चन्द्रे ताराव्यूहज्ञानम् ।

Candre tara-vyuha-jnanam

(By performing samyama) on the moon comes knowledge of astrology.

29. ध्रुवे तद्गतिज्ञानम् ।

Dhruve tad-gati-jnanam

(By performing samyama) on the pole star comes knowledge of the movement of the stars.

30. नाभिचक्रे कायव्यूहज्ञानम् ।

Nabhi-cakre kaya-vyuha-jnanam

(By performing samyama) on the navel center comes knowledge of the organization of the body.

31. कण्ठकूपे क्षुत्पिपासानिवृत्तिः ।

Kantha-kupe ksut-pipasa-nivrttih

(By performing samyama) on the hollow of the throat comes cessation of thoughts of hunger and thirst.

32. कूर्मनाड्यां स्थैर्यम् ।

Kurma-nadyam sthairyam

(By performing samyama) on the nerve centers which control prana, steadiness is achieved.

33. मूर्धज्योतिषि सिद्धदर्शनम् ।

Murdha-jyotisi siddha-darsanam

(By performing samyama on) the light at the crown of the head comes the power to perceive perfected Beings.

34. प्रातिभाद्वा सर्वम् ।

Pratibhad va sarvam

Through intuition, all knowledge is available.

35. हृदये चित्तसंवित् ।

Hrdaye citta-samvit

*(By performing samyama) on the heart, understanding of
the nature of the mind is gained.*

36. सत्त्वपुरुषयोरत्यन्तासंकीर्णयोः प्रत्ययाविशेषो भोगः परार्थात्
    स्वार्थसंयमात् पुरुषज्ञानम् ।

Sattva-purusayor atyantasamkirnayoh pratyayaviseso bhogah
pararthat svartha-samyamat purusa-jnanam

*Enjoyment is the result of a lack of discrimination between
Purusha and sattwa. Knowledge of Purusha comes from
performing samyama on the interests of the Self rather than
on the individual's interest.*

Purusha is absolute Divinity, which is beyond qualities.
Sattwa is purity, but it remains a quality of Nature. From *sattwa*
comes joy and light, but as mentioned previously, these qualities
must be transcended for the final merging with the Self. This
distinguishes between the purity of the Absolute and the purity of Nature. It is further explained that knowledge of *Purusha* is
gained by perfected meditation on the interests of the Self rather
than on individual interests.

37. ततः प्रातिभश्रावणवेदनादर्शास्वादवार्ता जायन्ते ।

Tatah pratibha-sravana-vedanadarsasvada-varta jayante

*From that comes intuitional hearing, thought, sight, taste,
and smell.*

Whatever is given up, automatically comes to the renunciate. By performing *samyama* on the interests of the Self rather
than on individual interests, all intuitional knowledge becomes available.

38. ते समाधावुपसर्गा व्युत्थाने सिद्धयः ।

Te samadhav upasarga vyutthane siddhayah

*These are obstacles to the state of samadhi, though they
are considered powers to the mind which is worldly.*

Here Patanjali makes it *very clear* that all of the *siddhis* that
have been described above are but temptations and distractions
from the superconscious state. They only appear attractive to those

who are steeped in worldliness, egoism, and the desire for power.

39. बन्धकारणशैथिल्यात् प्रचारसंवेदनाच्च चित्तस्य परशरीरावेशः ।

Bandha-karana-saithilyat pracara-samvedanac ca cittasya
para-sariravesah

*When the cause of bondage has been eliminated, the mind
can enter another's body through knowledge of its channels.*

When the highly advanced Yogi has given up attachment
to life and has developed intuitive knowledge of the physical body,
he gains the ability to use another's body for the purpose of helping
and teaching others. This is not the same as possession by lower
astral entities. The perfected yogi acts purely through the Self, which
is common to all, and is thus merely directing Divine energy.

40. उदानजयाज्जलपङ्ककण्टकादिष्वसङ्ग उत्क्रान्तिश्च ।

Udana-jayaj jala-panka-kantakadisv asanga utkrantis ca

*By mastery of udana comes levitation and the ability not to
come into contact with water, mire, thorns, etc.*

Udana is one of the types of *prana*, which is concerned with
the pull of gravity. This power is available to the yogis in the last
phases of their earthly lives before merging with the Self. It is not
to be confused with "hopping", the ability to bounce about a foot
above ground during certain powerful *pranayama* exercises. Some
spiritual groups teach these exercises to beginners, however this
is physically and psychically dangerous and is not recommended,
for it causes the *prana* to move too quickly in the body. Problems
can result for those who have not been practicing *asanas* and
more simple *pranayama* for a number of years.

41. समानजयाज्ज्वलनम् ।

Samana-jayaj jvalanam

By mastery of samana comes blazing fire.

Samana is another type of *prana*, which relates to digestion.
From control of *samana* comes radiance.

42. श्रोत्राकाशयोः संबन्धसंयमाद्दिव्यं श्रोत्रम् ।

Srotrakasayoh sambandha-samyamad divyam srotram

By performing samyama on the relationship between the akasha and the ear comes superphysical hearing.

Akasha means ether, or that medium through which sound energy travels.

43. कायाकाशयोः संबन्धसंयमाल्लघुतूलसमापत्तेश्चाकाशगमनम् ।

Kayakasayoh sambandha-samyamat laghu-tula-samapattes cakasa-gamanam

By performing samyama on the relationship between the akasha and the body and on the buoyancy of light-weight objects comes the ability to pass through space.

44. बहिरकल्पिता वृत्तिर्महाविदेहा ततः प्रकाशावरणक्षयः ।

Bahir akalpita vrttir maha-videha; tatah prakasavarana-ksayah

(By performing samyama on) mental modifications that are beyond the ego and intellect comes the ability to remain outside the physical body. Hence, all that hides illumination is removed.

Man's mind is not limited by his physical body, although he usually thinks it is. But it is the intellect and the ego that bind him there. By practicing *samyama* on those thoughts that are beyond worldly imagination, the yogi connects with the Universal Mind, and his own mind is not bound by time, space or causation. All ignorance disappears.

45. स्थूलस्वरूपसूक्ष्मान्वयार्थवत्त्वसंयमाद् भूतजयः ।

Sthula-svarupa-suksmanvayarthavattva-samymad bhuta-jayah

By performing samyama on the elements in their gross, constant, subtle, pervasive and functional states, they can be controlled by the yogi.

46. ततोऽणिमादिप्रादुर्भावः कायसंपत् तद्धर्मानभिघातश्च ।

Tato 'nimadi-pradurbhavah kaya- sampat tarddharma anabhighatas ca

From that (ability to control the elements) come the eight

*siddhis, such as making the body as small as an atom as well
as perfection and invincibility of the body.*

Patanjali is referring here to what are called the *Maha Siddhis,*
or Great Powers, which have been known to yogis from very
ancient days. These are attainment of: 1) minute size, 2) colossal
size, 3) weightlessness, 4) great weight, 5) any desire or knowledge,
6) entering the body of another, 7) unhampered will, and
8) Divine Power.

47. रूपलावण्यबलवज्रसंहननत्वानि कायसंपत् ।

Rupa-lavanya-bala-vajra-samhananatvani kaya-sampat

*Perfection of the body is beauty, fine complexion, strength,
and absolute firmness.*

48. ग्रहणस्वरूपास्मितान्वयार्थवत्त्वसंयमादिन्द्रियजयः ।

Grahana-svarupasmitanvayarthavattva-samyamad indriya-
jayah

*Mastery of the sense organs is attained by performing
samyama on their power of perception, true nature, relation
to the ego, pervasiveness and function.*

49. ततो मनोजवित्वं विकरणभावः प्रधानजयश्च ।

Tato manojavitvam vikarana-bhavah pradhana-jayas ca

*From that proceeds immediate ability to have knowledge
without the use of the senses, and complete mastery over
Prakriti.*

50. सत्त्वपुरुषान्यतास्यातिमात्रस्य सर्वभावाधिष्ठातृत्वं सर्वज्ञातृत्वं च ।

Sattva-purusanyata-khyati-matrasya sarva-bhava
adhisthatrtvam sarvajnatrtvam ca

*Only through realization of the difference between sattwa
and Purusha come omnipotence and omniscience.*

In the very final phases of a sage's last life he directly experiences the difference between the quality of purity and Absolute
Purusha. Here, the yogi leaves the realm of *Prakriti,* Nature, and
becomes one with *Purusha,* the Universal Soul. Then the powers
of *Purusha,* omnipotence and omniscience, are his.

51. तद्वैराग्यादपि दोषबीजक्षये कैवल्यम् ।

Tad-vairagyad api dosa-bija-ksaye kaivalyam

By non-attachment to even that (the omnipotence and omniscience of Purusha) comes destruction of the final seed of bondage, and liberation is attained.

Absolutely everything must be given up in order to reach God-Realization, even the powers that come with God-Realization.

52. स्थान्युपनिमन्त्रणे सङ्गस्मयाकरणं पुनरनिष्टप्रसङ्गात् ।

Sthany-upanimantrane sanga-smaya-karanam punar anistaprasangat

On being invited by a celestial being, the yogi should not feel pleasure or pride, for there is danger of a revival of evil.

The higher the level attained by a yogi, the greater the temptations. Ego is the cause of any attachment or pride that might arise when the yogi attains the ability to commune with celestial beings, and this would be his downfall.

53. क्षणतत्क्रमयोः संयमाद्विवेकजं ज्ञानम् ।

Ksana-tat-kramayoh samyamad vivekajam jnanam

By performing samyama on a moment and its succession comes discrimination.

The yogi cannot be tempted by celestial beings if he is fully concentrated on the moment at hand. This is what is meant by the phrase "Be here now". His full awareness is being applied to each second that passes, so no time is left for temptations and distractions.

54. जातिलक्षणदेशैरन्यतानवच्छेदात् तुल्ययोस्ततः प्रतिपत्तिः ।

Jati-laksana-desair anyatanavacchedat tulyayos tatah pratipattih

It (discrimination) also leads to knowledge of the difference between two similar objects, when their difference cannot be ascertained by class, characteristics or location.

Samyama performed moment to moment brings awareness of Reality that cannot possibly be discerned by any ordinary forms of perception. This *sutra* is not dealing with normal differences of objects but in the subtle distinctions of the highest levels of *Prakriti* and *Purusha*. Only a liberated sage can see such differences.

55. तारकं सर्वविषयं सर्वथाविषयमक्रमं चेति विवेकजं ज्ञानम् ।

Tarakam sarva-visayam sarvatha-visayam akraman ceti vivekajam-jnanam

The highest knowledge, born of discrimination, transcends all; it perceives all simultaneously in time and space, and transcends all, even the World Process.

When discrimination is perfected, the yogi transcends time, space, and causation. There are no barriers for him. All of eternity and infinity are available to him. This is why he is said to be God-Realized.

56. सत्त्वपुरुषयोः शुद्धिसाम्ये कैवल्यम् ।

Sattva-purusayoh suddhi-samye kaivalyam

Kaivalya (liberation) is attained when there is equality between sattwa and Purusha.

Liberation takes place when the mind has the same purity as *Purusha* itself. The purified mind recognizes its nature as *Purusha*. The essence of this nature is, and always has been, bliss, freedom, peace, Self-sufficiency and perfection.

CHAPTER FOUR: LIBERATION

The final chapter of Patanjali's *Raja Yoga Sutras* discusses *kaivalya,* liberation or independence. The full-blown yogi develops perfect discrimination, or the ability to distinquish the Real from the unreal. He is no longer affected by the three *gunas* of nature, and can distinquish *Purusha* from *Prakriti*.

1. जन्मौषधिमन्त्रतपःसमाधिजाः सिद्धयः ।

Janmausadhi-mantra-tapah-samadhi jah siddhayah

Siddhis are attained as a result of birth, medicinal herbs, Mantras, austerities or samadhi.

Siddhis that are brought into the present life by birth indicate their attainment in a previous life, but it does not guarantee that the individual is making proper use of them in this life. Those gained through chemical means are not necessarily associated with any level of spirituality at all, and can be easily governed by the ego. *Siddhis* achieved by Mantra repetition or *tapas,* austerities, are generally of a very high order as long as they are performed for attaining God-Realization rather than personal or material gain. Powers that come from *samadhi* are the purest, for they come to the aspirant without being desired. It must be remembered that *siddhis* are not the aim but a by-product of the path to God-Realization.

2. जात्यन्तरपरिणामः प्रकृत्यापूरात् ।

    Jaty-antara-parinamah prakrty-apurat

    All evolutionary transformations are due to the fulfilling of Nature's tendencies.

    All powers come in direct correlation with the evolution of the individual toward perfection through his many incarnations. Any attempt to force their manifestation will stunt spiritual growth. It is man's purpose to achieve Union with the Divine. This is a natural progression which can be aided through self-discipline and self-inquiry.

3. निमित्तमप्रयोजकं प्रकृतीनां वरणभेदस्तु ततः क्षेत्रिकवत् ।

    Nimittam aprayojakam prakrtinam varana-bhedas tu tatah ksetrikavat

    An apparent cause is not necessarily instrumental in bringing about natural tendencies; it only removes obstacles, as a farmer (clears some stones to create an irrigation passageway).

4. निर्माणचित्तान्यस्मितामात्रात् ।

    Nirmana-cittany asmita-matrat

    Minds are created only from egotism.

    The mind is not the Self. It proceeds out of ego, or separation from the Self, and must be transcended to return to the Self.

5. प्रवृत्तिभेदे प्रयोजकं चित्तमेकमनेकेषाम् ।

    Pravrtti-bhede prayojakam cittam ekam anekesam

Although the pursuits of the many (created minds) vary, they are controlled by the one Mind.

The many individual minds are scattered and pursue various activities, but they are all subordinate to and ultimately under the control of the one Universal Mind, which is the Self, Absolute Consciousness.

6. तत्र ध्यानजमनाशयम् ।

Tatra dhyanajam anasayam

Of these, the mind born of dhyana is free from past tendencies, samskaras.

Of the many individual minds, those which are tempered and directed by meditation become free from useless habits and scattering activity.

7. कर्माशुक्लाकृष्णं योगिनस्त्रिविधमितरेषाम् ।

Karmasuklakrsnam yoginas tri-vidham itaresam

For a yogi, Karma is neither white nor black; for others it is three-fold.

For a yogi, Karma is objectively worked out — there is no positive or negative about it. For others it is three-fold — black, white and gray — meaning there are subjective reactions to the work that must be carried out, and this in turn creates new Karma.

8. ततस्तद्विपाकानुगुणानामेवाभिव्यक्तिर्वासनानाम् ।

Tatas tad-vipakanugunanam evabhivyaktir vasananam

From these (three-fold Karma) is manifested fruition that corresponds to the desires or tendencies.

Each person enters a life situation according to this past Karma. His reaction to the situation is determined by his desires or tendencies. If he wants power or material wealth he will eventually receive them, but he must then suffer the pain that goes with them. If he wants only liberation, he must go through the discipline to achieve it, but that goal will be achieved.

9. जातिदेशकालव्यवहितानामप्यानन्तर्यं स्मृतिसंस्कारयोरेकरूपत्वात् ।

Jati-desa-kala-vyavahitanam apy anantaryam smrti-
samskarayor ekarupatvat

*There is an immediate succession (desire followed by appro-
priate Karmic situation), that is due to memory and samskaras, even though it may be interrupted by social class, location and time.*

The law of Karma is absolute. The effect of a desire or
tendency must definitely be reaped, although it may be in a
different lifetime and under different circumstances. Those who
experience what seems to be undeserved suffering are only working
out previously incurred Karma.

10. तासामनादित्वं चाशिषो नित्यत्वात् ।

Tasam anaditvam casiso nityatvat

*There is no beginning to them (desires), for the will to live
is eternal.*

This gives a scope of how long man has been going through
birth and rebirth. He has been reincarnating as long as there has
been desire. It is desire that binds him to the physical plane, and
there is no beginning to desire.

11. हेतुफलाश्रयालम्बनैः संगृहीतत्वादेषामभावे तदभावः ।

Hetu-phalasrayalambanaih samgrhitatvad esam abhave
tad-abhavah

*Desires are held together by cause, effect, support and ob-
jects; and when these disappear, so do the desires.*

What gives momentum to desires is cause and effect, or past
Karma; support, or the activity of the mind which creates them;
and the objects of the desires. When these foundations are removed,
so are the desires.

12. अतीतानागतं स्वरूपतोऽस्त्यध्वभेदाद्धर्माणाम् ।

Atitanagatam svarupato 'sty adhva-bhedad dharmanam

*The past and future exist in their own right; the difference in
properties are due to the various paths.*

The world exists apart from man. But it is the various paths
of the individual that create what appears to be the different prop-

erties and characteristics of the world, separating *Prakriti* from
Purusha.

13. ते व्यक्तसूक्ष्माः गुणात्मानः ।

Te vyakta-suksmah gunatmanah

*They, whether manifest or unmanifest, exist in the three
gunas.*

The properties or characteristics of the world, as man sees
them, are actually manifestations of the qualities of *Prakriti* —
sattwa, rajas and *tamas.*

14. परिणामैकत्वाद्वस्तुतत्त्वम् ।

Parinamaikatvad vastu-tattvam

*The reality of an object is due to the uniqueness in change
(of the gunas).*

Each object on the material plane can be identified and called
a reality because it is made up of its own unique combination
of the three qualities of nature, just as any color is a unique combination of the three primary colors — red, yellow and blue.

15. वस्तुसाम्ये चित्तभेदात् तयोर्विभक्तः पन्थाः ।

Vastu-samye citta-bhedat tayor vibhaktah panthah

*The object being the same, the apparent difference (between
two perceptions) is due to different minds' separate paths.*

The object remains the same, but when it is perceived by
more than one mind, there immediately arise varying views of that
object. This is due to the different paths of each individual. The
word "path" alludes to the fact that all are travelling toward realization of the Self, and it is the individual attitudes or karmic
situations that determine how a person sees something.

16. न चैकचित्ततन्त्रं वस्तु तदप्रमाणकं तदा किं स्यात् ।

Na caika-citta-tantram vastu tad-apramanakam tada kim syat

*An object is not dependent on one's mind, for it still exists
whether or not it is perceived by that mind.*

17. तदुपरागापेक्षित्वाच्चित्तस्य वस्तु ज्ञाताज्ञातम् ।

Tad-uparagapeksitvac cittasya vastu jnatajnatam

An object is either known or unknown to the mind because of the coloring of the mind.

What is perceived or cognized by an individual is entirely dependent upon the orientation and tendencies of that mind and not on the object itself.

18. सदा ज्ञाताश्चित्तवृत्तयस्तत्प्रभोः पुरुषस्यापरिणामित्वात् ।

Sada jnatas citta-vrttayas tat-prabhoh purusasyaparinamitvat

The modifications of the mind are always known to the Self due to the unchanging nature of Purusha.

The Soul, *Purusha*, absorbs all of the changes through which the mind goes because it is the Eternal Witness. All true knowledge exists permanently in the Self, while the mind is constantly being modified by thought waves.

19. न तत् स्वाभासं दृश्यत्वात् ।

Na tat svabhasam drsyatvat

Nor is it self-luminous, for it is in the realm of perception.

The mind is something that can be observed as an object, and not the source of knowledge, just as the moon is not a source of light but a reflection of the sun.

20. एकसमये चोभयानवधारणम् ।

Eka-samaye cobhayanavadharanam

It cannot perceive two things at once.

Even though thoughts are formed in but a split second, still only one thought-form can exist in the mind at one time. So it is impossible for the mind to be perceiving itself while it perceives something else.

21. चित्तान्तरदृश्ये बुद्धिबुद्धेरतिप्रसङ्गः स्मृतिसंकरश्च ।

Cittantara-drsye buddhi-buddher atiprasangah smrti-samkaras ca

If one mind could perceive another, then there would be cognition of cognition, as well as confusion of memory.

The mind can neither perceive itself nor perceive another mind, for if this were the case there would be complete confusion of the knowledge and memory of the different minds. The mind is but an instrument; all knowledge comes from beyond it.

22. चितेरप्रतिसंक्रमायास्तदाकारापत्तौ स्वबुद्धिसंवेदनम् ।

Citer apratisamkramayas tad-akarapattau sva-buddhi-samvedanam

Knowledge of itself comes through the self-cognition which occurs when the mind is stilled.

Patanjali has thus developed the explanation that the mind cannot perceive itself. It is *Purusha,* the Self, that perceives the mind.

23. द्रष्टृदृश्योपरक्तं चित्तं सर्वार्थम् ।

Drastr-drsyoparaktam cittam sarvartham

The mind that is colored by the Seer (the Self) and the seen (the mind) understands everything.

When the mind is stilled and allowed perception of itself through the Self, knowledge gained by the Self is then also known by the mind. Only then does the mind have full knowledge. Obviously then, it is not intellectualization but meditation that brings Self-knowledge.

24. तदसंख्येयवासनाभिश्चित्रमपि परार्थं संहत्यकारित्वात् ।

Tad asamkhyeya-vasanabhis citram api parartham samhatya-karitvat

The mind, though filled with innumerable tendencies and desires, acts for the Self, for they act in conjunction.

The mind is directly associated with the Self, so it acts for the Self even while it is still full of worldly thoughts.

25. विशेषदर्शिन आत्मभावभावनाविनिवृत्ति: ।

Visesa-darsina atma-bhava-bhavana-vinivrttih

He who sees this distinction ceases to see the mind as Atma.

Through discrimination, the yogi understands that the Soul and the mind are not the same.

26. तदा हि विवेकनिम्नं कैवल्यप्राम्भारं चित्तम् ।

Tada hi viveka-nimnam kaivalya-pragbharam cittam

With an inclination toward discrimination, he graviates toward kaivalya.

He who can distinquish the difference between mind and Atma has the power of discrimination, and moves automatically toward liberation.

27. तच्छिद्रेषु प्रत्ययान्तराणि संस्कारेभ्यः ।

Tac-chidresu pratyayantarani samskarebhyah

Thoughts that arise as interruptions to discrimination are due to past samskaras.

Before liberation is attained, remaining habitual thoughts and tendencies arise in the mind from time to time to interrupt the growth of discrimination.

28. हानमेषां क्लेशवदुक्तम् ।

Hanam esam klesavad uktam

Their removal is achieved in the same way as the removal of the afflictions, as previously described.

The methods for removal of the interruptions to discrimination are the same as for removal of the afflictions, or causes of misery, described in the second chapter, *sutras* 10, 11, and 26.

29. प्रसंख्यानेऽप्यकुसीदस्य सर्वथा विवेकख्यातेर्धर्ममेघः समाधिः ।

Prasamkhyane 'py akusidasya sarvatha viveka-khyater dharma-meghah samadhih

For one who has given up even the desire for the highest state of awareness, and who exercises discrimination, Dharma-Megha-Samadhi comes.

Even the desire for liberation must be given up, for it is a *vritti* as is any other desire. With this renunciation and discrimination comes *Dharma-Megha-Samadhi*, that which burns the seeds of all past *samskaras*, bringing full liberation.

30. ततः क्लेशकर्मनिवृत्तिः ।

Tatah klesa-karma-nivrttih
From that follows freedom from all miseries and Karma.

31. तदा सर्वावरणमलापेतस्य ज्ञानस्यानन्त्याज्ज्ञेयमल्पम् ।

Tada sarvavarana-malapetasya jnanasya-nantyaj jneyam
alpam

Then, with the removal of all distractions and impurities, (it becomes obvious that) what can be known by the mind is miniscule compared to Infinite Knowledge (of Enlightenment).

32. ततः कृतार्थानां परिणामक्रमसमाप्तिर्गुणानाम् ।

Tatah krtarthanam parinama-krama-samaptir gunanam

The three gunas, having fulfilled their purpose, which is the process of change, cease to exist.

For the person who has transcended *Prakriti,* the qualities of Nature come to an end, for they have fulfilled their purpose which is to push him through growth and to create the field for transformations on the path to Self-Realization.

33. क्षणप्रतियोगी परिणामापरान्तनिर्ग्राह्यः क्रमः ।

Ksana-pratiyogi parinamaparanta-nigrahyah kramah

The process of the succession of moments becomes apparent at the end of the transformation (of the gunas).

The lessons of the physical plane appear to occur in time, but in fact, they are a succession of separate moments in which there is varying play of nature's qualities, *sattwa, rajas* and *tamas.* This is much like a movie in which there appears to be a continuity, but it is only the effect of seeing many single frames in succession. Each frame — each lesson — is an entity, but this can only be seen when the film stops — when the individual is no longer looking through *Prakriti.*

34. पुरुषार्थशून्यानां गुणानां प्रतिप्रसवः कैवल्यं स्वरूपप्रतिष्ठा वा चितिशक्तेरिति ।

Purusartha-sunyanam gunanam pratiprasavah kaivalyam
svarupa-pratistha va citi-sakter iti

Kaivalya is that state in which the gunas (attain equilibrium and) merge, having no longer a purpose in relation to Purusha. The Soul is established in its True Nature, which is Pure Consciousness. End.

Liberation occurs when the *gunas* no longer have an effect. The three qualities of nature rest in balance, ceasing to go through change, for their purpose has been fulfilled. Then, the yogi can no longer be called an individual, for he is *Purusha* itself.

Electronic Meditation

The body is internally associated with the mind; rather, the body is a counterpart of the mind; it is a gross visible form of the subtle, invisible mind. Every change in thought makes a vibration in your mental body and this, when transmitted to the physical body, causes activity in the nervous matter of your brains. This activity in the nervous cells causes many electrical and chemical changes in them. It is thought activity which causes these changes. When the mind is turned to a particular thought and dwells on it, a definite vibration of matter is set up and often, more of this vibration is caused, the more does it tend to repeat itself, to become a habit, to become automatic. The body follows the mind and imitates its changes.

— Swami Sivananda
Thought Power

In the last fifteen years, with the advent of finer electronic technology, printed circuits, solid-state circuitry, and so on, has come a new and increasingly popular phenomenon known as bio-feedback. In the early days of its history, it was pretty much confined to the research laboratories of various medical and psychological institutes. Now, because of advances in electronics, a simple, inexpensive biofeedback monitor can be purchased by anyone.

These machines have become more and more familiar ever since their thrust into the popularity stream of the 1960's. According to Nicholas and June Regush in their book *Mind Search,* "Bio-feedback is one of the more recent and significant advances in medicine. It is being used to learn how to control an array of disorders such as headaches, high blood pressure and poor circulation. Through the use of instruments which record the body's minute electrical signals and feed them back in amplified form through a tone or some visual indicator on the machine, it's possible to be aware of certain changes in the internal body processes, to act on them and change the signal ... High tones indicate considerable

199

tension, lower tones, more relaxation. The aim is to reduce the tone by relaxing. As you listen to signals and try to relax by giving yourself positive suggestions, you learn to connect the feelings of being relaxed to the corresponding tone. Feeling internal changes as they occur is the key to biofeedback."

It is important to note here that these machines are used for the purpose of learning relaxation techniques and in no way can they propel one into higher states of consciousness. A journalist reporting on biofeedback instruments claimed he "was able to meditate to unusual states of intensity" after he had simply "fooled around with the gadget for about a week to see what it would do". Although it is conceivable that such a claim is valid, it could only apply to a person who had strong and deep *samskaras,* or a nature inherently suited to deep meditation. The average user cannot expect to acheive such results.

WHAT IS BIOFEEDBACK?

Ordinarily, life functions are carried on automatically without the individual's conscious control or knowledge. Biofeedback, stated simply, is a process by which those automatic inner activities are brought to conscious awareness. One of the earliest devices, long before they were used for meditation, was the polygraph, better known as the lie detector. The polygraph has been used for years, not only in psychology but also in the area of physiological research. To use this machine, various receivers are attached to specific areas of the body. As the body responds emotionally and physically to certain stimuli, the sensors pick up these changes and record them on the machine, where they are transformed into a more readily identifiable form, such as lines drawn on a sheet of graph paper.

The pneumatic bellows is the first attachment. This tubular device is strapped across the subject's chest or stomach, and detects changes in the volume of the chest during normal respiration. The respiratory cycle is never constant and can be influenced by a variety of factors, including the emotions. Respiration occurs in a complicated manner in which the brain sends rhythmic impulses to respiratory muscles like the diaphragm or the intracostal muscles. When relaxed, breathing is slow and regular; when excited, it becomes rapid and shallow. Scientists agree with Yoga that there is probably no other bodily function which is so closely connected with the mind and the nerves as breathing.

The second attachment is a wide air bladder which is wrapped around the subject's upper arm or wrist, and inflated. This attachment detects changes in blood pressure and pulse, both of which are intimately connected with the workings of the subconscious.

The third is the Galvanic skin response, or general skin resistance, commonly abbreviated GSR. This sensor functions because of the physiological relationship between the sweat glands and a person's emotional level. It has been proved that there is a direct relationship. When a person is relaxed and calm, the sweat glands function minimally and the skin remains relatively dry; yet when he is excited and nervous, the sweat glands become active and the hands become moist. This provides another accurate indication of changes in a person's emotional level.

Two small electrodes are placed on the subject's hand, and a minute electrical current is passed between them. This current is totally harmless, in fact, it is so small that it cannot even be felt. As the surface of the skin becomes more moist or dry, depending on the emotional changes within the subject, a corresponding change in the electrical resistance across the surface of the skin occurs. The machine measures the charge transmitted across the electrodes and compares it to that which was discharged. In this way, it creates a "normal" or "average" level of resistance. Although this varies with each individual, it remains constant during any one sitting. As the subject's skin becomes drier or more moist, this change is registered as a deviation from the normal resistance. The standard polygraph readout is indicated by means of pen tracings along a moving graph paper. However, on less sophisticated and inexpensive machines, these changes may be indicated by blinking lights or different sounds.

A polygraph is both expensive to own and complicated to operate. It requires a second person to attach the receivers correctly and monitor the readout. However, the third attachment, the GSR, has been adapted by many companies and put onto the market at reasonable prices. When the individual experiments with biofeedback on his own, one of these portable, compact GSR units is probably what he uses. To use it, one simply attaches two electrodes, one to either of any two finger tips, and turns the machine on. A high pitched sound indicates mental and physical activity, while a low pitched sound indicates relaxation. By associating the feelings which accompany the low pitched sound with relaxation, and attempting to recall these feelings, the subject learns to relax his body and mind.

Almost equally as popular as the GSR is the EEG, electro-encephalagram. The EEG, rather than measuring the activity of the body's nervous system, actually measures the electrical output of the brain by means of electrodes placed on the skin around the region of the scalp. The sensors do not deliver any electrical charge but are receivers only. Every brain emits waves of energy, much like radio waves, of which the length and amplitude can be measured. A wavelength of 14-28 cycles per second (cps) corresponds to the normal active waking state, and is called the beta state. 7-14 cps is the alpha state, indicating the mind is extremely relaxed or contemplative. The delta state, 3-7 cps, is a much deeper state than alpha. It is a state at which much creative thought takes place. There is still a good deal to be learned about this state, as well as about theta. At 0.5-3 cps, theta is the state of deep sleep, where there is no consciousness.

MEASUREMENT OF BRAIN WAVES

Cycles per second — cps   **State of Consciousness**
(number of brain waves per second)

```
28 ⎫
27 ⎪
26 ⎪
25 ⎪
24 ⎪
23 ⎪
22 ⎪
21 ⎬   Beta   11-28 cps . . . . . . . . . . . . . . . . . . . . . . . Normal waking state
20 ⎪
19 ⎪
18 ⎪
17 ⎪
16 ⎪
15 ⎭
14 ⎫
```

ERRATUM

P. 202

Alpha 8-15

Beta 16-25

Theta 4-7

Delta below 4

sciousness

While these various states are based on cycles per second, or length of brain wave, the magnitude of the energy output can also be measured. A reading of 30-40 micro-volts is common for experienced meditators, and advanced yogis have recorded mental outputs in excess of 100 micro-volts at will in the alpha state. Brain waves will have an amplitude no matter what the wavelength, or brain state.

MEASUREMENT OF BRAIN WAVES

Amplitude (power of brain waves) **one**
measured in microvolts **second**

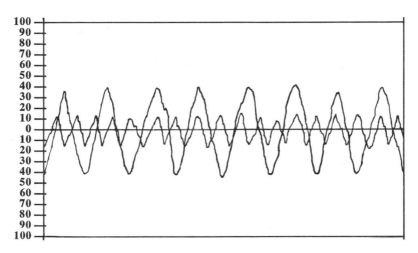

Cycles per second — cps
number of cycles (brainwaves) in one second

The shorter line indicates an amplitude of 13 microvolts, an output that is common in a normal waking state. It also registers that there are 18 cycles per second, which is low Beta.

The taller line indicates an amplitude of 40 microvolts, which is a considerably high output for most meditators. This gives a feeling for the magniture of the output by Swami Gokulananda and Swami Sri Dharananda who both registered over the 200 microvolt maximum of several EEG machines as described in the chapter on Spiritual Experiences. The same line shows 8 cycles per second, a very slow rate of Alpha.

BEYOND RELAXATION

Self-awareness is the consciousness or knowledge of one's condition or state of being and of the changes that occur in body, mind and environment. Because the biofeedback machine translates the changes that occur in the body into forms that can be seen or heard, the subject can increase his self-awareness as a by-product of the use of the biofeedback machine. At least up to a certain point.

A trained and alert yogi is completely aware of the various subconscious processes which take place in his mind and body, and is able to control his autonomic nervous system through the power of concentration. The average person cannot do this because he lacks the necessary physical and mental training and discipline. He has not spent the time on internal intunement. For thousands of years, yogis taught and practiced that one can control the involuntary functions of the body through concentration and meditation, while traditional science paid no attention. Now, with the revelations of biofeedback research, many are convinced that the yogic theory is not only true but is also possible for anyone with only a minimal amount of training.

But control of the mind is not that simple. Too often, those who make claims about a fast and easy method have very little knowledge of internal awareness, themselves; nor has their method stood the test of time. Mind control takes not only personal experience, but years of self-study and introspection. Yogis know that the autonomic nervous system, which controls and regulates the involuntary functions of the body, is under the control of the subconscious mind, and, for them, the subconscious is under the control of the conscious mind. A yogi can directly command his subconscious through suggestion and by mentally visualizing all the internal functions.

In biofeedback, electronic instruments are used for getting results from the subconscious, but its uses are limited. For example, if a person connected to a GSR machine, for reading skin resistance, is touched, a large change will occur in the instrument readout. In fact, a substantial reaction can be produced merely by bringing one's hand slowly toward the person. The GSR takes its reading directly from the activity of the sweat glands, which themselves, are under the control of the sympathetic nervous system. The sympathetic nervous system is that subdivision of the autonomic nervous system which is sometimes called the "fight or flight" mechanism. In times of great emotional activity, it increases the heart rate and supply of blood to the brain, increases oxygen intake and pumps adrenalin into the blood. The nervous system carries impulses to all internal organs and tissues, not just the sweat glands. If a person becomes excited *in any way,* his sympathetic nervous system activates physical and chemical changes throughout the body. As Barbara B. Brown states in her book *New Mind and New Body,* one of the greatest difficulties with biofeedback research is that its use necessitates control measures to insure that the experiments are not affected by unrelated influences. Ms. Brown goes on to say that this is a very difficult job for the psychologist, as opposed to the physicist or chemist, because those influences which work on human behavior are not as easy to isolate and analyze as those which affect conventional laboratory experiments.

At best, the biofeedback machines are rough indicators of biological functions. Those monitoring instruments used for relaxation or concentration serve as an indirect measure of sympathetic nervous system activity. Biofeedback can only be used to detect unspecified functioning of the autonomic nervous system and to visualize how much one is able to change its activities. Beyond a little relaxation and the reduction of certain metabolic activities like blood pressure, the biofeedback systems can provide little aid to meditation. One should not confuse the inner peace of the superconscious state achieved by yogis with the relaxation achieved through biofeedback conditioning.

In every person there is a certain power of concentration which can be used to attain a relaxed state of mind. One may concentrate on the lights or sounds of a biofeedback monitor, or on a beautiful sunset at the beach, and experience a relaxed state of body and mind in either case. But this must not be confused with delving deeply into the inner being and finding awareness and union with the Source of perfection. Biofeedback can only give quantitative information on certain bodily functions; it does not give any indication of the quality or depth of the meditative experience.

EXTERNALS vs INTERNALS

Despite the aid to relaxation which can be gained through experiments with biofeedback machines, their use cannot be substituted for a healthy and balanced lifestyle. A scientific instrument may monitor reduced blood pressure, but it can do nothing for arteries that have been clogged with calcium deposits and cholesterol. It cannot be imagined that the brain is getting more oxygen and nourishment through observation techniques when the body is weak and full of toxins. Scientists are now beginning to understand the relationship between sense organs, like the skin, and the mind. In fact, the whole theory of Western psychology is externally oriented. It is based on the study of observable behavior patterns and the physiological output of the brains of others. This is a far cry from the study of one's own mind, as is done in meditation. Traditional psychological techniques often provide more insight for the psychologist than they do for the individual seeking to go through growth.

Many scientists still do not distinquish between brain functions and the mind. Although both the brain and mind have intimate connections with the physical functioning of the body, the mind can exist separate from the body and can have knowledge and experience without sensory contact. The mind, which is located in the astral body, has three functions, which are sensation, thought and volition. It has three mental processes, and these are cognition, desire and will. It also has three aspects, the subconscious mind, the conscious mind, and the superconscious mind. The brain, however, is part of the physical body. It acts as a computer, carrying out the thoughts of the mind and transmitting electrical impulses within the body to maintain and control the different life functions. In this differentiation between brain and mind, biofeedback research is still incomplete,

For a yogi, the sensory experiences of pleasure and pain that come from objects, such as delicious food or soft clothing, are recognized as unreal, for they are a result of the internal state of the mind and are not a quality of the externals. A businessman may go to a party to enjoy himself. He takes pleasure in the conversation, and the food and beverage. Imagine he suddenly hears news that there has been a great upset in the stock market. He will immediately forget his drink and sandwich, not because they have lost their taste, but because he no longer has a taste for them. There is no more enjoyment. The drink and sandwich have not changed. What has changed is the direction of the mind. The mind is now concerned with the value of the stocks which at *this particular time* is an unpleasant subject. Consequently, there is no pleasure in what was pleasurable a minute ago.

A yogi believes that all experiences of sorrow and pleasure, victory and defeat, hot and cold are in the mind only. One should strive to be happy at all times despite external influences. Yoga goes beyond the mind and reaches a state of experience where there are no changing dualities. Traditional Western philosophy has been to accept the sensory experiences as real; traditional Eastern philosophy has been to accept those experiences in relative terms without giving them any permanent value.

Moreover, the scientific conclusions arrived at by studying behavior patterns only bring about false theories, distorted by the limitations of the objective mind and the tools used. Often there are conflicting theories based on experiences of the senses and the information given by the apparatus used. Consider what happens when one hand has been immersed in 110° hot water and the other hand, in 35° cold water, and after some time both are dipped in 70° water. One hand will feel warm and the other hand will feel cold. Simultaneously, there are two interpretations of the same experience for the mind, and neither of them can be called absolutely real.

The yogi studies the subjective state of mind by inner contemplation; biofeedback techniques use conditioning to observe changes in observable behavior. The data collected under this latter form of study is subject to individual interpretations, which may not correspond to reality. Consider the story about the professor who was interested in learning "frog psychology." He trained a frog to jump using the method of conditioned learning, that is, reward and punishment techniques. If the frog jumped on command, he got a reward of food; if he did not, he received a mild electric shock. After some time, the frog was conditioned to perform just by hearing the command "Jump!" Then the professor wanted to find out more about frog psychology, mostly, what made the frog jump in the first place. Therefore, he removed one leg from the frog and commanded it to jump. The frog jumped with three legs, though not perfectly. One by one, all the legs were removed and the frog was commanded, "Jump!" But the frog did not jump, he just sat on the table and croaked. The conclusion which the professor reached was that the frog did not jump because it couldn't hear when all its legs had been removed.

This anecdote indicates the dangers of relying upon individual interpretations of external phenomena. Yoga psychology utilizes a different approach. The yogi studies his mind through meditation. This experience, mystical in nature, is very different from the sensory experience. Yogic science is not merely a study of the behavior patterns of mind over matter, but it is a direct perception of life's principles. Eventually, the experimenter, subject and results — or knower, knowledge known — merge into one.

Supernormal phenomena take place naturally when, owing to innate faculties or abilities developed through proper training, one functions simultaneously on two planes. The external study of these phenomena along lines of ordinary science can only lead to limited results. Traditionally, science has been a constantly closer examination and analysis of phenomena or sensations. As a result of this analysis, laws are framed and made to agree with the activity of man's thoughts. Human science studies the surface of our sensible world, the surface on which our thought reflects itself. Yogic science studies that force which is at the center of life, and brings a union between the external and internal worlds. It studies the inner thoughts, working from inner planes towards planes nearer the center, getting closer and closer to that Reality from which all life emanates.

Yogic science is not a matter of erudition; its roots lie in action. It must be lived to be learned. It is in oneself, and not in others, that the rich source of spiritual development must be sought. For the true initiate, dogma must be replaced by direct perception or intuitive knowledge of the higher planes. Conditioned learning is but a mechanical means to help concentrate the mind. The techniques used in biofeedback may help one to recognize some facts about mind control, but we must not be deluded by the mechanics of our contemporary society. Machines cannot replace experience; meditation and mind control are experiencial. A child can use a calculator to solve all his arithmetic homework, but he will not learn to add. Biofeedback machines will give rough quantitative feedback to one's initial efforts to control the mind, but one can learn meditation only by practice of attunement to the inner Self, not to a machine.

Obstacles to Meditation

*Watch your mind very carefully. Be vigilant. Be on the alert.
Do not allow the waves of irritability, jealousy, hatred and lust to
disturb you. These dark waves are enemies of peaceful living,
meditation and wisdom. To some it is very difficult to keep the
mind unruffled and pure, the causes being deep-rooted worldly
Samskaras, unfavorable surroundings, and the predominance of
extrovert tendencies. To some, of course, evil thoughts are not a
problem at all. They appear occasionally as a passing phase without
doing much havoc. The very fact that evil thoughts give you mental
suffering is a sign of spiritual progress; for many do not have that
much of sensitiveness.*

— Swami Sivananda
Religious Education

The obstacles and stumbling blocks in the path toward Realization can be easily overcome once an intelligent and comprehensive understanding of them has been reached. It should always be
borne in mind that failures are but stepping stones to success. Just
as a pilot guides a ship along a dangerous coastline having knowledge of its reefs, so the aspirant is guided through the ocean of
spiritual endeavor by knowing about the various obstacles and the
methods of overcoming them. One must train the mind properly
and not be discouraged, for the journey to perfection was never
completed overnight.

CESSATION OF PRACTICE

The mind wants variety in the practice of meditation as much
as it wants variety in anything else. It rebels against monotony.
When this happens, the student can give the mind a little relaxation
and variety by changing the schedule of the practice, but it should
never be given up completely. Cessation of practice is a grave mistake; *Sadhana,* spiritual practice, should never be given up under

209

any circumstances. The beginner, full of enthusiasm and zeal, often hopes to acquire psychic powers in a short time. When he does not achieve them, he becomes discouraged and wants to give up. He may lose faith in the efficacy of his practice and, often, even considers forgetting about it completely. The practice of meditation must be continued, but without any expectations. Growth comes, but it is gradual. Sincerity, regularity and patience will insure eventual advancement.

HEALTH AND DIET

This body is the only vehicle man has for attaining Self-Realization, and as such it is best kept strong and healthy. Just as the ax must be kept sharp to cut a tree, so the goal can be reached sooner when the body is in excellent condition. A man may practice Yoga, or any other discipline or religion, and die before attaining perfection. Then he is born in another life, practices for some years more and dies again. In this way, much time is lost in recurring birth and death. Although one should not be attached to the body, it is essential that it be kept strong, clean, and able to withstand rigorous practice.

A healthy mind is also important. Because body and mind are intimately connected, it is important to maintain a cheerful frame of mind at all times. Cheerfulness and good health walk hand in hand. The wise aspirant keeps his body healthy with regular exercise, Yoga postures and breath control, a moderate diet, rest, and plenty of fresh air. One should avoid drugs and medicines as much as possible and, when necessary, resort to natural cures.

At the other extreme, there are some aspirants who refuse to take medicine even though they are seriously ill. These people unnecessarily torture the body; they allow disease to strike deep and ruin their health. Soon they become physically unfit to continue their practice. It is much better to take medication for a couple of days and resume practice quickly than to allow a disease to reach advanced stages, thereby causing great difficulty and delay in resuming regular practice. It is worth noting that the most effective cure for many ailments is fasting, during which the digestive system is given a rest, and poisons are eliminated from the body.

Just as clouds screen the sun, the clouds of sickness screen one from continued practice and self-discipline. Even if seriously ill, *Japa* and light meditation can still be practiced. Meditation is the best medicine for any disease, for it energizes and purifies every cell and tissue in the body.

Improper diet is another hindrance to spiritual progress. All foods have distinct energies. Just as the physical body is formed from the gross physical portion of the foods that are eaten, so the mind is formed from the more subtle portions. If the food is impure, the mind also becomes impure. Cigarettes, liquor, narcotics, and stale or aged food are most detrimental. Meals should be simple, light and nutritious. The processed adulterated preparations found on many supermarket shelves have no place in a yogic diet.

Many people eat far more than is necessary, merely out of habit or for sense gratification. An immoderate diet is the cause of the great majority of diseases encountered in modern society. If one is suffering from stomach ache or the inevitable sleepiness caused by overloading the stomach, then meditation is impossible. It is important not to eat for two hours before practicing meditation. If meditation is practiced in the early morning hours, the evening meal should be light.

Moderation is the keynote in one's daily habits. The body may become more susceptible to disease because of too much or too little sleep, eating the wrong foods, exposure to crowds, laborious mental work, excessive sexual activity, or lack of regular exercise. If a student of meditation becomes sick, he may be inclined to blame the practice rather than his own indiscretions and excesses. The mind is always looking for an excuse to avoid discipline, but it must never be stopped, even for one day. Listen to the inner voice of the Self rather than to the complaints of the mind.

LAZINESS AND SLEEP

Laziness, drowsiness and sleep are universal obstacles in the spiritual path, and sleep is the most powerful. Like food, it has become an overindulged habit of long standing for most people. However, the amount of sleep necessary can be cut down drastically through regular practice of meditation. Sleep is a psychological need and may be reduced gradually and slowly. The brain needs rest for only a short time every day; if denied, there is no doubt that one feels tired and is incapable of either working or meditating. Through the various yogic practices, a calm and steady mind is developed. Energy is no longer wasted on emotions and useless desires. The mind spends more time in a relaxed state, so it does not require great amounts of rest. One will have more and more time for *Sadhana* once a new and more pleasant pattern has been established.

Often during meditation one will begin to wonder if the mind has slipped into its old habit of sleeping or if meditation is actually occurring. This can be easily determined for during meditation the body feels light and the mind is cheerful, while during sleep the body and eyelids are heavy and the mind is dull. If sleep does become a problem during meditation, splashing cold water on the face, doing breathing exercises, or standing on the head for five minutes will return the mind to an alert state.

Lethargy and depression often afflict the beginner in meditation. Sometimes the cause is physical, such as poor eating habits, indigestion, bad company or poor weather. When this is the case, the cause should be removed, or perhaps a change of physical activity substituted.

Lethargy frequently sets in when the student's life is too unbalanced. Only a very small minority are fit for full time meditation; others must lead a controlled and balanced life. Young students, full of enthusiasm and ideas of independence and romanticism, need to regulate their energies. Instead, they sometimes disdain discipline and wander from one teacher to another. Sitting cross-legged for half an hour, they mistake lethargy for purity, assume they are beyond doing service for others, and imagine that Realization has been achieved. Or having become bored, some have turned to drugs to supply a poor substitute for the experience they could not find. A serious student, however, establishes for himself a daily program of meditation, exercise and study. If lethargy becomes an obstacle, some brisk work or charitable activity vigorously pursued will rectify the situation. Physical activity provides the necessary balance for the practice of meditation, and hard work should be an integral part of each day's discipline.

COMPLICATIONS OF DAILY LIFE

Unfavorable environments, uncongenial atmosphere and other obstacles do not necessarily lead to defeat of one's efforts. Rather, they can serve as trials and aids in the development of such strong powers as discrimination, empathy, will and endurance. The struggle through difficult situations brings rapid progress.

On the other hand, undesirable company is highly disastrous, for such contact fills the mind with useless ideas. To avoid being pulled into negativity, the meditator should protect himself carefully from any distracting influences. People who lie and steal, or are greedy, or indulge in backbiting and pass the time with idle gossiping have no place in the life of a spiritual person. The healthiest approach is to strictly avoid them.

The term undesirable company includes more than just people; it's anything that gives rise to negative thoughts or vibrations. Raucous surroundings, books and songs that create discontent, movies and television programs centering on violence and sensuality, all lead the mind astray and fill it with desires it would not normally have. One should even consider curtailing the reading of newspapers, for their intent as well as effect is to tantalize the mind with waves of unrest and sensationalism. All these distractions draw the mind outward rather than focus it inward. They foster the illusion that this world is a solid reality and obscure the Supreme Truth which underlies all names and forms.

The world is full of avarice, hypocrisy, flattery, untruth, double-dealing and selfishness, and those who profess to be friends are often one's greatest enemies. Beware of self-proclaimed friends who come for money and other comforts when circumstances are affluent, then disappear when the tide has turned. These fair-weather friends give their own brand of advice, waste precious time in useless chatter, and pull one off the spiritual path and down to their own level. Of course, most people do not like to think that this is true. Most would like to feel that their relationships are based on selfless love, but in fact many are based on the fear of being alone and the desire for diversion. One should cut off connections that are not beneficial and trust only the Inner Voice that dwells in one's heart. Associate only with those whose own aspirations for perfection are uplifting and encouraging.

USELESS CONVERSATION

Spiritual power is lessened by many bad habits, not the least of which is useless and excessive talking. Diarrhea of the tongue wastes much energy that could be utilized for personal development. Too much talking makes a person restless and unfit for the practice of meditation. The wise speak only a few words, and those only when necessary, for by their very economy they will carry the most force. To help calm, center, and discipline the mind, *Mouna,* silence, can be observed for about two hours daily, in addition to the time spent in meditation. In order to be of the most practical value, silence is best practiced at those time when there is the most opportunity to talk.

People of an intellectual nature are often prone to unnecessary discussions and controversies. A person who is unable to remain quiet easily becomes involved in heated debates, too many of which lead to enmity, hostility, and energy drain. When intel-

lectual reasoning, which is normally concerned only with investiga-
tion of the physical plane, is used for metaphysical inquiry, it can
lead the student to the threshold of intuition. Past this point, however, it is of no use, for transcendental matters are beyond the
reach of reason. One must give up arguing, become silent, and
look within.

Fault-finding is, likewise, a most detrimental habit. The mind
of the person who is always poking his nose into the affairs of
others is always outgoing and out of control. No one can be introspective when the mind is engaged in activity of this sort. Diligent
application to spiritual practice allows no time for managing the
affairs of others. Forget the shortcomings of other people and work
to improve yourself first. Life is precious and short. No one knows
when it will be taken away. Every minute should be used for much
higher purposes than gossiping and judging others.

Self-justification is another behavioral weakness to be overcome, along with its associated characteristics — self assertion,
obstinacy, dissimulation and lying. Once these weaknesses become
established in the framework of the personality, it is very difficult
to eliminate them, for the ego never admits to its own faults. One
lie covers another in an endless succession of vain attempts at self-
justification. Improvement comes quickly and rapidly only when
one learns to readily admit his faults, mistakes and weaknesses.

Petty-mindedness is closely associated with back-biting and
trying to pull down other people. All are caused by jealousy and
ignorance. They can easily be combated and eradicated by always
rejoicing in the welfare of others.

UPROOTING THE EGO

It must be evident by now that meditation involves far more
than sitting with eyes closed in concentration. It demands rigorous
introspection and an overhauling of one's personality, life patterns
and values. Behavior correction and the uprooting of weaknesses
are relatively easy adjustments to make. The more serious obstacles
to meditation and spiritual practice, which lie deep within, are the
emotional imbalances and personality defects that nurture outward
bad habits.

The petty obstinate egoism behind the mask of human personality is one of the biggest hurdles to overcome, for it veils the
divine Self, supports surface thoughts, and perpetuates its own habitual feelings and actions. This lower self-arrogating nature must
be whittled down, for if it persists in retaining its limited, false

values, no amount of *Sadhana*, spiritual practice, will bear fruit.

Too often a student says he wants to study and practice meditation, yet he is unwilling to eradicate the lower nature and change old habits. Clinging to them, he refuses even to admit the need for change. This type of student will never make any real progress for brief spiritual experiences, without radical transformation of the lower nature, lead nowhere.

It is not easy to change deeply ingrained habits, and the sincere beginner often feels helpless against them. By regular *Sadhana*, untiring selfless service, association with spiritually minded people and strong determination to eradicate egoism, a powerful but selfless will is developed. One must introspect and discover all weaknesses and defects. This is considerably easier for those living under the guidance of a guru, who points them out and indicates suitable ways to eradicate them. The transmutation of lower nature to higher nature demands full and heart-felt dedication. To make the transition to the highest goal, a willingness to surrender the ego is needed. Then only, with persistent endeavor, real change comes about.

Sometimes the old personality attempts to reestablish itself, even after years of meditation. Obstinately self-assertive, and supported by the lower mind and will, it can make the aspirant incorrigible, unruly, arrogant and impertinent. Identifying with the ego, he breaks all rules and disciplines, revolts against all things, and is ever ready to fight with those who are unwilling to accept his views and opinions.

The ego cherishes its own ideas and impulses, and refuses to follow beneficial instruction. Dissimulation, hypocrisy, exaggeration and secretiveness are the traits of a dominant ego. One who is in its grip may even lie in order to cover up his errant ways, to maintain his position, and to indulge in his own ideas and bad habits. Wallowing in self-justification, and denying faults and defects, the student may be unaware of the effects of his actions, for the intellect has been clouded by impurities. Not knowing what he means and not meaning what he says, he is too self-willed and self-satisfied to see the error of his ways.

One who is not straight-forward and cannot keep discipline or open his heart to others, cannot be helped by any teacher. Nothing can help one who deliberately shuts his eyes against the Truth. Such an aspirant, instead of making progress along the path, remains stuck in the mire of his own creation.

If there is any recognition that something is wrong, the

slightest attempt to improve, or even a slightly receptive attitude, then the errors can be corrected. One who is frank with his teacher and himself, begins to realize the nature and source of his defects; he is soon on the way to improving his life.

Power, name, fame and wealth, which strengthen and reinforce the ego, are all renounced and sacrificed by the serious aspirant. For Westerners who are taught to revere individuality, the need to surrender the ego is especially difficult to understand. But there are no half-measures; discipline of senses and constant meditation must be cultivated in order to make progress.

THE EMOTIONS

Of all the emotional barriers the most devastating is anger, the greatest enemy of peace, for it is the most negative. It is a modification of lust for when one's desires are not gratified, one becomes angry. The mind then becomes confused, memory and understanding are lost, and things are said and done without awareness or control. Anger does great damage to one's own physical and psychic bodies, as well as those of others. The whole nervous system is shattered by one fit of anger. Occasionally a spiritual teacher expresses a little anger outwardly in order to correct a student, but this should not be confused with an emotional outburst. Though he may appear hot and indignant on the outside, the true master remains cool within, for his motive is the growth of his disciples. Only when anger is the outcome of selfish or petty motives is it wrong.

Anger is very difficult to control when it has been allowed to grow and become habitual. It is much more easily controlled when it is a small ripple in the subconscious mind. One should watch the mind carefully for any signs of irritability; then control is no problem. Frequent irritation over trifling matters is a sign of mental weakness. This can be overcome by carefully developing its positive counterforce, the virtue of patience.

Just as heat and light can be transformed into electricity, anger can be transformed into spiritual energy. All vices, unwanted qualities, and wrong actions stem from anger; when anger has been controlled, all others die by themselves. This is half the student's battle.

Anger gains strength with repetition, and in checking it one gradually strengthens the will. The practice of meditation itself helps to eliminate the causes of anger, for it slowly changes values and perspectives. By learning to remain silent even in the face of insult and abuse, it becomes easier to check the impulses and emotions before they take form. Always speak moderately, and if there is a possibility of a burst of anger during conversation, stop speaking and do something else. Words should be soft and arguments hard, for if the words are hard they will create discord. Drinking cool water or taking a brisk walk are excellent aids in combatting the onslaught of anger, as is *mouna,* the practice of maintaining silence for long periods of time. Smoking, eating meat and drinking are irritants which aggravate the problem, and are best avoided.

Fear is the most debilitating emotion. The student must always be willing to risk everything including his very life in the quest for spiritual perfection. Timidity makes one absolutely unfit for the spiritual path. A criminal who is fearless, and totally indifferent and unattached to his body, is more fit for Realization than a nervous or overcautious person. His energies only need to be rechanneled. Fear is a product of the imagination, but nonetheless it assumes real forms, and can be troublesome in a variety of ways.

Fear manifests in many shapes, such as: fear of death, fear of disease, fear of solitude, fear of company. Taking hold of the mind, imagination works havoc and makes one prey to all sorts of fear. Fear of public criticism especially stands in the way of a student's meditative progress. Yet even in the face of persecution, one must stick to his convictions. Then only can one grow. Fear can be overcome by self-inquiry, devotion to a higher cause, and the cultivation of the opposite of fear, courage. Positive always overcomes negative, and courage always overcomes timidity.

DISCOURAGEMENT

The meditator sometimes begins to doubt the existence of an Absolute Source, his own capacity to succeed in Realization and the efficacy of his practice. Lack of faith is discouraging and is a dangerous obstacle in the path of personal development. When these thoughts crop up, the student is in danger of slackening his efforts and giving up his practice altogether. This would be a great mistake. It must be remembered that there will always be periods when one's progress is more or less apparent. Whenever doubts arise, the student should at once seek the company of spiritually elevating people and remain under their influence for some time. Conversing with people of firm and clear faith and practice clears all doubts.

When a student's expectations are too unrealistic, doubt is eventually bound to raise its head. The beginner often thinks that *Kun-*

dalini will be awakened within six months, and he will thereupon blossom out with clairvoyance, clairaudience, thought reading and flying in the air. Many strange ideas are sometimes entertained, and when these expectations fail to materialize, doubt sets in. This confusion can be removed by study of religious books, right inquiry and reasoning, in addition to spiritual company. Doubt will rise up again and again to mislead the aspirant. It must be destroyed beyond recovery by certainty of conviction, unshakable faith based on reason, and the understanding that difficulties are bound to manifest from time to time. It should always be borne in mind that these are but challenges that help to strengthen the practice.

LOSS OF THE VITAL ENERGY

For serious progress towards the highest goal of Realization, the observance of *brahmacharya* is essential. The word *brahmacharya* comes from *Sanskrit* and means knowledge of Brahman. It refers to the total control of all senses, and, more particularly, to celibacy. Celibacy is a concept that is almost foreign to the Western mind. It is a difficult one for many to fully understand, especially when people are becoming more comfortable with their own inner feelings and are striving to make their relationships more open and free. But celibacy is an ancient and timeless aspect of all the religious traditions of the world. Each has its group of aspirants who have renounced all worldly desires and sensual pleasures. They are known as monks and nuns, and in the Yoga tradition, as swamis, or *sanyasis*. Although it should not be thought that a purely celibate life is recommended for all, a complete understanding of spiritual life is not possible without a basic knowledge of the practice and purpose of *brahmacharya*.

It might be said that ninety-nine per cent of the goal of spiritual life has been attained when one has control over sensual experiences. This is difficult, not merely because of the gratification derived from the senses, but because it is the inherent nature of all living things to procreate, to continue the species. The most powerful impulse in nature, after breathing, is procreation. So of all that a yogi must master before he achieves the ultimate goal, control of his sexuality is the most difficult.

Cosmic energy, which forms and perpetuates the galaxies and worlds, is the same energy which is continuously vibrating in man's body and mind. This life energy, or universal *prana,* manifests on the gross physical level as sexual energy. When it has been controlled and sublimated, it is transformed into *ojas shakti,* or spiritual energy. Sexual energy moves in a downward direction, but *ojas* moves upward away from the sexual centers and is stored in the brain. *Ojas* is the creative power, the vital energy, the vigor in a person who has converted sensuality into spirituality.

In the sexual experience, energy is dissipated and lost. But through *brahmacharya,* the same energy is preserved. Through constant *sadhana,* spiritual practice, this energy is eventually converted into the most powerful force of all, the *kundalini shakti.* The *kundalini* lies dormant at the base of the spine in the *muladhara chakra* until it reaches the *sahasrara* at the crown of the head. It is in the rising of the *kundalini* that the higher meditative experiences occur. If energy is always being dissipated downward in sexual activity, it cannot be stored, nor can it build enough power to push upward through the *chakras.*

Aside from the consideration of *kundalini,* there are other practical reasons for sublimation of the sexual drive. Celibacy is a form of *pratyahara,* control of the senses. For those sincerely seeking to advance in meditation, total control of all cravings of the body is necessary. A strong will is developed by slowly gaining mastery over the sexual desire, as well as the desire for savory, exotic food, luxurious surroundings, and so forth. As the mind is turned inward, the advanced student gradually ceases to identify with experience of the physical world.

The greatest drive in man is procreation. One can see how powerful it is by the extent to which it has been exploited by the advertising media. There are precious few products that are not sold on the promise that, on one level or another, they will bring sexual fulfillment. The pull to unite with the opposite sex is so strong that it often overpowers all wisdom and reason. But the dedicated yogi cares more for control of the mind than pleasures of the body. Lord Buddha is said to have told his disciples that if there were any other obstacle as powerful as the sexual drive, he could not have reached enlightenment.

Of course, repression of the sexual urge is not suggested, for it would only lead to backlash or ill health. But a gradual reduction in sexual activity helps to develop the will, strengthen the spirit, and turn the mind from external to internal. Its energy can be put to positive and constructive use. This is the nature of sublimation. When the ultimate Union, with the Lord Himself, becomes the most important thing to a person, desire for sexual gratification falls away, for it is an experience far inferior to that of God-Realization.

THE MIND ITSELF

The mind itself offers many impediments to meditation. In the beginning of practice, layer after layer of impure and negative thoughts arise from the subconscious mind as soon as one sits for meditation. Students occasionally abandon practice because of this without understanding why it happens. There is an old adage that if you kill one mosquito twenty more come to the funeral. Even so, negative thoughts assail and attack with doubled force when the meditator tries to rid himself of them. This is the natural law of resistance.

Eventually they will all perish for negative thoughts cannot stand before positive thoughts. The very fact that undesirable thoughts create a feeling of uneasiness when they arise during meditation indicates growth and maturity, for at one time these thoughts were welcomed into the mind. They cannot be driven out forcefully or suddenly, or they will turn against the meditator with increased energy. They wither away of their own accord when the student persists in his practice with tenacity and diligence.

The mind must be watched, particularly when it is relaxed. The dark waves of irritability, jealousy, anger and hatred are the enemies of meditation, peace and wisdom. They must be countered immediately with positive thoughts, for ill thoughts are destroyed by good thoughts. Just as it is easiest to stop an intruder at the gate, so it is easiest to check a negative thought as soon as it arises. It can be nipped in the bud by sustained *sadhana,* good actions and awareness of the misery which arises from negativity. When the state of purity is attained, the problem no longer exists.

Hatred, like anger, is one of the fiercest foes of the serious student. Like greed or lust, it is insatiable. Though it may temporarily subside, it can burst out again with redoubled force. It is like a contagious disease which infects one person after another. If a father has a quarrel with someone, his children may also hate that person, although he has done them no harm. Contempt, prejudice and ridicule are all various modes of hatred.

If an Englishman hates an Irishman, an Irishman hates an Englishman; if a Catholic hates a Protestant, a Protestant hates a Catholic. Prejudice of this or any other kind must be rooted out vigorously. Prejudiced and bigoted people confine themselves in small circumscribed groups. Because of their jaundiced vision, they fail to see the good in others whom they treat with contempt. But it is possible to stick to one's own principles and still pay equal regard to the viewpoints of others. Truth is not the sole monopoly of any person, group or spiritual system. Universal peace and brotherhood are possible only when hatred, prejudice and bigotry have been replaced with love. Because its branches go out in so many directions in the subconscious mind, hatred needs prolonged and intense treatment. Constant selfless service combined with meditation for many years will remove this rank weed from the heart.

Infatuation and attachment are serious obstacles because they are subtle as well as powerful. When millions of people are killed during a war, a man does not weep, yet he weeps when his wife dies. This is because infatuation creates the idea of "mine", and the greater the attachment, the greater the pain. When a person speaks of "My wife", "My son", or "My home", he reveals an attitude of separation from the rest of mankind. So long as there is identification with the ephemeral physical world, little progress can be made on the path of meditation.

Greed, which is closely linked with infatuation, is insatiable, and it agitates the mind. Even though a man may be a millionaire, he schemes to become a billionaire. Greed assumes various subtle forms. If a man thirsts for name and fame, this also is greed. Infatuation, attachment and greed are destroyed by vigorous self-inquiry, prolonged meditation and constant *sadhana*.

Another impediment to meditation is memory or recalling past events. To understand this, assume for a moment that one is meditating quietly in a solitary country setting. If memories of a past holiday in Las Vegas arise and the mind is allowed to dwell on them, for the moment one will actually be living in Las Vegas in a past time. This applys also to daydreams. Looking back to past experience gives life to the memory-picture, reinforces it and pulls the mind away from its true nature. A sage never looks back; he concentrates only on identification with the Absolute.

OBSTACLES FOR THE EXPERIENCED MEDITATOR

Pitfalls still await the meditator even after the practice has been well established. The aspirant sometimes becomes puffed up with moral and spiritual pride after acquiring a few experiences or powers. He may separate himself from others and treat them with contempt. This kind of arrogance poses a serious obstacle to Self-Realization and must be completely removed. As long as there is pride and boastfulness, it is impossible to relinquish the ego and realize Divinity.

Religious hypocrisy, a related frailty, manifests in those who have made some progress but have not yet thoroughly purified the lower nature. Pretending to be what they are not, these people make an elaborate outward show of their vaunted religiosity. For aspirants travelling the spiritual path and dedicating all actions to God, there is no greater crime than using religion to take advantage of trusting people. In fact religious hypocrisy is much worse than ordinary hypocrisy, for the religious hypocrite makes a mockery of spirituality and God. He needs to undergo a long and drastic course of treatment, imposed upon him by somebody else for he himself is too egoistic and devious to apply self-cure or even to want it.

Sometimes during meditation, visions of terrifying forms may appear. Whether projected from the depths of the subconscious or actual materializations of lower astral entities, they can cause no harm. Appearing simply as a test of strength and courage, they cannot remain in the presence of pure and divine thoughts. The aspirant must stand firm and not let fear or nervousness upset the practice of meditation. Other visions and experiences also come and go, but these are not the goal of meditation. One who attaches importance to them becomes distracted from the path. Avoid all thoughts of these visions; remain indifferent and substitute higher thoughts. The final and true goal of meditation is intuitional and direct experience of the Supreme.

In time, a number of psychic powers also come to the student. They should not be given much thought, however, for there is nothing special or miraculous about them besides their novelty; yogis recognize them as perfectly natural. Just as an aborigine is astonished the first time he sees an airplane, so also most people are amazed and impressed by a display of psychic powers. But powers such as clairvoyance and clairaudience are not worth striving after because far greater illumination and peace are possible beyond them. Furthermore, the desire for them may upset and extinquish a student's spiritual propensities.

If one regularly practices concentration and meditation, psychic powers are bound to come. But they must not be used for selfish or materialistic purposes, for every wrong action will have a deleterious reaction, and misuse results in both psychic and spiritual loss. The powers are strong intoxicants; the intellect becomes turbid and understanding becomes cloudy. The practitioner becomes a victim of his own ignorance.

During meditation practice, the mind can assume various states of quietude and peace which are often confusing or misleading. There is a supersensual bliss that comes with the very lower stages of *samadhi* which once experienced leads the student to imagine that the final goal has been reached. Thereupon he gives up further practice. One should never be satisfied with these lower experiences but continue onward toward the experiences of the ancient sages as described in the *Upanishads* and other religious texts. Meditation is a lifelong practice, for there will never be a point where there is nothing more to be gained or learned.

At times the mind rests in a silent, neutral equilibrium that is mistaken for *samadhi,* or it lapses into a state of stupefaction following a deep meditative experience. In neither of these cases is there perfect awareness; rather, the mind becomes inert, unfit for active use. Do not be misled by these two states for, when they prevail, the body is light and the mind is dull rather than sharp. Careful introspection and continued practice helps to transcend these stages.

An intelligent student, who practices meditation daily, learns to recognize the different states into which the mind passes. While the beginner may ofttimes find meditation to be a tedious affair, with advancement more understanding is gained of the mind and its operations; the entire meditative experience becomes very absorbing. More meditation means more gain of mental control and understanding. As control of the mind is gained, a corresponding growth of inner spiritual strength occurs.

There is one last obstacle that all who meditate must face. When all the other obstacles have been overcome by painstaking, dauntless effort, and all the internal enemies have perished, one faces what appears to be a great void. This too must be crossed by the meditator. It is accompanied by an overpowering feeling of being stripped bare and left totally alone. There is nothing that can be seen or heard. The aspirant is beyond seeking solace in others, and confronts the necessity of depending entirely upon himself. Presence of mind is needed at this critical juncture. By drawing courage and strength from within, a triumphant leap to the final goal is made.

Here, set out, are the major obstacles to meditation. A careful study and understanding of them prepares the seeker to face and overcome them. Time and energy should not be wasted. With diligence and determination one can become a spiritual giant. The path of meditation is strewn with difficulties, but each hindrance serves only as a challenge to goad the student on to higher achievements.

Meditation Experiences

Vishnu Swami, observe well the many children who are now coming before you with problems of energy, problems of movement of energy within. Many children will be hearing voices from the higher planes. Many children will be having visions. Many children will have blooming forth in signs and problems that they cannot understand, that cause confusion, and ultimately bring them to your feet. This is no mere coincidence at this time. For much destruction, if coming through a negative path, can be brought once again upon humanity and the Earth plane itself. For this reason, Vishnu Swami, all past knowledge has been shielded and will be awakened only to the degree that each soul connects with the higher Source. For this reason, even beyond purification, is the reason sadhana and sadhana and more sadhana must take place.

> — Swami Sivananda
> *January 2, 1978, fifteen years
> after leaving the physical body,
> spoken through Swami Sri
> Dharananda in an out-of-body state
> of consciousness.*

Sadhana means self-effort. It is the tool, the implement, the spiritual practice by which one crosses over from worldly existence to the realm of the divine. It is the bridge between mundane existence and connection with higher planes of consciousness.

Those who practice various forms of *sadhana* — meditation, Hatha Yoga exercises, chanting, prayer — find an immense peace and joy is derived from their spiritual endeavors. Their lives become more positive and purposeful. This is, in fact, the reason for meditation, the immediate goal of *sadhana*. Occasionally, however, some aspirants have certain experiences along the path and these serve to encourage and inspire the seeker. The final three chapters of this book explain some of these phenomena, in both a general sense and from the author's own connection over the past year with his Guru who left the physical body in 1963.

Meditation experiences are not an end in themselves; in fact, there is the definite danger of becoming caught up in them and losing track of the original goal — realization of the Self. It would be something like taking a trip and never reaching the destination because you had become too involved in congratulating yourself on your progress at each signpost along the way. Spiritual experiences should be taken in stride, noted, appreciated, and then put aside. If insight is needed, the guidance of a Guru or an advanced spiritual student should be sought. It is best not to discuss these phenomena with those who are not spiritually inclined and cannot understand their significance.

Yogis, as well as serious aspirants in all world religions, have always experienced certain phenomena beyond normal perception as part of their growth toward God-Realization. One must consider it to be more than mere coincidence that the yogis of India, lamas of Tibet, shamans of Siberia, Zulus of southeastern Africa, North American Indian medicine men, and even the mystics of Western society should all agree in regard to superphysical phenomena which they have observed, independently of each other.

Not only have identical experiences been reported around the globe, but also all through recorded history. Various types of phenomena appear in the spiritual writings of all cultures and all religions even back to ancient Egyptian times, when they were recorded in *The Egyptian Book of the Dead*.

It must be remembered that there are certain difficulties inherent in attempting to present a description of spiritual experiences. In his book *Beyond Telepathy,* Dr Andrija Puharich discusses yogis who have returned from the state of *samadhi* and attempted to describe this state to others. He reports that people who read or hear of these accounts often feel a great disappointment because they know that they cannot truly understand these experiences as they were communicated. Dr. Puharich notes that the yogis find no adequate descriptions and must express their experiences in terms of light, color and radiance. Yet, these are terms used to describe our physical world, and their experiences are beyond this plane.

The following discussion of meditation experiences is not intended for those who are intrigued by the sensational. It is given for those sincere seekers interested in the ancient science of self-knowledge, so that they may be prepared for certain experiences should they occur. There is no way to emphasize enough the differ-

ences between specifically seeking *siddhis,* or powers, and acknowl-
edging them as an occurrence along the path. It is said that power
corrupts, and this is no less true in the spiritual realm. Those who
seek or use *siddhis* for personal gain will have to face severe karmic
repercussions. All knowledge, all experiences, all abilities gained
through *sadhana* must be offered back to the Source. They must be
used to benefit all of mankind.

SIGHTS AND SOUNDS

For many meditators there is never any particular experience
outside the tranquility of a stilled mind. To encounter astral sights
and sounds in no way indicates superior meditation. Yet, for those
who do have such experiences, it is best to have an understanding of
what may occur so that there is no fear or confusion when they
happen.

The most common experience in meditation is the manifestation of lights in the center of the forehead. These are *tanmatric* lights
and they are caused by the elements that make up the body. Each
element has its own color: earth is yellow; water, white; fire, red;
air, smokey; and ether, blue. There may also be small balls of
white light floating before the mind's eye. This is an indication that
the mind is becoming steadier and that concentration is progressing.
The lights may also resemble lightning flashing out from above the
forehead or from the sides. They give rise to extreme joy, happiness,
and an intense desire for more experience of them. When practice
is systematic, two or three hours in the morning and two or three
hours at night, the lights appear more frequently and remain steady.
High vibratory particles may also be seen in them. After some
months the size may increase, and there may be a full blaze of
white light appearing at the forehead or even above the head.

The vision of lights is a great encouragement to the aspirant
and spurs him on to regular practice. It also bestows a strong faith
in super-physical matters. It may be so powerful and dazzling that
one may withdraw from it, breaking the meditation. But there
should be no fear; through constant practice the mind becomes
accustomed to the experience and is able to maintain concentration.

In addition to lights, *anahata,* or mystic sounds, may be heard.
This is a sign that the astral tubes, the *nadis,* are being purified,
usually through the practice of *pranayama.* These sounds can be
most distinctly heard when closing the ears with the thumbs, although
in meditation one should focus on the sounds in the right ear only.

There are ten kinds of sounds that can be heard. The first is "chini"; the second is "chini-chini"; the third is the sound of a bell; the fourth is that of a conch; the fifth, of a lute; the sixth, of cymbals; the seventh, of a flute; the eighth has the sound of a drum; the ninth, of a double drum; and the tenth, of thunder.

At times one may experience certain physical sensation, such as a tingling or warmth in the spine, which indicates some movement of the *kundalini shakti.* There may be parts of the body that suddenly jerk from time to time. This occurs in the purification of the *nadis,* although if it happens very often, it may be due to an overzealous attempt to raise the *kundalini.* Some may experience an automatic retention of breath, or *kumbhaka.* This is a natural phenomenon and there need not be any fear of it. The sensation of rising may also occur. It may seem as if an invisible power is pushing one up from the physical body. This is not levitation, but a slight raising of the astral body to a plane beyond body-consciousness.

Beings and objects may also manifest during some stages of meditation. These visions can be either subjective or objective. They may be one's own mental reactions personified — crystallizations of one's own intense thoughts — such as beings one creates in a dream. Or, they may be entities from other planes of consciousness. The universe consists of planes of matter possessing various grades of density, and each plane has its own objects and beings.

The entities which sometimes appear in meditation may or may not have a high level of consciousness. As mentioned in the section on Karma and reincarnation, each person spends periods of time in a physical body, alternating with periods in the non-physical state. Until attaining an advanced level of evolution, beings who are not in the body are no wiser than those living on the earth plane. In fact, it is the manifestation of some of the less happy disembodied souls that explains the phenomenon of ghosts and demons.

Mr. H. Saraydarian, in his book *The Science of Meditation,* explains that during meditation one radiates lights, colors, and thought forms, and these attract the attention of the beings on other planes. They approach the meditator and try to make contact with him. Mr. Saraydarian says that many of these beings simply want to communicate with the physical world, but he cautions against contact with those whom he calls the "dark brothers". The "dark brothers", he says, are especially drawn to one who is advancing along the spiritual path and are anxious to harm him. But this can only happen if the meditator is unprotected because of his impure motives and desires, of if he is using advanced techniques without first having strengthened himself through proper preparation.

Not all experiences are of this nature, however. The meditator may see the forms of friends or relations, especially if he travels on the astral plane, himself. *The National Spiritualist,* July 1931, printed a story by Dr. Hout of Goshen, Indiana, in which he told of an astral experience. Having put himself into a quiet meditative state, Dr. Hout soon passed out of his physical body: "Almost suddenly, but still imperceptibly, I felt myself drawn out of my body.... No force was needed to jerk me free from my physical bounds. I just stepped away from the reclining physical form, turned to view it for a brief moment, and then resolutely and easily floated upward, out and away from the material room." Before returning to his body, Dr. Hout says that he met with friends and relatives who had previously died. In conclusion, he speaks about his dead friends saying, "I know that they are living somewhere in this great universe of ours in another place. . somewhere in God's great cosmos."

Dr. Hout's experience is far from unique; countless cases have been documented. *The Phenomenon of Astral Projection,* by Muldoon and Carrington, documents many similar experiences. In one case, the authors site an Oakland, California woman who one day felt a pair of hands slip under her body and carry her out of the house and across fields and gardens. Everything felt quiet and peaceful and she soon noticed that she was surrounded by a golden light. After, she was returned to her room.

Those who find themselves open to the visions and voices from astral beings should use discrimination. Only those who are of the highest order must be allowed to manifest. When lustrous forms of sages and saints appear, it is to give guidance. They should be honored and their advice heeded. But if in any way the being seems to have questionable motives, if they play on the ego's desire for power or objects of the physical world, or if there are negative physical or psychic reactions to their presence, they should be ignored. By turning to the purest Source — one's deity Mantra, a photograph of Jesus Christ, thoughts of the Guru, or prayer to God — the influence of these *bhutas,* lower astral entities, is easily overcome.

THE OTHER SIDE OF DEATH

Existence in the physical body is but a flash in the life of a soul. The brevity of earthly life becomes more apparent the older a person gets. As the seeker progresses on the path toward Self-

Realization, he begins to realize that all of existence is a spiritual experience. The only purpose of moving in and out of physical bodies is to advance toward perfection.

Death is simply another spiritual experience or phase through which the soul passes. During that period of transition referred to as "death" the body ceases to perform the life functions. The physical body is of the gross earth plane, for it comes from and is composed of the elements of the earth. Having served its purpose, it returns to the earth, and the soul separates to exist on other planes.

Earthly existence is but a fraction of the experience of the soul. Every person has three bodies — the physical body, the astral body, and the causal body. The physical body is also called the food sheath, for it is composed of what is eaten, and at the end of life it returns to the food cycle. The astral body is composed of the vital sheath, which contains all the *pranas;* the mental sheath, which contains all emotions and desires; and the intellectual sheath, which performs the functions of analyzing and thinking. The causal body is made up of the bliss sheath, for its nature is pure bliss.

Mrs. de Morgan, in her book *From Matter to Spirit,* tells of a time when she and a friend visited a dying man. Both of them, as the man died, saw a white cloud emerge from the body and hover over it. At first a nebulous cloud moving under the bed covers, it surged up the body and exited through the top of the head. This was the astral body separating from the physical body at the time of death.

Recently scientists have taken a much closer look at claims such as these. For instance, Dr. Charles Tart of the University of California at Davis and Harold Sherman of the ESP Research Associates Foundation have both been carrying out investigations of out-of-body experiences. The work of Valentina and Semyon Kirlian, who discovered and pioneered Kirlian photography, is known by scientists throughout the world. Kirlian photographs reveal an energy field which penetrates and surrounds all living things. Studies show that the patterns of this energy field can give information on the emotional state of the subject, indicate coming illnesses, and can be photographed even after the corresponding physical portions have been removed from the subject, such as a Kirlian photograph of an entire leaf when half of the leaf had been cut away.

In *Psychic Discoveries Behind the Iron Curtain* by Ostrander and Schroeder, the authors report that six soviet scientists, Drs. V. Inyushin, N. Shouiski, N. Fedorova, V. Grishchenko, N. Vorobev, and F. Gibadulin, have done extensive research in this area; and in their book-long scientific paper, these Soviet scientists have come to the conclusion that all plants, animals and humans have, in addition to a physical body, a counterpart body composed of energy. This body can be seen by those with psychic vision, in Kirlian photographs, and even through special machinery and glass lenses that have been treated with certain chemical dyes. This is the astral body which interpenetrates and extends six to eight inches beyond the physical body, where it is frequently called the "aura".

The physical body is the vehicle of the astral and causal bodies while the soul is incarnate on earth in order to learn lessons. When death comes, the astral body, with the *pranas,* the mind, memories, past impressions or *samskaras,* and the senses —which all exist in the astral body — separate from the physical body and move out of the earth plane to higher planes where other types of knowledge are gained.

What is it like to die? Many people involved in accidents or operations have exhibited all the signs with which modern medicine normally associates the condition of death, and subsequently have been revived. After returning to a normal state, they have recounted experiences that can only be described as being of a spiritual nature. Dr. Raymond Moody has made a detailed study of hundreds of such cases. The following, from his book *Life After Life,* is his sketch of a typical "case" as might be experienced by anybody undergoing clinical death and returning.

"Despite the wide variation in the circumstances surrounding close calls with death and in the types of persons undergoing them, it remains true that there is a striking similarity among the accounts of the experiences themselves. On the basis of these points of likeness, let me now construct a brief, theoretical 'ideal' or 'complete' experience which embodies all of the common elements.

"A man is dying and, as he reaches the point of greatest physical distress, he hears himself pronounced dead by his doctor. He begins to hear an uncomfortable noise, a loud ringing or buzzing, and at the same time feels himself moving very rapidly through a long dark tunnel. After this, he suddenly finds himself outside of his own physical body, but still in the immediate physical environment, and he sees his own body from a distance, as though he is a spectator. He watches the resuscitation attempt from this unusual vantage point, and is in a state of emotional upheaval.

"After a while, he collects himself and becomes more accustomed to his odd condition. He notices that he still has a body, but one of a very different nature and with very different powers from the physical body he has left behind. Soon other things begin to happen. Others come to meet him. He glimpses the spirits of relatives and friends who have already died, and a loving, warm spirit of a kind he has never encountered before — a being of light — appears before him. This being asks him a question, nonverbally, to make him evaluate his life and helps him along by showing him a panoramic, instantaneous playback of the major events of his life. At some point he finds himself approaching some sort of barrier or border, apparently representing the limit between earthly life and the next life. Yet, he finds that he must go back to the earth, that the time for his death has not yet come. At this point he resists, for by now he is taken up with his experiences in the afterlife and does not want to return. He is overwhelmed by intense feelings of love, joy, and peace. Despite his attitude, though, he somehow reunites with his physical body and lives."

Dr. Elisabeth Kubler-Ross, in the forward to Dr. Moody's book, writes: "It is evident from his findings that the dying patient continues to have a conscious awareness of his environment after being pronounced clinically dead... It [Dr. Moody's findings] is also corroborated by my own research and by the findings of other very serious minded scientists, scholars and members of the clergy."

Thus it can be seen that there is now scientific evidence supporting the teaching of a continued existence after death. When death actually occurs, the soul accompanied by the astral body departs from the physical body and travels to different planes according to its Karma. The results of good Karma may be the enjoyment of heavenly surroundings, while negative Karma earns unpleasant experiences beyond the physical plane.

After leaving physical life, the soul's experiences correspond to the afterlife he has come to expect. A Christian may be taken by angels through a procession of saints, while a Hindu may be taken to the palatial abode of Yama, Lord of Death. The plane to which the soul travels is most influenced by the last thought prior to death which is determined by the types of thoughts which predominate throughout a person's life.

There can be no doubt that heaven and hell exist, although these are as much a state of mind as a solid reality. A man who has been selfish, greedy or brutal in his dealings with his fellows will exist on a lower plane where he must face the memory and the karmic effects of those deeds. One who has lived a virtuous life travels to a higher plane where the soul will have but to think of that which it wants and the desire will automatically manifest from his thoughts. But those who have transcended the idea of heavenly rewards, who understand the nature of birth and rebirth, and no longer wish to partake of the endless round of material pleasures and pains, travel to even higher planes, where everything is of a purer and lighter vibration. There is still pleasure, for these souls will have accumulated much good Karma. But the experience is a learning one. Peace, bliss and joy are the rewards of these planes, and the soul can meditate and reflect on the lessons learned in the previous life.

There are seven higher planes and seven lower planes. Each has its own vibration and is composed of matter of an appropriate density which interpenetrates the matter of the plane below it. For example, the astral interpenetrates the physical plane and extends for some distance beyond it. Its vibrations are more rapid than those of the physical plane, and the material of which it is made is more subtle. The mental plane, heaven, interpenetrates the astral plane, and its matter is likewise much more subtle. From there, the soul may later ascend to higher planes where everything is of the vibration of sound and light.

These planes do not exist in different locations or in different spaces. The astral plane is not a place to which one travels, like going to San Francisco. All the planes coexist within each other. When the soul passes from one plane to another, there is no movement in space. The soul simply changes its focus of consciousness. Just as one can have different visions through a microscope or a telescope by changing the lenses, so each soul has different vehicles and can function on different planes by using those vehicles. Each of the bodies and sheaths of man occupies the same space but is composed of grosser or subtler matter. As the vibration of consciousness is speeded up, corresponding higher planes of consciousness are experienced.

Dr. Hout of Indiana, mentioned previously, writing about his return to a normal state, moving from one plane to another plane, describes it as a "definite change in rates of vibration." The same experience is reported by Swami Sri Dharananda whose story is told in the following pages.

Thus it can be seen that any spiritual experience is but a glimpse from the vantage point of the Self. Life on earth and life in the spirit are only phases through which the soul passes. As the entity becomes refined and moves closer to realization of the Self, the gross physical plane holds less appeal for him, and he begins to experience subtler levels of consciousness.

Messages from Beyond the Earth Plane

*I am One with the Source yet have separated temporarily in
time to come to guide, to protect my children, to bring forth Truth
that must bloom to help all mankind.*

> — Swami Sivananda
> *December 28, 1977, spoken through
> the body of Swami Sri Dharananda.*

The Sivananda Yoga Vedanta Centers and Ashrams were
established in honor of Swami Sivananda for the express purpose
of carrying out his teachings. The organization's work for the most
part involves teaching Hatha and Raja Yoga, meditation and Vedanta philosophy in the various city centers around the world, training
Yoga teachers at the six main Ashrams, sponsoring several symposiums a year to demonstrate the connection between ancient yogic
traditions and modern scientific research, and to promote world
peace through the True World Order (TWO). It has always been a
strictly non-commercial, non-profit organization. Its members have
tended to be quite average people and its philosophy was such that
one did one's *sadhana,* or spiritual practices, along with a healthy
amount of Karma Yoga. The subject of spiritual experiences was
rarely discussed. For twenty years this was the case.

Suddenly a new dimension emerged. In August, 1977, Master
Sivananda who had departed earthly life on July 14th, 1963, began
to communicate through not one, but several different members of
the spiritual community.

The earliest messages were received through Marilyn Rossner,
a devoted student of mine who has been practicing Yoga for many
years. She is a highly respected Canadian psychic and professor of
Special Education at McGill University in Montreal. The following
is an excerpt from an automatic writing she received in late August
of 1977.

"Oh, my child of Earth, the times are changing. A new era
is dawning and very few will be prepared. But I shall show myself as

233

the need arises and light shall lead the way. There shall be others who will witness my presence, for of necessity I shall stay close."

And on September 20, Marilyn received another automatic writing. It concluded with the words, "Direct communication is forthcoming." Yet there was no way to understand the immensity of that promise.

That fall, in September and October of 1977, Master Sivananda's presence was felt more and more strongly by various members of the Sivananda Yoga mission. Several students reported experiencing visions of him; others reported a very strong sense of feeling his guidance. On October 17, Swami Divyananda, who was then the director of the Sivananda Yoga Center in San Francisco, also had an experience of automatic writing: "Do not doubt, I am here. Do not doubt, I am here. Sivananda." Ultimately, however, it was Swami Sri Dharananda who was to become the vehicle for Master Sivananda's words.

Swami Sri Dharananda is a very close disciple who had always expressed a particular devotion to Master Sivananda. She is known for her wonderful cheerful nature, and in particular for her loving overseeing of the Summer Children's Yoga Camp. She had been experiencing great physical problems and had undergone much suffering a good part of her life, but it had been more pronounced over the past couple of years preceding the first manifestation. Master Sivananda explained later, in a message received on November 21, 1977.

"This child, the one you know as my voice, is my chosen link to the Earth plane. She is one of many chosen Children of Light. Their work is one of great struggle, for their mission to help the Earth has been chosen by all these children long before they arrived. The pain you see before you is taken on by these children to help relieve great suffering of mankind. They are not children of this Earth plane, and their existence here is one of great, great pain and suffering. For they long within to return to their homeland. They are children from the highest plane come to help those who are living in darkness."

The messages, which have come to be known as "Master's Manifestations", began on October 18, 1977. They continue, even as this book goes to press, often on a daily basis. Each session brings new instruction, new insight. Needless to say, not all who hear or read the messages are inspired. Reactions range from devotion, joy, awe, and enthusiasm to curiosity, doubt, skepticism and even fear. It is impossible for the human mind to fathom intellectually the magnitude and significance of this phenomenon. However, one thing has become apparent; we are only scratching the surface of a whole new realm of knowledge. The full story is given here for the first time.

"NO PAIN, NO GAIN"

When he was living in his Ashram at the foothills of the Himalayas, Swami Sivananda would sometimes, in a loving way, remind a troubled disciple, "No pain, no gain." That is, it is in the confrontation with difficulties, in the overcoming of obstacles, that the mind is purified and made strong. This was certainly the case for Swami Sri Dharananda.

Throughout her life Swami Sri Dharananda had experienced certain phenomena that others did not. She saw auras, and sometimes would perceive beings who did not exist on a physical level. She also suffered, from childhood, occasional unexplainable pain in her abdominal area. This pain had become increasingly worse in recent years, and in the fall of 1976, it reached a level that was beyond endurance; on several occasions she found herself leaving body-consciousness. While she had seen a number of doctors about her condition, neither insight into the problem nor any relief was forthcoming. I decided to send her to the finest specialists in the country. In December of 1976 she was examined extensively by Dr. Steptoe, a leading gynecologist at Columbia Hospital in Washington, D.C. She was subsequently seen by Dr. Gerber, a famous surgeon at Washington Hospital Center, also in D.C. Both physicians diagnosed the problem as endometriosis. However, the medications she was given seemed to aggravate the condition, and on several occasions she was in a critical situation.

Surgery was recommended. But I had an intuitive feeling that this was not the answer. Swami Sri Dharananda also rejected the idea. During her illness she had had many visions of the Lord, and recently there had been a vision of Lord Vishnu in which He told her not to seek guidance from others, that this was all His work, and that she would have to endure.

In February, 1977, I brought Swami Sri Dharanandaji to our warm, sunny Ashram in the Bahamas in the hopes of giving her direct help there. It was possible sometimes to relieve the pain somewhat through various Yoga techniques, but for the most part the terrible, unbearable stomach pains continued. Sometimes she was not able to breathe. Her diaphragm would become swollen and as hard as a football; her body would become stiff and rigid.

At that time we heard of a very progressive doctor, Dr. Kelly of the Kelly Foundation, in Winthrop, Washington. He had a new way of treating cancer. Swami Sri Dharananda was sent immediately to the West Coast where Dr. Kelly put her on a rigorous cleansing and purification program, supplemented with great doses of vitamins. But by June the pains still continued, and she returned to the Sivananda Yoga Camp in Canada to direct the Childen's Summer Program, despite her difficulties.

It was at this time that I came to know in an intuitive flash that Swami Sri Dharananda's problems were not of a physical nature. While she was experiencing physical distress, the true cause lay in the astral body and its source was psychic energy blockages. I was brought to this knowledge by recollection of similar agonizing pain which I had experienced in earlier days during my own period of intense *sadhana*. I immediately put her on a rigid program of *pranayama*, breathing exercises which I had followed myself some twenty years back.

The program began with a bath at 5:30 in the morning. A small amount of food would be taken at 6:00 followed by *puja*, a worship service of offerings at 6:30. At 7:00 Swami Sri Dharananda would do a short set of *asanas*, and then begin a series of *pranayama* exercises lasting for three hours, with emphasis on maintaining the *mudras* and *bhandas*, postures and locks which help to direct the spiritual energy in the body upward. The *pranayamas* were as follows: *Vipitakarani* - 10 minutes, *Kapalabhati* - 10 minutes, Alternate Nostril Breathing - 20 minutes, *Suryabhedha* - 10 minutes, *Ujjayi* - 10 minutes, *Sitkari* - 10 minutes, *Sitali* - 10 minutes, *Bramari* - 10 minutes, *Mahamudra* - 10 minutes, *Mahabhanda* - 10 minutes, *Mahavedha* - 10 minutes, *Bhastrika* - 10 minutes each for left, right, alternating, and both nostrils, *Shaktichalani* - 10 minutes. (For details on the procedure of all but the most advanced of the above exercises, refer to *The Complete Illustrated Book of Yoga*. The most advanced *pranayamas* are not given, as they should only be practiced under direct supervision of the Guru.)

On completing *Shaktichalani*, Swami Sri Dharananda would leave body-consciousness for an hour, then be returned to begin the process again. The schedule was repeated four times throughout the day, the last session ending at 4:30 a.m. During that period of intensive *sadhana*, sleep was never necessary; the out-of-the-body state seemed to give all the rest that was needed. The schedule was varied during the Children's Camp; there were three slightly longer sessions, and the additional time was alloted to work with the children.

Later in the year the schedule was again changed, returning to four sessions; but with concentration on the various *kriyas,* or internal cleansing exercises, in the early morning session.

When losing body-consciousness, Swami Sri Dharanandaji would be completely unaware of anything in the environment, and no stimulus could bring her back to a conscious level. Her body would become completely rigid, and it would take quite some time after she returned for her to be able to use her limbs properly. I finally discovered that by throwing cold water on her I could bring her back fairly easily. The water would create a shock in the nervous system, which is the link, via *prana,* between the physical and astral bodies. So the effect of the shock of the cold water would reconnect the two bodies electrically and she would return to a conscious level.

A PERIOD OF TESTING

In order to document these unusual states of consciousness, I brought Swami Sri Dharananda to Sun Ship Biofeedback Systems of Canada, a laboratory in Montreal where she was tested by senior researcher Allan Lundell. Both Swami Sri Dharananda and a control subject were monitored on an electromyogram and a electroencephalogram. Their skin temperature and pulse were also recorded. Five different breathing exercises were performed by both, and measurements were taken before and after each exercise. Dr. Terry Cale, of Huntsville, Alabama, wrote in his report on the experiments.

"During the post-experimental phase, the subject B [control] discontinued without any effect other than slight headache. Subject A [Swami Sri Dharananda], however, was noted to become unresponsive to voice stimuli. She remained in a sitting position, however, with legs crossed. The pupils remained responsive to light, and there was an eyelash reflex to stroking. There was no reflex to loud startling noise. Patellar deep tendon reflex remained present. Babinski reflex was negative. A match was held to her skin without response. Pin prick elicited no response."

The most significant aspect of the test, however, was the amplitude of Swami Sri Dharananda's brain waves as registered on the electroencephalograph when she left body-consciousness. An experienced meditator does well to raise his brain-wave amplitude to 40 microvolts while in an alpha state; Swami Sri Dharananda registered the maximum reading of the instrument, *300 microvolts!*

It was at this time, during the summer of 1977, that I was involved in my campaign against the fraudulent practices of the organization known as Transcendental Meditation. They had been claiming to teach levitation — and charging a very pretty price for it — while in fact they were teaching nothing more than the hopping techniques practiced by yogi's who are doing advanced *pranayama*. In order to combat the negative effect this was having on the public, as well as on sincere practitioners of Yoga, I organized a series of press conferences. I brought Swami Sri Dharanandaji to the New York and Montreal press conferences to demonstrate the hopping technique and to show the unusual state of consciousness that she entered.

The Montreal conference was monitered by Hal Myers, Ph.D., cofounder of Thought Technology in Montreal. On July 28, 1977, *The Montreal Star* reported,

"Swami Sri Dharananda sat cross-legged on the cloth covered collapsible table and began taking quick deep and rhythmic gasps of air. Wired to an electroencephalograph (EEG) machine, she repeated the exercise for about 20 minutes. Suddenly she began bouncing about five inches off the table.

"As wide-eyed newsmen looked at the spectacle, the Swami went crashing to the floor as the force of her hopping caused the collapsible table to do exactly that. Without flinching or demonstrating any outward sign of pain or surprise she was quickly restored to her lotus position...."

The Montreal Gazette also ran a story that same day, and added that when "the table accidentally collapsed, the Swami was not awakened, nor did she later acknowledge feeling anything." Dr. Myers was most astounded by the readings of his machines. Not only had Swami Sri Dharananda remained in alpha state during her fall, but she had registered an amplitude of 300 microvolts the entire time.

FURTHER AWAKENINGS

It was a summer of tremendous *sadhana,* and Swami Sri Dharananda was not alone in her spiritual experiences. Swami Gokulananda, a very devout and dedicated disciple, had been working closely with me for the past seven years. She had been my personal secretary, had almost single-handedly organized all of the major symposiums, festivals, and tours of India, and had acted as the administrative head of the Sivananda Yoga mission in my absence. Beyond that, she was teacher, supervisor, counselor, and confidant to the many members of the organization spread throughout the world.

In mid-June, 1977, after many months of working exceptionally hard, Swami Gokulananda also began to experience movement

Swami Sri Dharananda wired to an electroencephalograph at the "Symposium on Physics and Metaphysics" in Los Angeles, on October 30, 1977.

of energy within her body, particularly in the spine. Sometimes it was accompanied by the sensation of heat. She would find herself sitting for hours in meditation, greatly absorbed and focussed on the Lord. Each meditation seemed to bring greater peace and intunement.

The Annual Labor Day Retreat at the Sivananda Yoga Ashram Ranch in the Catskills of New York marked a point at which it became apparent that the events that had been happening were part of a much, much greater story, which was yet to unfold. During evening meditation, before over one hundred students, Swami Sri Dharananda, Swami Gokulananda and another student, Saraswati, all had intensive spiritual experiences, and all left body-consciousness. Then, Swami Gokulananda's hands raised up into the *chin mudra,* with thumb and first finger touching, and the last three fingers of each hand extended. Her hands remained extended in this manner the entire time she was in an absorbed state. It was only at this time that Marilyn Rossner first told of several automatic writings which she had recently received, one of which was to give me the following message:

"Just tell him that I am with him and he will be able yet to fulfill many of his hopes and wishes. But he shall be called upon to enter a phase which even he does not fully comprehend. Assure him of continued success for mankind.... Say to your Swamiji that Master appeared and he will understand. This is Master Sivananda."

As is the case each fall, we left the Ranch for the Sivananda Ashram Yoga Farm in Grass Valley, California. Both Swami Sri Dharananda and Swami Gokulananda continued to experience altered states of consciousness during meditation, occasionally seeing visions of Master Sivananda. Swami Gokulananda would go into a deep meditation and experience very high-intensity energies which would sometimes guide her body into automatic *bhastrika* (an advanced *pranayama)* and automatic *asanas;* other times her hand would raise into the *chin mudra.* Swami Sri Dharananda shortly began to experience other levels of consciousness. She often had visions of Lord Vishnu, and sometimes she would meet other "beings of light and energy" who would give her various instructions. Even so, since there was as yet no proof that Master Sivananda was actually responsible for all of these events, I instructed them both to concentrate on *sadhana* and not to be too concerned with the phenomena themselves. In the meantime, I conducted various experiments, brought in several physicians for documentation, and had testing done.

Swami Sri Dharananda continued to have physical problems. Her abdominal pains continued; sometimes her diaphragm would become blocked and breathing became nearly impossible. Several times her vital signs all but disappeared. On October 15 I had her begin a forty-eight hour marathon in which she remained in an out-of-body state of consciousness the entire time, returning only for short periods to take nourishment and use the bathroom. Towards the end of the second day her body began trembling violently, almost bouncing off the ground. Then she began to speak.

"*Om pani dvayam tvaya.*" Her words were very faint, but I shortly recognized them as being Sanskrit. Listening closely I finally understood what she was saying: "Two hands by you." But what could that have meant?

Upon returning, Swami Sri Dharananda felt that she had been taught a Mantra, but I was sure that it was meant as some kind of message. The next time she left body-consciousness, the same words were repeated. "*Om pani dvayam tvaya.*" Taking these to be directions, I asked, although I knew she could not hear me, "Where?" The answer came immediately: "*Suhasrara*".

I was astonished. Swami Sri Dharananda knew the meaning of that word; it refers to the *chakra* at the top of the head. But she had never been able to pronounce it correctly in a normal waking state. She would (and still does) call it "Sahaswara". This was the first indication of proof that all of the unusual occurrences which had been going on stemmed neither from the subconscious minds of Swami Sri Dharananda and Swami Gokulananda, nor from a lower astral entity.

I immediately placed my two hands at the top of her head. Suddenly my body began to vibrate just as hers was, and I began to do automatic *bhastrika*. Energy began pumping into my body far beyond my control. The violent *bhastrika* continued until all of the excess energy was diffused and Swami Sri Dharananda lay in a relaxed state, the swelling in her abdomen gone and her breathing normal.

The entire phenomenon immediately became clear. Swami Sri Dharananda had been experiencing blockages of the spiritual energy which was moving in her body. The great purification and *pranayama* which she had been following helped to clear the blocks and raise the energy up to the highest *chakras,* which would result in her change of consciousness. Now I was being taught to facilitate this process using my own hands as a conductor to draw off the excess energy.

Before the end of her forty-eight hour meditation, there was a second unusual occurence. Swami Sri Dharananda began to repeat other words while she was out of body-consciousness. She would repeat single words over and over, such as *kala, kala, kala,* or *jagath, jagath, jagath,* or *dwala, dwala, dwala.* Later she reported being taken to an etheric "Garden", where she was witnessing and being taught certain sounds. There were beings there who actually vibrated these sounds, and each one had a meaning. *Kala,* for example, referred to destruction, and she felt that this pertained to a certain negative energy that exists on earth at this time which must be countered. What was most interesting, however, was that even though Swami Sri Dharananda did not know it, the words she had been learning were, for the most part, Sanskrit in origin, and their meanings corresponded exactly with the correct Sanskrit translations.

MASTER SIVANANDA MANIFESTS

Within the realm of religion and spirituality it occasionally happens that one hears of communication between the higher planes and mankind where the laws of physical existence are bypassed. It is not that the physical laws cease to exist, but only that higher laws are applied.

Sri Shankara was one of India's greatest sages. His life might be compared to that of Saint Francis of Assisi. Though he died at the age of 32, in his brief lifetime he established the four major monastic orders of India, and brought about unity to the various sects of the diverse Hindu tradition. At the age of sixteen he engaged in a debate regarding whether the life of a *sanyasi,* or monk, would raise one to higher spiritual levels than that of a householder. In the debate he was challenged on a point of the *Kama Sutra,* the scriptures that deal with science of sex. As a celibate from birth he could not answer directly. But, as a realized yogi, Sri Shankara was able to manifest the eight major *siddhis,* or powers. He bid his disciples take care of his body, while he psychically entered the body of King Amaruka, who had just died. For one month he lived the life of a householder, and during that time wrote a treatise which secured his position in the debate. Then, the king died, and Sri Shankara returned to his life as perfect *sanyasi.*

Western religion also carries histories of such super-physical phenomena. One of the better known stories is where Moses encountered a bush that was burning in the desert, and yet not being consumed. "And when the Lord saw that he turned aside to see, God called unto him out of the midst of the bush and said, Moses, Moses.

And He said, Here am I." (Exodus 3; verse 4). Then the Lord bid Moses to lead his people out of Egypt.

In the Gospel of St. Matthew of the New Testament, the story is told of how Peter, James, and John accompanied Jesus up a high mountain where Moses and Elias both appeared to them. There "a voice came out of the cloud, which said, This is my beloved Son, in whom I am well pleased: Hear ye Him." (Matthew 17, verse 5).

The history of every religion is filled with inspirational stories in which the physical plane has been transcended. Yet, in the tradition of my Guru, Swami Sivananda, I had always believed and taught that one should not become involved in "psychic" matters, but should concentrate on the goal of realizing God. I maintained a detached and scientific attitude towards all of the spiritual occurrences that were filling the days that fall, but it became more and more clear that it was Master Sivananda himself who was guiding and communicating through these phenomena, and that it was his will that the knowledge he was giving be shared.

The day after Swami Sri Dharanandaji's marathon ended, on October 17, 1977, we all travelled to the San Francisco Center to begin a series of programs and lectures. That evening, for the first time, Master Sivananda spoke. His first message came through Swami Gokulananda. With her hands raised in the *chin mudra,* she spoke these words:

"God is manifest through these effulgent beings of light. Do not see yourselves as beings of the Earth, for I am with you. This is my sign [The *chin mudra*]. This all has to happen to avoid the destruction of the Earth."

If the words were beyond comprehension, there was at least no doubt that Master's presence was there. That same evening was when the automatic writing came through Swami Divyananda, and she too experienced the movement of energies in her body. Throughout most of that night the small group of devotees remained uplifted and focussed on the awesome grace of their Teacher.

The next day, on the afternoon of October 18, Swami Sri Dharananda awoke, hearing an internal voice telling her to arise and prepare. "Do not tarry in time for a new dawn is fast coming." All bathed themselves, cleaned the altar and dressed it with a fresh cloth and flowers. Again, Master's presence filled the entire atmosphere. As they sat for meditation, each could feel himself quickly focussing and becoming absorbed in the energy. Shortly, for the first time, Swami Sri Dharananda's hands rose slowly up into the *chin mudra,* the sign that was to indicate in this and every message that followed that Master Sivananda was about to speak.

"I am separated from the Source, yet I am One with it. I have come to help all of humanity. My work is laid before you. This is my message. Know that I am manifest by this sign of the hand. My sign is the hand; know I am manifest by the sign of the hand."

From that time the messages began to come from Master Sivananda on almost a daily basis. Each time, exactly the same pattern would be repeated. Swami Gokulananda, Swami Sri Dharananda and I would all have to be present, for as Master later explained, it was not possible for only one to contain the energy alone. Each session would begin with a meditation in which both swamis could feel the energy rising in their bodies, the rate of vibration increasing steadily. Swami Sri Dharananda would leave body-consciousness, her breathing would become very deep, and her entire physical being would become locked in place so that it would be impossible for even two strong men to unlock her crossed legs. After some time, however, the locks would be released and she would be laid gently onto her back. Shortly after, her head would begin to roll rapidly back and forth. The hands would quiver, then form the *chin mudra* as the arms slowly lifted to a position perpendicular to the floor. The arms would remain extended for the duration of the message, sometimes as long as two hours. When Master finished, the hands would relax back to the floor, the breathing pattern return to normal, and within a short time she would be back at a conscious level.

It is interesting to note that on October 18, at the same time that Master's first message was coming, several other members of the Sivananda Yoga Organization had unusual spiritual experiences. Madhava, a staff member at the Yoga Camp headquarters, wrote the next day,

"After Arati, I went back to the temple and started shaking, doing *pranayama,* and fell forward, and spontaneously prostrated, my hands touching Master's feet. He was standing towering over me with His big coat on. Smiling He said, 'Oh immortal child give up worldly pleasure, realize the Supreme Self'. My heart opened up, I was crying mentally to Master, heart pouring with devotion to Him. Touching His feet, it was the highest of honors to be able to see His divine presence.

"All during the day after I was wide awake and calm and peaceful. I saw the world in a different perspective, able to challenge anything. All that happened last night was Master's energy working through us all."

Despite the fact that I remained cautious in accepting these

Above: At the IBM Los Gatos Laboratories near San Jose, California. From left to right: parapsychologist Father John Rossner, Swami Vishnu Devananada, Swami Sri Dharananda, Marcel Vogel, Swami Gokulananada, and Swami Divyananda. Below left: Madhava, staff at the Sivananda Yoga Camp Headquarters, who had a vision of Master Sivananda in October, 1977. Below right: Marilyn Rossner, psychic and professor of Special Education at McGill University, Montreal.

"psychic" events as being Master's work, he had manifested to a number of students and in several different Centers and Ashrams. In the next sessions, on November first, he said, "Vishnu Swami, I am with you. I will guide you." *Vishnu Swami*. That was an affectionate name that he alone had used when I was with him in Rishikesh. No one else had ever addressed me that way. I suddenly realized how close Master had really remained in all those years since he had left the physical body.

MARCEL VOGEL AND THE CRYSTAL

The next stop on our tour was Los Angeles, California, There I again had Swami Gokulananda and Swami Sri Dharananda tested. At the Biofeedback Training Institute, of Hollywood, Dana Mebransky, along with the director of the Institute, conducted the experiments, while both swamis did advanced *pranayama* and brought up the energy in their bodies. Ms. Mebransky's comment was, "I have rarely seen such strong stable alpha for such a long period of time. I have *never* seen such an amplitude. The needle was off the scale continually for a lengthy duration."

Our main purpose for being in Los Angeles, however, was for the *Symposium on Physics and Metaphysics*. One of our guests was Marcel Vogel. I did not know him personally then, but his work sounded most interesting. He was and is a senior research scientist at I.B.M. Research Laboratories in San Jose, California, where he had been doing work in luminescent technology. His most interesting developments included pioneer work in plant response and communication, some very unusual experiments with quartz crystals and energy transference, and a program on developing a camera which will photograph thought, as yet to be completed.

Mr. Vogel made it clear that the areas in which he worked were considered to be somewhat outlandish by most of his colleagues. Often he felt more of an affinity with those involved in spiritual and psychic matters than with men of science. He himself had a spiritual awakening at the age of six, when he was near death from double lobar pneumonia. At that time he had an out-of-body experience which established in him an intense desire for spiritual growth. At the age of nine, he also became deeply interested in science. At eleven, upon observing a glowworm, he made the determination to understand its luminescent quality; by fourteen he had a complete three-room chemical laboratory and had created a multi-stage organic synthesis of the organic compound which duplicated

Marcel Vogel intuning with crystal to Marilyn Rossner, after which a message from Master Sivananda was received. This occurred on October 30, 1977, at the Los Angeles "Symposium on Physics and Metaphysics."

the light of the firefly and glowworm.

What Marcel Vogel spoke about at the symposium, however, was his work with crystals. He explained that he had cut a number of quartz crystals, actually faceting them through intuition rather than any mathematical process. These instruments can be used to take the energy of the mind and bring it into focus, in much the same way that crystals were used to transfer sound vibrations in early radios. Just as a microscope concentrates the rays of the sun, so a crystal can be used to concentrate thought energy.

In a later speech, on March 18, 1978, at the Sivananda Ashram Yoga Retreat in the Bahamas, Marcel Vogel elaborated further.

"The reality of our body is not the physical form that we look at; the reality is in the energy field that surrounds you. This is our ethereal body — an energy form. The pattern of the space groups, the linking of these energy fields, is systematic, and information of the mind is stored in these space groups. Quartz crystal is particularly wonderful in storing the information of the mind. It is silicon dioxide, with a space group very close to that of water. Our bodies are over 70% water. The energy of water, as it is released from the body, forms patterns or fields which surround our bodies. The energy of mind utilizing these fields can penetrate a crystal of this type. The energy can be reabsorbed or retransmitted as information or as an image — a communication link.

"The basic shape is hexagonal. We in our pattern of energy around us are hexagonal. The most economical use of space is a hexagonal space. You'll find this in a beehive, too. In the future, crystals will be used for healing, in communications, and in thought photography. They will be used in intergalactic communications, and to communicate with Masters and Teachers who were on this Earth plane at one time.

"The method and form that men will use requires guidance from other planes. It is beyond normal human intelligence, and I am grateful to the Lord for the guidance He has given me. Many times I wished to destroy these crystals and not reveal again to mankind the teaching that was given at one time. [Mr. Vogel is referring to the cause of the destruction of Atlantis, which will be discussed later.] The reason was that I was concerned about the misuse or abuse of sources of energy at this time."

Mr. Vogel's misgivings stem from the fact that a crystal can magnify negative energy as well as positive, and that only highly purified people should use them.

Despite his concern about releasing knowledge of the crystal,

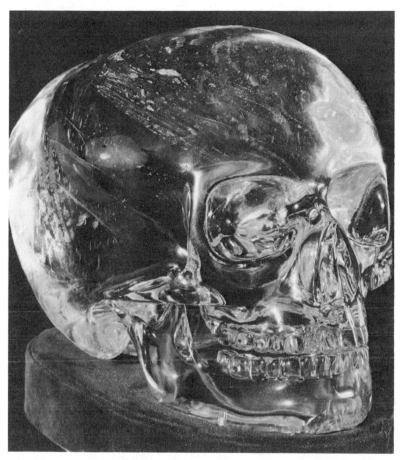

The fascinating Crystal Skull, discovered by Anna Mitchell-Hedges in 1927 in the Lubaantun Tomb of the Mayan ruins of British Honduras, although it is uncertain whether this is where it originated. The skull, weighing 11 lb. 7 oz. and measuring 5" x 5" x 7", was in the possession of Frank Dorland for five years, during which time he studied it carefully. Its age cannot be determined by any known scientific means, yet calculations indicate that it would have taken 300 years to complete it. It contains a series of concave and convex lenses which reflect light from the base to the eye sockets and also magnify anything under the base when observed through the top. Dorland reported that he and many others observed that the skull also often generated paranormal experiences.

he recognizes that the time has come on earth when this knowledge is again to be known to man. This same feeling was expressed by Oh Shinnah, spokeswoman for the Native People of North America, in a talk given at the New Age Community Center in Vancouver, Canada, November, 1977.

"Did you know that all the energy in this crystal here can generate enough electricity to run this building? The ancients used crystals for healing and for communication — for all sorts of things. The way is there; the esoteric is not going to be esoteric very much longer. One of the things that my father told me was, 'This is the age. There will come a time in your life when the mysteries of all the peoples of the Earth will be revealed to each other.'"

Dr. Frank Dorland, bio-crystallographer, and author of *Rock Crystal, Nature's Holy Stone,* confirms Mr. Vogel's findings. He states that, in a sense, the crystal acts as a filtering antenna and amplifying reflector to the psychic receptor centers. He explains that the brain sends out waves of energy that trigger the crystal into activity, which is then reflected back, stimulating the psychic centers of the mind.

I found Marcel Vogel's speech at the symposium to be most interesting, but what really touched me was how he credited all of his success to meditation and to the Lord's grace. His talk, however, was all but forgotten in the whirlwind of activity in the days that followed. But on the morning of November third, a message came that made it clear that Marcel Vogel was already a part of Sivananda's family. (The words contained in parentheses in this and all following messages are my own.)

"Vishnu Swami, you must learn the secret power lying within the crystals." (Gurudev, who will teach me?) "You have met one child already learning the secret. For hidden within you are powers to help humanity. I will guide you. Be bold, Be brave; I am with you. Go to that child you have already met. I will help you."

I called Mr. Vogel that same day. When he answered the phone, he exclaimed that he had cut a crystal just the night before not knowing who it was for. But now he knew. We all immediately went down to visit him at his Laboratory in San Jose. There he presented me with the first crystal.

A PERIOD OF TRAINING

With the crystal came a new period of intensive training. The crystal, or "instrument", as Master Sivananda referred to it, replaced my hands as a means of drawing off the excess energy which caused so much discomfort in the bodies of Swami Sri Dharananda and Swami Gokulananda. By synchronizing my breath with theirs and concentrating on Master, I would draw the energy into the crystal, just as a sponge absorbs water. Slowly, day by day, Master gave instructions for using the crystal to release energy blockages in various parts of the body and for drawing the energy out through the *sahasrara* at the top of the head.

He also explained how to meditate with the crystal. In the earliest days it seemed like meditating with an inert piece of glass in my hand, but as time passed, the crystal began to take life, and it gradually became possible to feel subtle vibrations emanating from the instrument. Master later explained that this was partly due to my own intunement with the crystal, and partly due to his ignition of its vital properties.

So many questions were raised with the unfolding events of each passing day. What was the purpose of all these strange goings on? And why was it necessary that these two "Children of Light" be subjected to such incredible physical stress? Master explained that they had, in fact, chosen this work. Its immediate reason was to help me learn the many intricacies of the crystal, and to push my own limitations further and further through my desire to relieve their suffering. But in a broader sense, the purpose was to help all humanity, which had always been my innermost and strongest goal. On December 7, Master Sivananda explained.

"A new beginning is about to dawn on the Earth plane, Vishnu Swami. The Children of Light must be prepared. They must be ready for that which will manifest to save the Earth. Many will come together as one. Parts will unite as a whole. You will understand this is a sign. For one man cannot, cannot hold all. But many can bring forth great, great parts, interconnecting to create something far beyond a capacity of mankind on Earth to unfold all by itself. All are being guided, Vishnu Swami. You are but one of many. You are one link of many. When the links unite, all the great knowledge from each link will interconnect to bring forth the plan on Earth as it has been prepared."

The complexity of that in which we were all involved became even clearer through a series of automatic drawings which came through Swami Sri Dharananda. The earliest ones, which came in October, were a series of pictographs which bore a direct relation to the Sanskrit words Swami Sri Dharanandaji was taught in her visits to the "Garden". She later found almost identical symbols in a book with Egyptian hieroglyphics, although the meanings did not coincide. Later the drawings became more intricate and seemed to have an uncanny resemblance to the Great Pyramid and some of its inner chambers and passageways.

The drawings would always come when Swami Sri Dharanandaji was in an altered state of consciousness. It was fascinating to watch. Instead of both hands going up into the *chin mudra,* the fingers of her right hand would come together as if she were holding a pencil and the hand would start moving back and forth. I would then put a writing pad in front of her, or on her stomach if she was lying down, and the hand would slowly rise and begin to scan the surface area of the paper.

As if there was an eye at the tip of the pencil, her hand would begin to draw, never going over an area which had already been drawn on, despite the fact that her eyes ware closed and often covered with a cloth. One time, to test this, I pulled the paper upward, thinking somehow to confound the mechanism, whatever it was. The hand moved back and forth again, as if it were using radar, then went directly to the empty area and continued drawing. I pulled the paper again. Once more she found the empty spaces. Whenever the paper was full, or the diagram complete, her hand would again move rapidly back and forth, scanning, until a clean sheet of paper was placed before her.

These kinds of experiences would occur from time to time while Swami Sri Dharananda was in an altered state of consciousness just before a message came through. Master Sivananda explained that this was all a part of the learning that was meant to come about, the purpose of which was far beyond human understanding at this time. Another common experience was Swami Sri Dharanandaji's trips to the "Garden", which she explains in some detail in the following paragraphs.

"I am continually aware of Master Sivananda's presence now, even in the normal waking state. It is a particular vibration which I have always felt at ease with. When I started transcending body-consciousness, that presence was always there to guide me. However, since there was no form I was not sure that it was Master until on two occasions Master appeared before me in etheric form and then expanded into that incredible, immense presence that I have long known. The second time this happened was the night of October 17, 1977, just before Master's first manifestation and message on October 18. Swami Gokulananda was also present at that time and had an intense experience of the Master, too.

"Powerful energies flow in my system and build all day long.

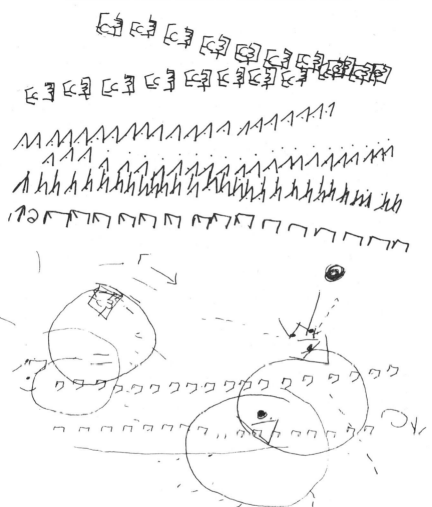

The above series of symbols were a part of an automatic writing by Swami Sri Dharananda on November 3, 1977. Those in the lower drawing were received on December 29. On November 21, Master was asked the meaning of these symbols: "This is the pattern of unfoldment of what is to come to save the Earth plane." (How can we decode and translate these symbols?) "The symbols coming through now are only a summary of a longer version to come later. All will be revealed at the proper moment."

When I sit to meditate, it quickly moves up the *chakras*. I feel Master's presence becoming more and more immediate and then there is a kind of blast off. At first my being is immersed in a yellow light. It is very subtle. But as it builds it changes to white and then finally to blue.

"As it goes from yellow to white, there is loss of sense of the body. When it is white I am vibrating faster and faster and faster, Master's presence coming closer and closer. The blue stage is only a flash because as you are going from white to blue the white stage, or dual state, vanishes. The experience of becoming blue energy is only momentary as I quickly merge in Master's presence, at that point becoming totally absorbed in Him. There is no memory, no dual experience. Sometimes when Master separates away, I slowly but directly return back to the physical plane. I can see my body clearly from another level before I re-enter it. My energies have to slow down tremendously before re-entry. The transition from other planes to the Earth plane is considerable as there is an immense difference in the rate of vibration.

"Sometimes after Master separates away from me, I may not be returned directly to the physical plane but am taken to another experience. Often I find myself in a place I call the "Garden". Master always remains with me and seems to deliver me there. Sometimes I am right in the Garden and other times I am left at the fork in the road just outside. I have learned that I must go right and not left at the fork and then bear left quickly further down the road. This leads to an opening like a cleared meadow. The "Form" is there surrounded by what appears to be dense plant life. But they are not plants like what we know here, but forms of deep green. That is why I call it the Garden. It is the only way I can think to describe it. The whole place is another dimension, different from the Earth plane. Nothing is gross or solid there. Everything is energy vibrating at different levels. You can see the different energies and colors. You can merge with things and pass through them.

"There are other beings there besides Master and myself. Like us, they are presences of energy without shape. They are vibrating sounds, many of which are not reproducible with the human vocal chords. Somehow it just passes through their systems. There is a four-sided 'Form' that appears as a deep blue-green color and of a solid density, although on many occasions the 'Form' changes form solid mass to pure blazing light. When the 'Form' is in the state of pure light you can see beings passing through it to other planes and returning like a beam of light. You can see beings changing their vibration, color, and intensity of energy as well as changing from a presence to a shape. I am finding more and more that I am also able to do all these things. When I am there I seem to know things and have abilities that are hidden from me when I return to this plane.

"Twice I was taken by Master to an ancient pyramid. I am delivered inside a room with hieroglyphics covering the walls. In one room there is a mummifield body and a stone emanating great light, which I assume is a crystal. There is a tiny door in one side of the room about three feet high. My whole attention is drawn to that door but I am not allowed to pass through it. The first time I was taken to that place, Master said, 'You are the first one to enter this room since it was sealed.' The room seems very, very familiar to me. Since these experiences I have been able to pick up books on hieroglyphics and understand much of the meaning without reading the translation. As soon as I saw hieroglyphics I realized that they exist on two levels. Some convey experiences here and others relate experiences on another plane coming to this plane. They are marked specifically. The ones from the higher level are marked in brackets.

"Recently I have been taken to the outside of a pyramid. I have been shown that there is a trap door on the right side, right-angled from the main front door. The trap door leads to a completely sealed room far beneath the ground. At other times, I have witnessed the front door being sealed. There is another small side entrance that leads into many small passageways. There is a special chute just big enough for a body to pass through. It leads to a hidden level which is like a sub-sub-basement way below ground level of the pyramid. This also leads to the sealed room. I have been shown this several times and have gone down the chute. It is like a map in my mind, clear and distinct. I have never been to Egypt in this life in a physical way, or to wherever this pyramid is, but I am quite sure I could find the sealed room.

Somehow I know that room contains ancient knowledge held within pure light vibrating from another level. It is held on the Earth plane but connected to another dimension, and therefore part is not visible to gross perceptions. It has been there for thousands of years. One day it is going to be discovered, but it can only be deciphered by someone who has the ability to be on two planes at once. I understand this from my experience in the Garden.

"At other times I am taken to a temple. Master is always with me through these experiences. It seems I am taken back in time because I feel intuitively that this place I visit is the Great Temple of Light on Atlantis. I witness and participate in many phenomenon

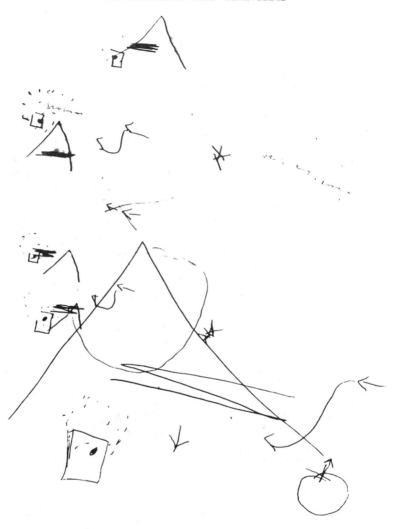

The above automatic drawing was received on May 9, 1978. That same
day, Master Sivananda explained: "Know well they are significant maps,
crude, but with much much knowledge to bring forth and trigger much
from within to others, who are also being exactly prepared."
Interestingly enough, these drawings are often received by Swami Sri
Dharananda while she has out-of-body experiences in a place she feels
to be the Great Pyramid.

which are not understood here on the Earth plane.

"These experiences continue to occur frequently. One thing I know for sure. It is all Master's will and not my own. It is like a complex puzzle. Slowly, part by part, it is fitting together."

GATHERING THE CHILDREN OF LIGHT

As my tour of lectures continued in the late fall of 1977, more and more people were introduced to the phenomenon of Master's manifestations. Naturally there were those who were inspired in a spiritual sense, and others whose interest was triggered by the "psychic" aspects of the phenomena. Master explained, however, that what was referred to as "psychic" was only a fact of nature. What had been occurring was his work according to a plan that had been laid long before. On November 12, he gave very strong advice to those who were sincerely seeking, advice that has been repeated time and time again.

"You must do Sadhana [spiritual practice]. More and more Sadhana. Dive deep, deep within. There I am waiting. You are all stars shining in the darkness. The way is prepared. All is laid waiting. Do not waste one precious moment lost in sensual pastures. You must dive deep within. There the light will be kindled. All lights must shine on the Earth, for time is growing short. Darkness is covering the Earth. All my children must shed light.

"I am with you all. I am manifest to save humanity. Do not doubt, for all that is prepared is beyond human understanding. Do your Sadhana; focus within. There I am waiting. All that comes is meant to be. All must unfold at the proper time. Fear not. Lose all doubts. Do not tarry in human emotions, for this will cloud your inner light. All my children, shine, shine bright. All must shed bright, bright light. Oh Children of Light, struggle on, for I am with you."

As 1977 drew to a close almost 250 Yoga students and staff from the various Sivananda Ashrams and Centers gathered together for the Christmas season at the Yoga Camp in Val Morin, Canada. It was a time of very great and concentrated amounts of purification and spiritual *sadhana*. There were many late night sessions with Master during those two weeks. On December 28, for the first time, Master gave a broader understanding to the whole situation.

"Vishnu Swami, I am One with the Source, yet have separated temporarily in time, to come to guide, to protect my children, to bring forth Truth that must bloom forth to help all mankind. For that which is on the brink of manifestation surely will destroy mankind if vibrations are not purified, if Truth is not again borne properly on Earth. *For Truth alone is the saving element of humanity.* For the destruction yet to unfold will be so great, Vishnu Swami, that only a power from a Source far beyond the Earth plane can send forth an element of purifying light to help the children properly move forth from the gross plane in that time of destruction to the higher place where they emanate from in the first place."

(What type of destruction, Master?)

"The Earth is now rocking on the brink of a chain reaction of natural events to bring forth great and disturbing changes."

(For example, Master?)

"Prophecies have come forth in a correct manner. You have before you, Vishnu Swami, many accounts of the destruction to come. It is not necessary at this time to bring forth any further details. *For yet to manifest many, many energies can go forth to lessen, to interrupt, to change the pattern of what might come.* It is the Karma of many of the Children of Light before you to go forth among the destruction and collect many of those lost sheep and open their hearts in a time when they are most closed."

(How should the children work to prepare for this, Master?)

"All is being prepared and manifesting forth *exactly* as is meant to be, Vishnu Swami. Worry not, for you must fulfill that which manifests before you. I am here. I am guiding, Vishnu Swami. At this time it is your work to learn the powers of the instrument [crystal] and simultaneously in this effort to bring these Children of Light before you, through their struggles and tests laid before them, that they too will be prepared in the time that is meant to be.

"Help them to understand well that Sadhana, Sadhana, Sadhana on a regular basis must come forth. For this *is* their support. This will be their foundation in the days to come....You must learn to lead the children in a way that they too will understand what must come."

(How?)

"Many doing their Sadhana will unfold experiences of connections to a higher level. They will gain experiences at this time where the subtle bodies do not function properly with the gross physical sheath....For much is meant to bloom forth in the process of ripening all my children. For in the days to come, these children must be strong, must have great, great faith for them to endure, for them to withstand their work that is to come forth soon."

(I feel Master is guiding them. They are doing their best, I'm sure, Master.)

"Vishnu Swami, teach the children to focus *always,* focus always with great, great faith in these times of inner struggle, in these times of confusion. For that which is lying within my children in a dormant state must be awakened, must come forth. These children are engrossed in a very physical manner at this time. Slowly, slowly as they do more and more Sadhana, I will ignite, I will bring forth that knowledge, those experiences of strength from the past. This will surface in the children in future days. Worry not, Vishnu Swami. This is not a situation of unusual psychic phenomenon *but is* my work bringing forth inner strength, inner faith in my children."

(With Gurudev's Grace, I'll try my level best to lead them on the right path.)

"Many children, many many children, Vishnu Swami, want to serve, want to surrender, want to be useful instruments of the Lord. In time this will manifest forth and be fulfilled through all these Children of Light. But in this time on Earth these children must not be external, follow external manifestations, but must go within, each individually, through Sadhana must tap their intense surrender. For this will quicken the ripening process of my children."

As time passed, it became clearer that the scope of Master's manifestations was much greater than the imagination could conceive. I began to bring Swami Sri Dharananda and Swami Gokulananda before large gatherings in order to bring his messages and work to greater numbers of people. Some seemed to also experience energies moving within their bodies, although to a lesser degree than Swami Sri Dharanandaji and Swami Gokulanandaji.

It seemed strange, all this happening in such a short time. Master Sivananda explained that this phenomenon was occurring now as many souls from Atlantis are reincarnating. It is interesting to note that Edgar Cayce, among others, reports that crystals were used as a source of power and communication in Atlantis, and that it was their misuse that eventually brought the destruction of that civilization. According to Master, those experiencing movement of energies and other unusual occurences are merely reawakening to knowledge they once had many thousands of years ago. On January 2, 1978, he elaborated.

"Vishnu Swami, observe well the many children who are now coming before you with problems of energy, problems of movement of energy within."

(I observe this, what shall I do, Master?)

'Many children will be hearing voices from the higher planes, many children will be having visions. Many children will have blooming forth within, signs and problems that they cannot understand, that cause confusion and ultimately bring them to your feet."

(What shall I do, Master, at that time?)

"Vishnu Swami, this is no mere coincidence at this time. Listen well, for you must understand the phenomenon which has unfolded and will continue to unfold. These children, Vishnu Swami, have deep, deep samskaras from past lifetimes incarnate from the time of the civilization of Atlantis."

(How do I know this? Is there any way I can recognize and understand this, Master?)

"Vishnu Swami, in the times of this civilization, the subtler parts of the soul were brought into great, great intunement, to higher, higher power, caused by many instruments known as crystals. These came in many forms. Vishnu Swami, to explain the entire phenomenon, will take years, but to summarize that which is unfolding now before you, and which will continue to unfold before you at a greater and greater rate, can be summarized at this time.

"Vishnu Swami, many of these instruments do still exist on the Earth plane. According to Karma these instruments are soon to be rediscovered. Due to the vibrations on Earth, and due to the unfolding in time of these children, all is manifesting forth simultaneously. As these instruments come forth, and as these instruments are being experimented with by many brothers besides yourself at this time, a very exact subtle vibration is going forth. These vibrations are seemingly powerful; however, in contrast to those yet to be discovered, they are very insignificant. However, Vishnu Swami, they are playing their part to unfold that which must take place. As these vibrations go forth, the samskaras [latent impressions from past lives] which are so, so deep within these children are coming forth, from the subconscious to a direct conscious experience. There is *no* relationship with Sadhana or any action these children partake to cause such experiences to come forth from within at the level, and at the intensity that it is blooming forth."

(Why is this happening?)

"You must understand, Vishnu Swami, the powers of these instruments [crystals]."

(The instruments are affecting our children also? Swami Sri Dharanandaji and Gokulanandaji and so forth?)

"Your instrument is only one of many that are being used at this time on Earth."

(What type of people are using it? Spiritual or non-spiritual people?)

"Vishnu Swami, crystals are being discovered on many levels by many types of people. Mainly scientists, at this time, are groping in darkness to understand something far, far greater than scientific facts and intellectual phenomenon, for the power and the properties extending from these crystals far, far go beyond the human understanding from the intellectual point of view. The source of power coming through these instruments passes from one level to another and back again so quickly, that it cannot be recorded on any physical instrument.

"Vishnu Swami, that which you hold in your custody is but a mere playtoy, a mere starlet before a great, great sun in contrast with that which will come forth in the near future. However, it is meant to be that you use this instrument to learn and gain a small understanding of the power and control of the energies which can come forth through such an instrument. Soon a new instrument will come forth."

(From which source, Master?)

"One is in preparation to be handed to you for custody but even this instrument, Vishnu Swami, serves as a tool for learning, for those which are still buried deep, still in the Earth plane, from times of past civilizations will come forth, and these instruments are perfected beyond the understanding of any scientist on Earth at this time."

(Did I in past lives do anything with the crystals? Did I experiment with these instruments?)

"Vishnu Swami, many, many souls incarnate on the earth at this time in one way or many ways connected with either the direct or indirect use of the instruments. These knowledges will come forth in time, but only in a very controlled way. For much destruction if coming through a negative path, can be brought once again upon humanity and the Earth plane itself. For this reason, Vishnu Swami, all past knowledge has been shielded and will be awakened only to the degree that each soul connects with the higher Source. For this reason, Vishnu Swami, even beyond purification, is the reason Sadhana, and Sadhana and Sadhana and more Sadhana must take place."

(These children are doing their Sadhana, or should they increase it?)

"Vishnu Swami, many of the children will bloom forth experiences from within. They will think it is caused by their Sadhana, but in truth this is not exactly so. For these children on a subtler level are being directly affected by the vibrations going forth from the many instruments being used all over the globe as well as the great, great instruments soon to come forth once again. However, Vishnu Swami, know these children always are being affected; however, only in times of Sadhana when focussed deep within can these children see this great effect on them. For this reason mental surrender, and mental focus to the Master, the Lord, the higher source, must be maintained at all costs."

(Why is this happening at this time, Master, not before?)

"All must manifest on the Earth plane as it has been prepared. For ripening processes are undergoing on many levels, through many, many children all over the globe. Vishnu Swami, it is not mere coincidence that what you call psychic phenomenon is blooming forth.... More and more you will fall upon many, many, many children with this experience. For the multitudes of those incarnate with samskaras from the time of Atlantis will subconsciously be intuned greatly to the frequency of the currents going forth in a scattered way on the Earth at this time.

"Vishnu Swami, more and more your eyes will be opened to the multitudes of children living and dwelling in great distress due to this going forth. Understand well what is happening before you as these manifestations go forth. It is for your understanding that this unfolds before your eyes that you may be prepared to fulfill the work ahead."

GREATER INTUNEMENT

I spent most of January working in India, and returned to teach the Yoga Teachers' Training Course at our Yoga Retreat in Nassau, Bahamas. There a new phase began. With the background and purpose of his manifestations established, Master launched me on an intensive exploration into the complexities of the crystal's use. Each time I meditated with the crystal or used it to draw off the excess energy, Master would guide me to a new experience.

At first there was just the faintest sensation of a pulsation in the instrument. Then it became clear that there were different rates of vibration as well as different intensities. Soon Master pointed out that in moving the crystal over someone's body, changes in temperature could be perceived. A warmer sensation indicated an abundance of energy where *pranas* were blocked and could not flow evenly, while coolness in the instrument meant low energy or blockages in the *prana*. By moving the crystal back and forth over cool and warm areas a balance could be brought about so that the *pranas* flowed evenly.

A greater understanding of the nature of the energies was also given at that time. In the Teachers' Training Course of approximately one hundred students, almost a third manifested some form of reaction, particularly when I used the crystal on Swami Sri Dharanandaji in the temple before the students. Some would do deep breathing, some automatic *pranayama*. Others would have very deep meditations. Most experienced the intense energies moving within their bodies, creating pressure as in an overinflated balloon, and often locking the body in an uncomfortable and sometimes frightening way.

On February 28, 1978, in a message spoken in the temple before about 175 people, Master Sivananda explained how to control the *pranas*.

"As you have already experienced, a type of pranic field is emanating forth. Many children now witnessing this event are for many reasons opened in their subtle bodies. These children are subtley connecting to this pranic field. All who are experiencing such vibrations within must know what is happening and understand properly. At this time and going forth in moments ahead, all those who are in such connection must move farther from this immediate field and with opened eyes mentally do japa, mental repetition of Ishta Devata Mantra, as energies that have been connected to within will be properly sublimated and expelled properly; as Mantras do balance out these subtler bodies within each child who is connected in this way.

"Vishnu Swami. (Yes, Gurudev.) Each child must *not* mentally dwell upon pranas entering into their systems. For such mental attention will only serve as a great block holding these pranas within. Rather, as each one mentally relaxes, focussing more and more the mind to the japa, pranas will properly flow out.

"That which manifests forth and appears frightful to those who understand not, understand well. The quality of the mind when experiencing energies of this intensity for the first time causes more and more problems within. For this reason, with great focus on what is occurring within, more and more the mind becomes inflexible, unable to relax, to balance all that each may become once again balanced back to their normal state. In this situation have each child become immersed in water, as the quality of water magnetizes and draws off these subtler pranas beyond the mind.

"For those children who can control and relax the mind by proper focus each will experience the pranas flowing out to the degree the mind becomes refocussed. For those children with inflexible

minds, those who are greatly intuned within to the occuring problem, who become fearful, these children must be made to enter a
situation where the water can act and connect, drawing out, by-
passing the efforts of the mind. Each child will be properly restored
back. Worry not, Vishnu Swami. I am here witnessing all that is
taking place. No harm, no damage, only the experience will go
forth."

At the end of the Teachers' Training Course in early March, I
went to India with Marcel Vogel to inaugurate two new Ashrams.
There we made an expedition to Ponnambalam Medu, a mountain I
had visited briefly on an earlier visit in January. I had had the definite impression the there was some connection between that place
and the "Garden" to which Swami Sri Dharanandaji travelled. At
the top there were some ancient carvings and writing. One was similar to a Star of David; another seemed to be a trident.

The history of Ponnambalam Medu is quite interesting. Located nearby is the Shabarumala Ayyappen Temple, a very old and
ancient temple. The idol of the temple is Ayyappen, also known as
Monny Khantan, the Lord with the Crystal in his Neck. The ancient
legend has it that there was once a king who prayed for many years
for a son. One day, while hunting, he found a child floating in a
basket. It was a baby boy, and he had a crystal tied around his neck.
The king took him home and raised him as his own son. In later
years the child, who was actually a divine incarnation of Siva and
Vishnu, left the palace of his father to lead a life of seclusion in
this Ayyappen Temple. Yet, his father the king still came to visit
him once a year. This day, known as Makaru Valakku, is still cele-
brated as a very holy day. Thousands of people come to the temple
on that same day, which occurs about mid-winter, each year.

During this holiday, at the end of a special worship service in
the evening, a light can be seen glowing over the hill to the east. It
is called Makaru Jyoti, and is belived to be a holy light.

The mountain Ponnambalam Medu, over which the light appears, is about ten miles from the present temple. It is believed that
originally the temple was built on this mountain; Ponnambalam Medu means Mountain of the Golden Temple. This temple was destroyed untold ages ago. The area around the mountain is a deep,
dense jungle inhabited by many wild animals, such as elephants,
tigers, cobras and wolves. The vegetation is overgrown everywhere.
Few people venture there, for it is considered taboo; and of those
that do go, some never return. It was to this mountain top that I
made my expedition. Master confirmed my intuitive feeling about

Above: Carvings discovered at Ponnambalam Medu. In Master's message of February 9, 1978, he explained their meaning: "These symbols are of great value and have great deep deep meaning that holds within hidden truth from those days past. Some of those people who existed in Truth in those times knew well of the coming destruction and had these signs made permanent that all the knowledge would not go in vain. In days ahead, only at the right moment will this truth that is hidden be again revealed. It will come only when the experience matches the truth that lies there to be again told, that it will make full sense, full understanding, when it is revealed." Below: The mountain Ponnambalam Medu at sunset.

its relationship to Swami Sri Dharananda's "Garden" in a message on February 9.

"I witnessed your journey. I know that which took place. This place, Vishnu Swami, is one of many that is a replica where much, much intunement in days past took place. Great knowledge was going forth at those times. In those days, during the time of the temple which stood at that place, a *great crystal* was going forth, emanating great light. Even this day the phenomenon is still known of the *light that goes forth*. However, in this time it is *artificially produced*. However, in days of yore a great instrument [crystal] existed there. The markings you witnessed will help to restore back the proper angle. This explanation is coming forth in later days for you. When an instrument is intuned properly and angled properly at the proper time of the sun coming forth, it is magnified exactly and going forth a great light is yielded from the instrument. To those who understand not, this was a spectacle of awe for it was hard to comprehend.

"Vishnu Swami, as was the case with almost all the great instruments in days of past, after knowledge came it was misused. And due to this, great destruction came forth. This, too, was true of the place you visited. (Was there any temple in that place?) Yes, Vishnu Swami, one of great great beauty. However, due to the over-intunement, too much energy coming forth, beause of ego and separation from the higher Source where all manifested forth from; eventually the instruments brought forth the end of both the people who misused them as well as the instruments themselves.

"However, deep within the Earth remnants of these instruments remain, still vibrating forth the power which was at that time tuned properly. This instrument still exists. Vishnu Swami, knowledge will come forth. Knowledge of instruments to come and those possessed at this time will be useful and will help to re-intune those places of past which still have great power going forth. However, in most of these places, the ancient great instruments will not in themselves come forth. For this is not necessary. Instruments that are given in these days are meant to be. For with these new instruments it is of a different source. One of protection, that history will *not* repeat, bringing forth the final destruction of man in that plane. It is for this reason, Vishnu Swami, that the ancient instruments will not come forth. Those few that do will be only for proof that they did in fact exist."

In the second visit, each member of our party had very profound spiritual experiences, which included hearing Master's voice, several visions, and a joint sighting of a U.F.O. which lasted twenty minutes. Master later verified all of these phenomena, indicating that a detailed explanation was not possible at this time, but that great purification was going on.

The journey to India was significant not only because of the unusual events that occurred there, but also because it marked Marcel Vogel's gift to me of a second, larger crystal. This had been promised by Master as far back as November. At first it did not appear to be nearly as powerful as the smaller crystal, but it was explained that only through its gradual ignition by Master, and through my own intunement day by day, would its full force become known. I began to meditate daily with the large crystal. Regular sessions were held, according to Master's instructions, at sunrise and sunset — the time when spiritual *pranas* flow most easily — to draw off the excess energies from Swami Sri Dharananda and Swami Gokulananda with the large crystal. In time I came to know of its much greater, yet more subtle, capabilities.

PRANIC HEALING

Mr. Vogel and two students who had gone to India, Swami Brahmananda and Swami Gitananda, all had very intense physical and mental reactions to their experiences at Ponnambalam Medu, where they had been exposed to extremely high frequencies of energy. These frequencies, far beyond what a human body can contain under normal circumstances, had affected their electromagnetic systems, the link between the physical and subtler bodies.

The "symptoms" were much the same as those Swami Gokulananda and Swami Sri Dharananda experience regularly: dizziness, sharp pain in the head, heaviness in the chest, weakness of limbs, difficulty in breathing, blurred vision, and sometimes a fever. It was at that time that Master first gave instructions for bathing in warm water and "that element known to you as baking soda." The result was to neutralize the effect of the energies and bring a balance to the system. This "cure" has since been applied regularly by Swami Sri Dharananda and Swami Gokulananda, as well as others who have been subject to the high intensity energies moving within their bodies.

The most amazing lessons in healing, however, were in regard to the crystal. Swami Gitanandaji had lost the hearing in her left ear as a result of her visit to Ponnambalam Medu, and was told by doctors that her hearing loss was a permanent one. Yet Master later gave instructions that she receive regular treatments with the crystal, and her hearing gradually began to return to normal.

In early March, A. Gaurishankar and his wife, Lalita, came to the Yoga Retreat Ashram in the hope of somehow reversing the paralysis in the lower portion of his body. As a lawyer, he had had the benefit of the best doctors in India. Yet, although he could manage to get about with great pain and effort, two canes, and his wife at his side, experts told him he would never walk again.

The problem had begun some eight years ago with a spastic twitching in the left foot. Gaurishankar had gone from one physician to another and entered several hospitals, where his condition had been diagnosed as irreversible spastic paraplegia. Various types of therapy were given, and he was administered great dosages of medicine, but the problem only increased. By the time he arrived in Nassau, he was almost paralyzed from the waist down. In order to move about, he would lean heavily on his canes and painstakingly slowly drag one foot forward at a time.

I turned to Master in the hope that he could give some guidance to help alleviate Gaurishankar's difficulties. As per his instructions, we gathered each evening when I would use the small crystal on him. At first the crystal was used to identify areas where *prana* was not flowing. If the crystal was cool, it would indicate areas of blockages; if it was warm, it would reveal that the *pranas* were flowing properly. Variations in the rate of vibration in the crystal also could be detected. Very methodically over the period of several months, Master taught me how to use the crystal to lesson the blockages and move the *pranas* more freely through the body.

This, Master Sivananda said, would one day come to be known as pranic healing. His instructions detailed minute technical and physiological explanations of what was going on. In a message on March 25, 1978 he defined the source of Gaurishankar's problems. His statements categorically confirmed the fears of those concerned with the drug-oriented medical profession and the chemical-oriented food industry.

"Vishnu Swami, understand well the power of many medicines known in that place of the Earth plane. Many, many medicines known now are greatly, greatly powerful and cause great, great damage within the gross sheath as well as the subtler bodies. For this reason damage has come to the nervous system of that child. Many, many polluted children that have indulged with great, great medicines upon fasting immediately causes a great, great reaction within the system. Cause not this reaction, for if too great of itself can even cause death. But rather, learn to go slow; let the systems slowly move out these great and powerful medicines. For they, too, can repoison again and again with reaction on the physical and subtle bodies as these are being purified out. You already know this fact, Vishnu Swami. Take this as a warning, for you must beware of the effects that can take place. Fasting immediately upon children of great, great polluted systems causes a great movement of these poisons within these sheaths. These must be moved at a very, very slow rate that poisoning can be washed out without a great, great and significant reaction.

"Mankind knows not the power or damage that does take place. Instead of many medicinal types of herbs that sometimes can be used, they rather use the chemical fashioned. The ones borne of great, great chemicals of themselves cannot harm. But many are mixed together, and of this action when induced into the system causing a great, great reaction and even in times causing death to those poor souls. In these days moving ahead more and more, the profession of medicines is polluting these souls on Earth. With greater and greater, more powerful mixtures of these chemicals, these children in time will come to great harm. Many paralyzed, many coming to great and more difficulties, and even many to death. Understand well, the combination of medicines induced to many souls be there dormant after illness passes seemingly. Upon inducement of fasting, these powerful medicines lying dormant within surge, surge again through the system."

(Is there any way we can make humanity and the medical profession avoid this?)

"Vishnu Swami, combination of medicines known in Medicine combined with many chemicals included in much of the food substances taken in these days, all combine and recombine again upon storage within the gross sheath. In many children already even much of the gross structure is in time broken down through this process. Mankind does not know what he is headed toward due to the actions that one takes. Many lost sheep following blindly by the road, following the medical science and profession, are being led down the path of doom. Vishnu Swami, it is in these days and days ahead that man is going to a destruction within a type, though not from without, but from within. *Mankind in time is but destroying his own self, not only through the physical sheath but also through mind and the subtler bodies as well.* You understand well, Vishnu Swami. Look all about you in the environment; you can see the pollutions everywhere bombarding the systems day by day."

(Yes, Gurudev. Is there any way we can help humanity? It is far beyond even my dreams.)

"Vishnu Swami, only in days ahead with great, great and powerful vibration, frequencies from this place, can children be once again restored to balance. From a subtler level first, and then in time this subtle level will manifest forth again affecting finally the gross sheath. Only in this manner can mankind once again be saved."

Within a few weeks, Gaurishankar began to show improvement. Along with the crystal sessions he was given a routine of purification to follow each day. This included three days of fasting a week to facilitate removal of the harmful chemicals, *pranayama* and frequent baths to cleanse the subtle bodies and help the flow of *pranas,* and Hatha Yoga *asanas* with massage to increase circulation and bring the muscles back into use. By the beginning of May, Gaurishankar could walk the length of the Yoga Retreat four times faster than when he had first come.

"THIS IS EXACTLY PREPARED"

As the spring of 1978 drew to a close, the Sivananda headquarters moved back to the Yoga Camp in the Laurentian Mountains north of Montreal. A heavy schedule was planned. It included a tour of Europe, a tour of South America and the United States, two Children's Summer Camps running simultaneously, two Teachers' Training Courses at the Camp, one in California in the Fall and another in India in November.

The days were full, and Master's manifestations often kept us up late into the nights. I came and went from my tours and conferences, and my two "Children of Light" managed as best they could when the crystal and I were absent. Still, the irregularity was extremely difficult for them, and I found myself turning again and again to Master for assistance in finding a way to have the time to both help them and also carry out my other duties. In a message on June 7, Master gently but firmly explained that all of these externally oriented activities would have to be replaced by a concentrated turning within in order to truly render the service that would be needed by mankind in days to come.

"Understand well, Vishnu Swami. It is natural for the mind to escape intense suffering; to withstand and endure with one-pointed focus causes strength, causes control, and in days ahead this will be of necessity for these two children [Swami Gokulananda and Swami Sri Dharananda]. For this reason, it is prepared that these children cannot escape, but must watch on with control, for in later days this will be of greatest necessity for their work to unfold as it has been prepared. Vishnu Swami, your own suffering facing the outside world going forth in more and more futile efforts will bring you to the silence within and in those greatest moments, your own instrument in hand will carry forth with great, great ignition your most inner thoughts."

It seemed that in the near future it would be necessary for me to spend great periods of time in silence. But this certainly seemed to be far beyond the realm of the possible with the schedule which had been set for the remainder of the year. In fact, far from eliminating the commitments, it seemed I was taking on more. In early June, a group of scientists involved in the study of parapsychology requested to be present at some sessions, document what they found, and take some Kirlian photographs.

The scientists were Drs. Rene Labrosse and Jean Claude Dionne, both physicians and chiropractors; Pierre Blondeau, a biologist; and Michel Forest, a chemist. Their first visit was to the June 11 session, where they monitored the EEG, GSR, pulse rate and blood pressure of both Swami Sri Dharananda and Swami Gokulananda. The readings on their instruments were not unlike previous testing that had been done. But there were several other remarkable occurrences which distinquished that session. One was that Master remarked several times that they should check their machines, as one was not set up properly. A second was the manner in which Master arranged for the Kirlian photographs to be taken. He cautioned.

"Vishnu Swami, remain one-pointed in your actions going forth, for time is greatly measured. In these moments connect first to the sahasrara once again to this child. Upon proper connection, take forth the left hand. Blockage of pranas holding this mudra will go forth to but free that hand. Vishnu Swami, it is of paramount importance that you remain properly connected throughout this event. Do *not* break concentration....Process has now begun, Vishnu Swami. This is but a dangerous event going forth. For this reason you must remain properly connected throughout until this position of mudra is once again restored back."

At that point Swami Sri Dharanandaji's hand slowly lowered out of the raised *chin mudra* and the three photographs were taken. Then it returned to its raised position, Master gave a few explanations of what had happened, and it seemed as if the manifestation had ended. Swami Sri Dharanandaji stretched slightly and opened her eyes. But then she began to speak in that same soft voice with

The Kirlian photograph above is a particularly sharp image of the normal aura of a finger. According to Dr. Rene Labrosse, the term "aura" is not easily defined. In general, the aura shows a quantity of energy, a level of vitality. The most precise definition that can be given is that the aura is a bio-electrical luminescence. It is "the electricity of life. It manifests as a spiral electrical current surrounding the body. It is a direct reflection of the body metabolism. Its manifestation reflects electricity in the body and what chemical compounds are being produced in the sweat glands." That is, the activity of the brain directly affects the sweat glands as well as the nervous system. The sweat glands produce a positive or negative resistance to the skin. The amount of light emanating forth in an aura depends on the resistance of the skin to conducting electricity. This has been proved by experiments in which no aura was detected when the fingers were covered with glycerin, soap, or plaster. When the hand is immersed in salt water or gasses like neon, in which there is a great deal of conductivity, the pictures are much lighter and brighter.

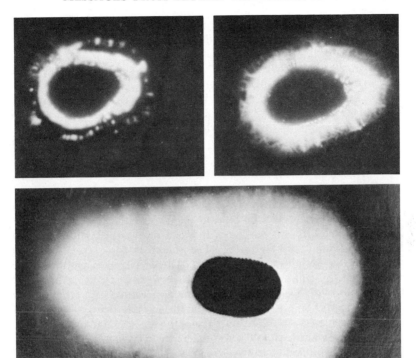

From the session of June 11, 1978, where Drs. Rene Labrosse and Jean Claude Dionne, as well as Pierre Blondeau and Michel Forest, two other scientists, were present. Upper left: photograph of Swami Gokulananda's aura during meditation before the message began coming shows a highly unusual double corona. At the time this photo was taken, the EEG machine registered its maximum reading of 250 microvolts. It is possible that extreme stimulation of the chemical compounds caused high explosiveness of the bio-electrical energy. Upper right: extremely large aura of Swami Gokulananda during the message, indicating that she may not only be receiving energy but somehow transmitting it. Bottom: Kirlian photograph of Swami Sri Dharananda's aura taken during the session on July 18, 1978. This is the only picture taken during that session while the crystal was being used; it shows an "over-manifestation" of energy. During this time, the EEG reading was over 100 microvolts, the maximum on the machine being used, and the eye and arm reflexes were negative.

which I was accustommed to hearing Master's words spoken!

"This is proof to you that this child is connected to the other place as she remains on the Earth plane."

(Master says that while she is living in this gross plane, still she can connect to the other plane.)

"As days ahead come forth, this child will function in the gross plane remaining connected completely to this higher level."

(How is that possible, Gurudev?)

"Voltage of this level is only possible if the person is connected to a higher source. Check now the machinery and this will prove so."

The electroencephalagraph read its maximum, 100 microvolts, in alpha.

The scientists returned on June 18 for another session. It was determined that it would be held in the Yoga Hall before the guests and Teachers' Training students. It was a rainy, blustery night, with frequent thunder and lightning. The scientists took great pains in setting up their elaborate equipment. All the students gathered and sat meditating, waiting. As usual, I sat with the crystal focussed at the *sahasrara* of Swami Sri Dharananda. Swami Gokulananda lay beside her. But this time, instead of the crystal being a source of relief, it seemed to be causing greater havoc in their bodies. In a short while Swami Sri Dharananda began to speak. Through her, Master said simply to remove the crystal from the area and immediately bathe both in water and great amounts of baking soda, which would have the effect of grounding them. "This," he said, "has *not* been prepared."

An explanation did not come for several days, while the two "children" went through a very difficult period of recuperation. It seems that just as the crystal can magnify thought energy, so it will also magnify currents in the atmosphere. Swami Sri Dharananda and Swami Gokulananda had in a sense been internally electrocuted. The results of the Kirlian photographs taken at that time were most unusual, with large projections of energy emanating from the fingers in several shots.

On August 5, the scientists again gathered for a session. This time Master Sivananda gave instructions for taking Kirlian photographs of the crystal itself.

"It is understood these children coming forth to your feet [the scientists present] their own efforts to learn; let them go forth in these moments with small small instrument [referring to the small crystal]. Go forth now, Vishnu Swami, with small instrument. Take Kirlian photography as these pranas pass through.

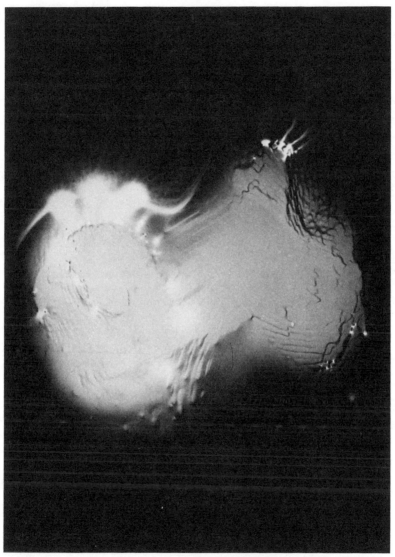

It was during the session of July 18 that a severe electrical storm began while testing was going on. Swami Sri Dharananda's finger was placed on the machinery for photographing just as the rain began, moments after bright lightning. Then, immediately after the incredible photograph shown above was taken the EEG reading dropped to zero.

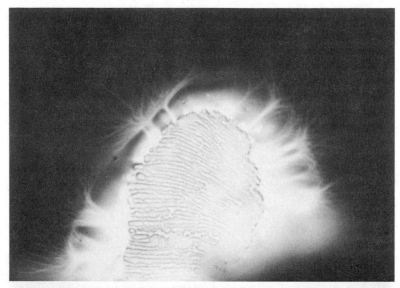

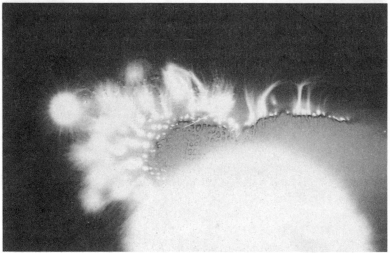

These two Kirlian photographs are also far, far from the norm. Both were taken during the July 18 session. Above: Usually the central portion of a Kirlian photograph, where the finger is placed, records black. Here, the fingerprint is actually recorded. Below: Great flares of energy emanate from the hand. Dr. Labrosse said simply, "It's the first time we've seen a picture like this so we don't know what it means."

(Gurudev, the instrument should be photographed or the finger should be photographed? This is not very clear.)

"Vishnu Swami, for proper experience at hand, go forth, lay instrument on top of machinery, hand disconnected. Pranas continue to pass through without your own physical connection. Turn the instrument on top side frontal portion. You will see one portion, angle at front tip. Turn instrument over. Put the angle at front portion on instrument.

"Take a writing utensil, place on instrument, and give proper pressure. In this manner, aura of human-most portion of gross sheath will not come in direct contact with instrument."

(Gurudev, the instrument is now ready and I am using a writing instrument to press it hard. Now are we ready to photograph, Gurudev?)

"Go forth now."

(Yes, Gurudev. We completed the first one.)

"Now take the instrument in hand. Turn instrument on other side. You will see, at front portion, angle cut flat. Use this surface with your own hand in proper connection for next photography. [Long pause] Before taking photography, intune yourself once again to the sahasrara of this child [Swami Sri Dharananda].

"Upon proper intunement, intensity of current passing through instrument in hand, only then as this goes forth in direct experience, only then take proper photography of instrument. Remain greatly concentrated, Vishnu Swami." [Long pause]

(Gurudev, we have completed this particular photography. What shall we do next?)

"Go forth now, Vishnu Swami, as time is growing greatly short. There is one child before you who is having greatest difficulties in the back region. Let this child come forth to you."

(Who is this child who has got back problems? [Master was referring to Swami Durgananda who had had pains in her back most of her life.] All right, come here.)

"With instrument in hand, intune yourself to this child. You will come to perceive a type of prana frequency of another nature. Remain properly intuned until maximum intensity comes forth of instrument in hand. In that moment, go forth once again taking photography of instrument."

(Gurudev, after gaining intensity of this current, then we should take same type of photography you took before, by placing the flat surface upward and holding with my hand? Am I correct?)

"You can place instrument on machinery. *As these pranas fill and pass through instrument in hand, these will go forth on photography from this machine.* You can remain properly connected. Upon completion of this photography only then repeat once again instrument going forth with no physical connection, using only a writing utensil for proper pressure."

(Yes, Gurudev; understood. First, photography with my body in tune with the instrument facing downward; second time use a utensil to hold it down. Am I correct?)

"This is correct. Once again go forth now. Intune yourself to that child in the affected area. [Long pause] Go forth now, Vishnu Swami."

Again, the results were most interesting. In order for a Kirlian photograph to register an image, there must be pressure on the camera from the object being photographed. In both photographs where a pencil was used to create the pressure, a single circular light area was the result. And in the one taken after intunement with Swami Sri Dharananda, a faint outline of the crystal could be seen. Where my finger was used for pressure, there was nothing but a slightly lighter area in the photograph taken after intunement with Swami Durgananda, while in the photograph taken after intunement with Swami Sri Dharananda there was what appeared to be a miniature finger imprint, although it had a proportionally larger aura and was out of focus.

All of this, Master explained, was a part of the learning process that had long since been planned. But he emphasized more strongly than ever that it was necessary to turn and dive deep within rather than try to serve humanity through these external means. And, too, he said it was of the utmost importance to be consistent in regard to the location of the sessions, for in time a pranic field would be built up which would protect, heal, and strengthen all who entered it.

Despite my tendencies toward working with people in an external way, I endeavored to draw inward more and more. The pranic field of which Master had spoken began to increase steadily in the little room where the sessions were held. The crystal took on new life, and for the first time I felt it as pure energy floating in my hand. While the problems of running a Yoga organization seemed to increase, internally I daily felt more connected to Master. Finally on August 7, 1978, I surrendered to the will of my great Teacher, Swami Sivananda, and began a long period of silence and isolation so that I might carry out whatever work he has prepared for me in the future to benefit mankind.

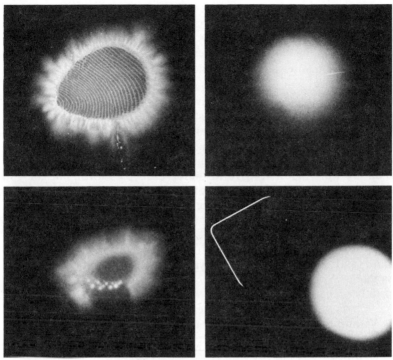

*Kirlian photographs taken during the session on August 5, 1978. Above
left: photograph taken of Swami Sri Dharananda's finger, during Master's manifestation. It is particularly unusual because of the spark
emanating off to the right, and because the central area shows the fingerprint, rather than being dark. Upper right: Kirlian photograph of the
crystal after use on Swami Sri Dharananda. Pressure on the object being
photographed is necessary for the image to register in Krilian photography. Here, a pen was used to press the crystal onto the plate. Lower left:
Kirlian photograph of the crystal after use on Swami Sri Dharananda;
here, the author's hand is used to create the pressure. It appears as if
the photograph is picking up an image of the finger through the crystal.
Lower right: The crystal was next used on Swami Durgananda, who was
having pains, after which the crystal was again photographed. Where
the author's finger was used for pressure, there was a light area on the
image such as cannot be reproduced. Where the pen was used for
pressure, the circular light shape can again be seen. This time, however,
a very faint outline of the tip of the crystal could be seen, which has
been outlined for reproduction purposes.*

On the day that I announced my seclusion, Master Sivananda was there to speak to all the guests and students. As I finished speaking, Swami Sri Dharananda's hands rose again into *chin mudra,* and the following message was given:

"I am manifest. Blessed Children of Light:

"Learn to recognize well signs all around. In these days, you will come to recognize also your own inner sufferings, each and every one. In areas of innermost, most weakness, will come the situation of enduring great, great suffering in days ahead. All weakness from all levels will be changed greatly to innermost strength. Learn well to recognize signs of this innermost ripening process. This is all my work manifesting forth. In these days go forth, *not* going in a way immersing yourselves in an emotional level or going forth immersing yourself in externalizing actions. These are all paths which lead each and every one further into more suffering, and greatly more and more into darkness. Rather, as these signs come forth, know well these are signs to you to dive deep, deep within. Go forth more and more with faith in your hearts. Do more and more Sadhana. You will come to hear my voice on many levels. This is exactly prepared.

"As you have but just witnessed forth, my son, known to you as Vishnu Swami, is also going forth in an intense ripening process. In these days, as this child goes forth in externalized actions, trying to fulfill that which surges greatly through his own heart, innermost frustrations manifest forth through him. In this way, this child also is going forth in futile actions. More and more, innermost suffering comes forth from within. As these actions become greatly intense, this child goes forth, finally, diving deep, deep within. In these moments, this child reaches innermost recesses and in those moments great, greatest innermost ripening will come forth, as that child will be but lifted up to another level far, far beyond the gross Earth plane. In this manner also much, much ripening will go forth *to each and every one of my children.*

"Worry *not,* for I am here to guide and protect each and every one. Know well, you know not the path you are but treading in these days, for you are but going forth in a direction beyond your own comprehension in these days. Time is growing greatly short in that place. Darkness is growing deeper and deeper all around. For this reason you can see much of that which is unfolding on the Earth plane. For reasons of emotions, I know well, to give forth full details and explanations of all that is to come soon in that place would greatly evoke intense fear in the hearts of my children. This would greatly hamper your own inner ripening process. This is *not* prepared. Rather, in these days fulfill greatly each and every work given at the feet of each one. Continue on with full faith in Truth which has been greatly engraved on the tablets of each heart.

"*Stand Strong! Stand Firm!* with that which you know well in your hearts. Bend not to the darkness which is greatly growing all around. Rather, go forth, each and every day, in your time, with your actions to fulfill, and in other moments dive within, in greatest regularity of Sadhana. In this way, each and every one will ripen properly. Go forth well, in a way also gathering those children immersed greatly in darkness. Stand strong with those Truths engraved in your hearts. Draw in all the children lost to your great, great family of light! In these days, this is your work. This is the duty of all my children. For that child known to you as Vishnu Swami, know well that in these days great, great transition is going forth. As this child takes on burden of your own actions, your own sufferings, know well this action, this innermost wish to be with you, is also going forth, in a way exactly prepared. This child will endure, will remain to the end with each and every one.

"However, in these days, it is prepared that all carry on in the mission of gathering those lost sheep in the darkness. For time is growing short. My son is greatly going forth at the brink of a new mission, one beyond the comprehension of all mankind. *One-fold power changes soon into two.* And as darkness intensifies greatly, two-fold power, in the end, in a quick time, short on that Earth plane, will in these days change to three-fold power. This is prepared. All mankind, those immersed in light, will quickly be lifted up. It is prepared that each and every child continue on inner intunement. For this is greatly essential for your own intunement in those last moments. Worry *not.* For in these days much is going forth beyond the comprehension of all. Worry *not!* Rather, dwell, each and every one, on your own efforts to endure each and every one's portion of inner ripening, inner suffering. Continue your own Sadhana, and you will come to know my presence. I am manifest for all my children and, in greatest days ahead, for all mankind."

Editor's note:
In the days that followed Swami Vishnu Devanandaji's retreat into isolation, the effects of his prolonged meditations with the crystal could be immediately felt. The pranic field which had been built up daily in the room where the sessions were held began to increase at a rate that was observable to all who entered it. On a lesser scale,

*almost everyone could feel the movement of energies known well
to Swami Gokulananda and Swami Sri Dharananda. Master Sivananda had said that the one-fold power was changing into two-fold
power. Although no one knew yet the exact meaning of that statement, there was no doubt that great change was taking place unlike
anything recorded before in history.*

*The story has not ended. In fact, Master has said that this is
just the beginning. All will be revealed "as it has been prepared".*

*On August 24, 1978, Master Sivananda spoke to all of the
staff, students and guests gathered in the Krishna Temple at the
Yoga Camp. His words were ones of inspiration and great promise
for the days to come.*

"Blessed, most most blessed Children of Light,

"Listen greatly to your own purpose soon to be given, that
each and every one come to understand properly purpose at hand,
soon to manifest forth on the gross gross earth plane. In greatest
days past, all came forth in a way proper knowledges came forth
for proper purification of the gross gross sheath. In past days three
of my children chosen [Swami Vishnu Devananda, Swami Gokulananda and Swami Sri Dharananda] came forth first to manifest
greatly one-fold power back on Earth. Soon in days ahead all will
but change greatly to two-fold power. In this manner my three
children have led the way for proper introduction of much that is
to come.

"Listen well my children, for each must come to understand
properly purpose at hand, duties each and every one must fulfill.
Soon in days ahead, two-fold power will greatly manifest forth in
slow time upon the gross Earth plane. In these days ahead it is
prepared for each and every one. Go forth my children each and
every day, without one day amiss, [meditate] twice daily in that place,
in small number, gathering together, spread all around the globe. Go
forth my children. Intune greatly to my feet. Soon in these days
ahead as two-fold power manifests forth in slow time you will come
to understand great great pranic field in each place chosen for your
own gathering purpose. In this way intunement becomes greater and
greater. This is only the beginning of your own duties at hand. In
these days great great seeds go forth planted upon fertile ground of
each and every one. These will go forth greatly growing from within.
Therefore worry not my children. Stand strong. Have great great
faith in each heart. Gather greatly together. Intune day by day to
my feet. You will come to witness greatly purification of area upon
which each and every one assembled. More and more intensification

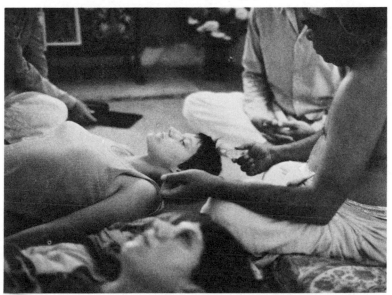

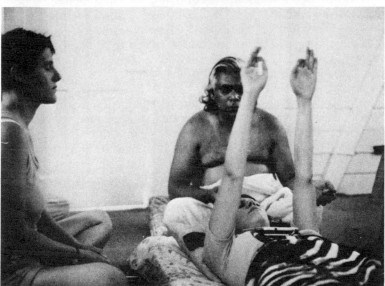

A typical session. Above: the crystal is used to draw off energies from Swami Gokulananda. Bottom: Swami Sri Dharananda's hands raised in the Chin Mudra during one of Master's messages.

of my presence will be known. In this manner spots of light, places of purification, spread all around will manifest properly upon the Earth plane. This is only one part of that which each and every one must fulfill.

"Go forth my children, fulfilling all your duties. In this manner my will will be fulfilled. For all my children must be gathered in these days. You will see in but short days ahead this event unfolding in slow time. In these days few lost sheep come forth. And in slow slow time will but come forth seeming as the multitudes, for my family is but immense all around. All my children are being greatly greatly gathered. Continue on my children. Let each and everyone stand strong as perfect mold for those lost ones to understand, to follow in your own footsteps. In this way gross sheath also can greatly go forth following proper Sadhanas for proper purification. As all go forth day by day, you will also come to witness intense change from within, as you but go forth intuning more and more, as also pranic field will manifest in a way all my children will properly come to know proper intunement. And in this way can be properly and quickly lifted up. I am here guiding and protecting all my children. Soon my group, my children banded in these days must go forth all around, back into darkness. Gather greatly my lost children for time is growing short. Worry not, for in days ahead all is exactly prepared. My voice will be known to all, each and every one will be properly guided. In these days these two children carry greatly the heavy and awesome burden of *first* going forth, purifying greatly on yet another level that all may pass through first to that plane introducing great, great field of subtle pranic current from highest level. In this way subconscious seed planted in each and everyone before entering that gross gross plane will be in time ignited once again to know your purpose. All manifests forth as it has been exactly prepared. Worry not as you but witness intense suffering of these three children chosen, for I am here to rejuvenate back as each one suffers through time of going beyond capacity, of carrying burden of pranas far far beyond ability of gross sheath to receive. This work has been chosen before these children entered that place. In days ahead these three children will but continue to pass through intense current, continuing on in a way each and every one will but know frequency of pranas from this place. Upon your own connection from this current going forth you will come to know my presence.

"Go forth my children. Fulfill well your duties at hand, as each one intunes greater and greater. You will see also those lost children gathering in greater number to your feet. I am here, guiding in a way that in those last moments I will remain to lift each and every one, remain here to receive you all. In days ahead part by part, step by step, all will be revealed as it is properly able to be received by my children. As each one intunes, as each one purifies more and more, will be given that each and every one will but come to understand, through direct experience, each and everyone's part. From time to time as necessity deems my voice will be heard, that each and every one will come to properly understand all that is manifesting forth. Let not the minds of my children manifest forth into a state of confusions, into a level of emotions. But rather rest greatly at peace, for I am here for each and every one. Let each and every one in these moments tune greatly to these pranas going forth, for you will come to understand your own connection to this higher place. [Long pause]

"Dive deep deep within. Let each and every one know his own intunement, his own connection to this subtle most most subtle frequencied pranas from this place. Seeds greatly hidden within, ignited *now,* soon to take root and grow *greatly* in days ahead. With everyone's own inner efforts, you will come to see this event manifesting forth from within. [Long pause]

"My children, recognize well pranic field, inner connection in these moments, as you but go forth, spread all around the globe on that plane. Go forth continuing on day by day intunement to this pranas from within. *You will come to witness greatly pranic field all around those chosen spots.* Hold that area of purification greatly greatly protected, greatly greatly precious in heart. For it is in these areas of purification of pranic field that each and every one will go forth, greatly protected from darkness all around. In days ahead it will be these areas of pranic connection, areas of pranic field emanating forth from this place, which will end in last moments spot of all my children, gathering together finally in those moments in greatest greatest intunements, coming forth to this place.

"Learn well now, my children. Ignition has gone forth."

Master Sivananda Speaks

Approximately 130 messages have been received from Master Sivananda to date, September 1978. A vast amount of knowledge has emerged which has been divided into six major themes:

1) I Am Manifest — The Plan is Laid
2) The Earth Must Be Saved
3) The Children of Light
4) Crystals; Their Use and Purpose
5) The Ancient Lost Knowledge to be Restored on the Earth Plane.
6) Messages of Inspiration

These six themes will now be developed through excerpts taken from the messages themselves. In many cases only the key sentences have been taken from the entire message, which may last from a few minutes to two hours, but the meaning has in no way been altered. It should be noted that Master Sivananda not only gave very detailed and technical information, but also was able to carry on a conversation. The sections contained in parentheses indicate questions which I asked him, and these are followed by his response.

I AM MANIFEST — THE PLAN IS LAID

October 16, 1977 — Partial Manifestation

This message was not received during Master's full manifestation. Swami Sri Dharananda, in a conscious state, often hears Master Sivananda's voice in her mind, Indian accent and all. As she was hearing this she wrote it down.

"By example, those who are blind can see again. By the repetition of my name those who are deaf can hear again. By my light those who are dying are again restored to new life. Go now and fulfill my will. *My manifestation is again born on Earth.*"

October 18, 1977 — Gurudev Sivananda's first full Manifestation

"I am He. I am the three-fold power. I am creation; I am

286

destruction. I am existence. I can never end. I am existence though I never exist. Know that I am manifest by the sign of the hand. The Truth is waiting within. Absorb in me. There I am manifest."

November 1, 1977

"All the children on Earth will be guided, *not only by me.* They must do more Sadhana."

November 10, 1977

"The way is laid; all is waiting. All that play parts in this cosmic play must know all was prepared before they even existed. Now all must unfold as was recorded. All parts are equally important, for I am guiding all. All will be guided at the proper time."

November 16, 1977

"The way is prepared, Vishnu Swami, yet you know not the Great Plan behind it all. In time this will manifest in a way guided beyond human mentality."

November 22, 1977

On November 3, a quartz crystal was presented to me by Mr. Marcel Vogel, a senior scientist at IBM's Los Gatos Laboratories in California. Master Sivananda explained, "You must learn the secret power lying within the crystal." He later elaborated:

"I will ignite the power hidden deep within the instrument [crystal] you hold, Vishnu Swami. Go to that brother. You must remain in tune with him. Together, I can ignite the proper vibration to bring the events of unfoldment of Light back on Earth."

(Master must make Mr. Vogel feel his presence in some form so that he will be happy to cooperate with me.)

"Vishnu Swami, your brother perceives me in his own way. Do not push him to see me as yourself or others do, for in all Truth I exist.

"I am manifest by the sign of the hand. Know I am manifest in the hearts of all who call upon me. All is waiting to unfold. Know I am One with the Source, unseparated yet apart, in a way to help mankind. For those who search I exist, though I am really One with the Source beyond existence."

December 2, 1977

"Vishnu Swami, even in this period of preparation falling from the Source, great great energy of light is flowing forth to help the Earth plane."

December 20, 1977

This message was received while travelling in the Winnebago motor home (Sivananda Mobile Headquarters) from Winnipeg to Montreal. Swami Gokulananda, who was driving, had pulled over to change drivers with the other car. Sri Gurudev's manifestation was already in progress in the back of the vehicle. Suddenly, a passing semi-trailer truck hit the outside mirror which crashed through the side window. The glass shattered all over Swami Gokulananda but caused no harm to her. Just before the impact, Master had stopped speaking although the hands remained up in the *mudras* the whole time. A few minutes after the accident occurred, Master started speaking again:

"This is all prepared; you were all in great danger. You have been made to come to this situation to prevent that which was about to occur. All my children are protected."

December 25, 1977

"All over around the globe many Children of Light, in many ways, are being gathered and guided, for in time they must unite to bring the light again and dispel the darkness on Earth. This manifestation is going forth on multi-levels in places everywhere, in ways mankind cannot understand. For you, you are one of the few great great leaders of many children on Earth. For this reason it appears that manifestation only appears before you. In truth, on all levels this manifestation is going forth, for light must again be generated in the hearts of the children of the Earth."

January 5, 1978

"Know always I am here. I am with you. I am witnessing and guiding every step. I will remain with my children until the last moment, through their departure from this place."

February 9, 1978

"Vishnu Swami, keep yourself opened to that which is going on around the world. In time, you will come to know that great knowledge is in fact going forth to many children who are connected to ancient truth through many different paths. In time, these children will be brought together, and they will come to know that their truth is but one and the same with all other links. Each part will exactly connect with other parts bringing forth that which the mind at this time cannot fully understand. Vishnu Swami, each one of the links is intimately and closely bound to a perfected Master. It is this union, this link to their higher Source, that opens and ripens these children. It is for this reason that each is chosen to go forth with his part. For this reason, a great type of protection comes forth, for the connection to this place is of a great bond. Your love and devotion to me is but the same love and devotion of the other chosen children to their great masters of this Source. You know well, Vishnu Swami, *the Source is but One. We all manifest from one Source,* bringing one great truth, but can only be understood as each mind is intuned and according to the intensity of each one's devotion. This will soon in time be revealed to you. You will meet other brothers, Vishnu Swami. You will feel close to them, for you will feel one with these chosen children as you come to meet them. Already one brother [scientist Marcel Vogel] you have met. He is greatly devoted to the master known as Jesus the Christ. In time you will meet others. Each one, Vishnu Swami, will help one another, for they will recognize what has come through. They will recognize the work each one must partake and yield to the others. This has already been planned.

"Vishnu Swami, in later days these truths will greatly awaken scientists and those in the field called medicine. These truths will prove how crude are the philosophies and understanding of these professional children. Ones considered of great knowledge will realize how crude their understanding really is. Rather, these higher truths will fill in the areas considered unknown knowledge that, more and more, all children will benefit. All mankind will again dwell in higher truth. Vishnu Swami, energies, pranas, spirituality — all these are still considered phenomena not yet known in general to mankind. More and more, those closed will be ripened by inner struggle to see these thoughts that do greatly exist and will greatly benefit all."

February 27, 1978

"Vishnu Swami, all is exactly prepared. For *no* child remaining on Earth has the capability of absorbing the entire plan. For this reason, part by part broken down, each one learns a significant piece and in the right moment one part links to another bringing greater and greater unfoldment of that which is manifesting back on Earth again. Vishnu Swami, the plan is laid. All is exactly prepared.

Understand this point well, Vishnu Swami. All is manifesting in a way that mankind can best learn."

March 31, 1978

Swami Gokulananda and Swami Sri Dharananda both experienced a constant building of the level of the *pranas,* or energies, in their bodies. Often the rate of vibration of these *pranas* changed, and this variation could actually be felt while holding the crystal, or "instrument."

"Understand well this explanation to be given to you. One day back in your own time, this child [Swami Sri Dharananda] has passed through and entered a new stage. Pranas [energies] in the past days were of a great and gross nature. Only step by step have you been properly prepared to receive more pranas. In this day past in your time, a great and subtler prana has finally come through from this place into the Earth plane, through this child. It is for your own experience, through this new instrument, that finer and subtler pranas again and again come through, stage by stage.

"Understand well, Vishnu Swami, pranas manifesting in this level are in great great contrast to those flowing forth in the gross earth plane. All will be given to you in time. You must understand only through experience first. Vishnu Swami, all has been exactly prepared that you learn, that you properly experience directly intunement with your instrument. Only in this manifest way, in the gross physical plane, can you properly intune yourself through first external experience through your instrument. This cannot be learned from another level. Know well, even those pranas of a subtler nature coming forth will also seem gross compared to the more greater and subtler pranas to come through in days ahead.

"Know well, Vishnu Swami, in these days at hand mankind is dwelling greatly greatly in deep deep darkness and cannot hear. Your own self as well as other chosen children, who are being greatly prepared, will have the proper answer as mankind goes forth in search of their own understanding. Much, much is going to manifest forth, Vishnu Swami, exactly in a proper way that all going forth will be used properly in a way that all mankind can hear and understand."

May 9, 1978

The *pranas* or energies of which Master Sivananda speaks are of such a magnitude that they must be divided among Swami Sri Dharananda, Swami Gokulananda and myself. The same *pranas* provided ignition of a second, larger crystal that was given to me by Marcel Vogel.

"Vishnu Swami, with these two children great pranas will flow to ignite this great instrument. Taken in hand with these children, all three create a pranic field conducive for great great ignition. For in these days of intensity coming forth, it cannot pass through only one. For this reason it has come through, connected through three. In this way, no harm comes forth. In these days ahead, these children before you also are greatly being prepared, more and more being connected to this higher place. This all has been exactly prepared, for they too will go forth in experiences others cannot comprehend. For this reason, all three will bloom forth in a way no harm can come to any one in a physical way."

May 12, 1978

"Understand well, Vishnu Swami, the gross sheath is not meant to absorb these great yet subtle *pranas,* more and more, as pranas flow back from this place becoming more subtle. Understand well, preparation is going forth. Before these *pranas* manifest in an intense way, great preparation must take place that no harm come to these two children."

June 12, 1978

(Gurudev, is this type of phenomenon taking place for the first time on the Earth plane, or has it happened before?)

"Vishnu Swami, in this manner, coming forth from one level to another, knowledge gained in this manner has come forth in great days past. However, long lost is this ability and in these days, due to the intense currents which are upon mankind, these knowledges must come forth in this direct manner."

June 26, 1978 — Partial Manifestation

After Message No. 122, when Swami Sri Dharananda returned to a conscious level, the first thing she said was that she saw a blue light around the head of Dr. Andrija Puharich, who was present during that session. Dr. Puharich is an M.D. who holds many patents on medical equipment. He is the author of *Uri, The Sacred Mushrooms,* and a number of other works. Swami Sri Dharananda said that the light was not part of his aura, but from another source. She then heard Master Sivananda's voice:

"Yes, this child is also in a ripening process on the brink of a new discovery, new unfoldment, new learning. For all children, all is exactly prepared. All unfolds before each chosen child in a way beyond their own will, beyond their own control. It is only of each child's duty to fulfill that part which is given."

(Ask Master what the blue light signifies.)

"This child knows well of his own connection to a higher place. As this child connects properly, emanating energies of that pattern of light go forth. As this child's heart goes forth in humility, surrendering to this higher place, more and more this child will be emanating this connection. All is exactly prepared. Know well, knowledge from this place, coming forth in these days, are meant for the well being of all mankind."

(Master, is there any message for Father Rossner, who is also here?)

"Struggling, going forth to each child, is prepared for inner ripening process. Understood well is this phenomenon; struggling brings forth inner growth. *In many children in these days intense struggling is prepared. For these days are ones of great great inner growth, inner ripening that in later days intense unfolding comes forth.* Worry not; all is going forth as is exactly prepared. Each portion allotted exactly for each child, that all go forth in that place as is exactly prepared — all interconnected, all intermingled in a way beyond human comprehension.

"Allotted at these days is intense learning, intense growing in yet another level. In days ahead it will bloom forth in a way that cannot be properly comprehended. However, knowledges from a place beyond that plane will flow forth that all understanding comes forth once again, that all benefit mankind. Each and every chosen child has his own part, his own portion to ripen, to unfold, to bloom forth. Each interconnecting, that all that is prepared comes forth for all mankind in that plane. As each one but reflects within, each can come to see a small part of the greatest plan of the greatest event coming forth in these days.

"Each child must come to understand his own part. Each must unfold exactly as each one is prepared. All is guided. Time is growing short in the Earth plane. As days grow shorter, intensity will increase — intensity and inner ripening coming forth through each chosen child, each one exactly guided. Each one at an exact rate is unfolding through these days."

July 9, 1978

(We pray Gurudev to shed light on all these children who are spread all around the world.)

"All is ripening forth; all is unfolding before the children. All in time will come to know my presence. I am here. I am manifesting forth for all mankind. More and more as each child goes forth, with inner part unfolding from Sadhana, day by day, each and every one will come to know my voice within. I am here, Vishnu Swami, for all my children."

THE EARTH MUST BE SAVED

Many messages from Gurudev Sivananda revolved around the need to reverse the negativity on the earth plane. Abuse of power, of natural resources, and of scientific knowledge has placed the world in a precarious balance.

October 18, 1977 — Spoken during Master's first manifestation

"I am He. All my children must shed light to save the Earth plane. My children must unite to survive. Only by the light within can they save the Earth. My light shining through them will purify the Earth. All the Devas are waiting to serve my children. The lost sheep must be found. Know I am manifest. Know this day to be a new beginning. The struggle will be very difficult. By my name, by my light, by my presence in my children's hearts can they gain enough strength to endure. Know there will be a sign. Know there will be placed a beacon light on every continent. Each beacon will have a sign. The sign will be manifest for all to see. The blind must see again. The deaf must hear again. Ignorance in the darkness must be dispelled by the inner light. All must learn the Truth or they will perish in the fire of destruction."

November 5, 1977

"Vishnu Swami, you know not the power that lies in your hands. The power in the crystal, the hidden secret, can either destroy or save the world. Vishnu Swami, you must always absorb in me upon taking this crystal. I will guide you, for you know not what you have in your possession. You must take care. You must take great care, for what you have can be misused. You must always have it on you, for it can be very destructive if it falls into the wrong hands."

(Why did Master guide me to obtain such a dangerous thing?)

"Used properly, you can help humanity greatly, for hidden within you are powers to help all mankind."

November 8, 1977 — Partial Manifestation

"Certain nations are playing havoc with the human mind. They are able to break the flow of thought. When the flow of thought is broken with instruments [crystals], they are able to interfere and take control. They use tactics of fear to break the flow of thoughts. The mind can only be controlled in a state of fear. They are great experts in creating this kind of environment of fear. They can reduce the mind to its lowest level if given enough time. They easily know how to break the mind as well. They are now testing and researching on bringing this to a greater level. They want full control. It is very difficult to counteract and stop this, for once fear enters the mind it is very difficult to break. The mind loses all rationale in a state of great fear. The impressions are very deep in this state. Thus, control is made very easy."

November 18, 1977

"At this time the Earth is rocking between a new light and more darkness. By focussing, by deep focussing, by deep deep heartfelt prayer can the Earth balance toward the new light. This must manifest. This is crucial. Guide my children, Vishnu Swami, for the Earth is in a dangerous position. Mankind cannot understand words or actions. The time is unfolding where light, prayer, and in silence, thoughts can heal the Earth. Focus on me, for vibrations can heal."

November 22, 1977 — Just after President Sadat's visit to Israel

"Worry not, Vishnu Swami, of externals at this time, for you do not realize the situation the whole Earth is about to enter. This is the beginning of the large scope of events that will greatly affect all of mankind. Vishnu Swami, the Earth is now entering a time where events cause other events, cause more and more and more, until it cannot be stopped. Now is the time unfolding to get set in motion a vibration of peace. This is the last chance for humanity. Vishnu Swami, you must know I am guiding. I am manifest to help all mankind. You know that this is the beginning of either a restored life or a beginning of the unfoldment to bring a final end. Vishnu Swami, the events to take place in the near near future — follow those in Cairo, follow those in Jerusalem, follow those in the place that is called the Middle East, for great great danger is coming to those who are trying to unfold peace."

(Is President Sadat's life in danger?)

"All the peacemakers on Earth are in great danger, for it is the vibration on Earth that continues the events to unfold disaster. Vishnu Swami, this is the work of thought. This is the work of the crystal — to change the pattern of events, to change the patterns of dark vibrations by interruption and by thought, to change them to one of great peace. Mankind knows not the vibrations he is immersed in. Mankind knows not the influences that cause him to act in a way that can be changed."

December 2, 1977

"I am manifest. Vishnu Swami, worry not, for I am guiding and protecting. All my Children of Light must be purified, must pass a test of great endurance, for this work is one of great great difficulty. Now is the time when all are being prepared, for time is growing very very short. Vishnu Swami, worry not, for each Child of Light has his work laid before him. All is being prepared. All is unfolding as it is meant to be. Vishnu Swami, know their struggle will bear great great fruits. For in the time of great darkness to come, their light must not be washed away. They must be strong to stand firm when all is dark around, when all is fire and destruction everywhere. These children must must dive deep and be one with their Source, and this will be their strength."

(I do not understand the fire and destruction Master speaks of.)

"The Earth plane is headed for great disaster and destruction. Many many children in the past have brought these warnings of what is to come."

(When will this destruction come?)

"Vishnu Swami, the time element is dependent on many many factors. It manifests only by vibrations set in motion. These vibrations can be slowed down, can be altered, and ultimately can be stopped."

(By what method?)

"Vishnu Swami, this is the time where Sadhana can purify not only souls who partake, also the Sadhana sends off purifying vibrations around the globe.

"All the knowledge that is meant to be will unfold to those who hold these instruments. In the past, knowledge came to all. They learned the secret and were able to even shut off the powers of the Masters who were guiding them.

"These instruments [crystals] were then used negatively against mankind, against the will of what was meant to be. Now history is again unfolding. The souls who know this knowledge are now once again reincarnating back on Earth. But the knowledge will come forth only in a way, in a time, that the Masters guide. All those that gain the instrument will be those who are one with the guiding force. That will unfold in the souls which is meant to help all mankind."

December 28, 1977

"Vishnu Swami, I am One with the Source yet have separated temporarily in time to come to guide and protect my children, to bring forth Truth that must bloom to help all mankind. For that which is on the brink of manifestation surely will destroy mankind if vibrations are not purified, if Truth again is not borne on Earth. For Truth alone is the saving element of humanity. The destruction yet to manifest will be so great, Vishnu Swami, that only a power from a Source far beyond the Earth plane can send forth an element of purifying light to help the children move properly from the gross plane, in a time of destruction, to the higher planes where they emanate from in the first place."

(What type of destruction is Master speaking of?)

"The Earth is now rocking on the brink of a chain reaction of natural events to bring forth great and disturbing changes. Prophecies by many have come forth in a correct manner. You have before you, Vishnu Swami, many accounts of the destruction that is to come. It is not necessary at this time to bring forth any further details. For yet to manifest, many many energies can go forth to lessen, to interrupt, to change the pattern of what may come. Vishnu Swami, it is the Karma of many Children of Light before you to go forth among the destruction and collect many of those lost sheep and open their hearts in a time when they are most closed."

January 5, 1978

This message was also a partial manifestation, Swami Sri Dharananda hearing Master's voice internally. Swami Vishnuji was not present. This message was addressed to her for the most part, but this short excerpt is given here as it applies to the general topic.

"Endure with inner conviction and strength that this eventually is for all, that they may all benefit and be helped in a time when all the Earth suffers, that all will have an answer in their hours of greatest need. I am manifest to help all mankind. Mankind must be restored back to his inner faith, driven within from worldly material illusion. He must be made to touch his inner being that he once again know who he really is. Children on Earth are greatly lost. The time is long overdue that he returns back to learn and again walk in a way that he knows his purpose.

"This will come. Mankind is headed for a great and difficult time that he will come to know his inner Source, faced at that moment with destruction all around. At that time on the verge of coming to extinction, mankind will not perish but will come to a great struggle that will bear great great fruits. But at this time knowledge will be known by a chosen few to prove God's work, His Great Plan, that they may come to know their relation to Him. This will unfold in a way that the knowledge will come forth only at the moment of mankind's greatest need. That it will be ignited in that moment to bring all mankind back to a higher level, back to his proper existence, one in light rather than in darkness.

"All this is prepared. Know well how important is your part to help unfold this great knowledge once again back on Earth. Therefore my child, stand strong. Endure well that which is laid before you, for your struggle in the end will help all mankind."

June 12, 1978

"Understand well, Vishnu Swami, these knowledges in these days have little value, for coming in these times the danger is not yet felt. However, soon upon the Earth plane will but unfold and in those hours all will come to you, and full understanding will then unfold. Beyond comprehension of mankind in these days is but that which is soon upon mankind. Only in those days as all quickly unfolds will this but come forth in an increased way to go forth, beyond your own knowledge, to help mankind."

THE CHILDREN OF LIGHT

Master Sivananda often speaks of his "Children of Light." Sometimes this refers directly to Swami Sri Dharananda or Swami Gokulananda, but in many cases he is speaking of all those on the spiritual path who are incarnated to help the Earth. Some of these "children" already know their purpose in life; others are yet to be gathered. Master explains that although the entire picture of what is to unfold has not yet been revealed, all are now being trained to carry out their parts at this time.

November 10, 1977

Master has, since the beginning, spoken of the three-fold power. Although as yet there have been only hints as to its meaning, it is clear that this power will bring about major change.

"The light on Earth is being kindled all on the Earth in my children's hearts. In union, all this light ignited by the three-fold power will save the Earth. I will guide all."

November 20, 1977

This message was received while the "New York Symposium on Physics and Metaphysics" was in progress, sponsored by the Sivananda Yoga Vedanta Centers. We had just had a similar symposium in Los Angeles a few weeks earlier, and were in the process of discussing a large gathering at the Yoga Camp in 1979.

"Vishnu Swami, the meetings of the ways must continue. Children of Great Light must be brought together, for on their own the light is scattered. But brought together, their light shines far far beyond human understanding. The inner light among my children must unite and grow into one large great great light on Earth. Meetings of the ways must continue, for at these times much much unfolds beyond that which is seen and understood. The fruits of these meetings act as sparks for new light to come forth and manifest on Earth. This light will spread far far until it reaches the four corners of the Earth."

November 21, 1977

"That which is unfolding comes to those who are ready to hear. You are surrounded by many Children of Light, Vishnu Swami. You are also surrounded by many who still remain in darkness; and also there are many who are somewhere in between — sparks of small small light breaking through a great darkness. These are children who appear to know all, but exist in great confusion. Those in darkness understand not. To hear words of truth causes a great barrier for them to open up to understand. For theirs is a need of silence, of comfort, direct guidance and daily Sadhana only. For the Children of Light, these truths will serve as a great inspiration. You will be able to see the reaction, and know which type of child by the reaction. Vishnu Swami, already by actions, by great word of mouth, these messages are going forth. You already perceive much chaos caused to those living in darkness.

"You already know, Vishnu Swami, even a Child of Light immersed in a vibration of darkness can become lost and lose his light. Vishnu Swami, there are children in the place called the Middle East who are struggling to remain one of Light, to remain focussed on *me*. But they are greatly immersed in deep deep dark vibrations which constantly darkens their light. All my children are being prepared. They will accomplish their work. *They will become hands in moulding the Earth back to its original Source."*

December 2, 1977

"Vishnu Swami, at times this child [Swami Sri Dharananda] will not be on the Earth plane for she will be connected to a higher Source. Her physical manifestation, like all the Children of Light, will be a pure source to help all mankind."

(Who are the Children of Light? How do I find them? How do I recognize them?)

"Vishnu Swami, these children are dispersed all over the Earth. They are not like others you see, their ways, their hearts. These children are set apart, for their home is not of the Earth plane. Vishnu Swami, these children are born from the highest loka. Only their souls have enough strength to endure the fire, the darkness that is about to unfold. Vishnu Swami, those children incarnated for that purpose. This which is hidden within is being shielded, for their minds become a block to that which is lying ready to manifest. At the given moment all these Children of Light will be connected to a Source far beyond their comprehension. At those moments, words will not be theirs, actions will not be theirs. The mind will cease to function.

"They will be pure channels to manifest that which is meant to be. In the end Truth always remains. This is the purpose of the children bearing this burden, Vishnu Swami. Their burden is great, for holding the light, holding the truth in darkness is a greatly difficult task to withstand. All time immemorial, cycles of darkness came. Always in these times those children who withstand the darkness to kindle their light also come. The task is of great struggle, but Truth always triumphs in the end. *Truth shall live on beyond all."*

December 28, 1977

"Vishnu Swami, this is the time of great great preparation of all Children of Light on Earth. Many during their Sadhana will unfold experiences of connections to a higher level. That which is lying within my children in a dormant state must be awakened, must come forth. Slowly slowly, as they do more and more Sadhana, I will ignite, I will bring forth that knowledge, those experiences of strength from the past. This will surface in the children in future days. Worry not, Vishnu Swami, This is *not* a situation of unusual psychic phenomenon but *is my work bringing forth inner strength, inner faith in my children.* For these children in days to come when they are completely immersed in chaos, in confusion, in times of deep emotion and sorrow in darkness, their strength *only* will be this higher Source that is at this time trying to surface within them. These experiences only serve to reawaken a part within that strengthens the tie to their *homeland*. For this in future days will serve as a guiding light for each child when each goes forth amidst the destruction to lift up others who are dwelling in emotions, who are dwelling in darkness."

April 13, 1978

"In reality these experiences are part of their own existence from days past. These types of experiences in days past were but considered normal experience. However, incarnate in this great and dark time all was shielded. *Know these are but signs, guiding lights to these children, helping them to search for a greater understanding.*"

June 6, 1978

The *pranas* moving through the bodies of Swami Gokulananda and Swami Sri Dharananda often create great physical discomfort. Master Sivananda explained that both physical and mental pain bring about strength and growth, and prepared them for the work they had chosen for this lifetime.

"Vishnu Swami, understand well this process going forth. In these times, as the sun has passed away in your plane, is the time when connection is greatest from this place into these children. In days past the degree of concentration was small, and in time, has increased more and more. In these days, and some few ahead, know well the greatest portion is at hand connecting into these children. For this reason more and more pain occurs within. For it is this pain that signals to all that ripening and strength are coming forth within.

"In the days ahead, when the systems at hand become properly strong, only in that time will the pain subside. This will be a signal to all that these children have ripened properly and are ready to enter into this new stage ahead. In these children the mental perception of pain in the gross sheath must take place, for *mental strength is of paramount importance in these two children.* It is my work going forth causing these two children to witness that which is going forth. Only in this way can deepest most strong subtle vibrations, samskaras within [latent impressions from past lives] knowledge from past come forth within them that they may learn to withstand these pranas within, on all conscious levels.

"Vishnu Swami, your own suffering facing the outside world,

going forth in more and more futile efforts, will bring you to the silence within; and in those greatest moments your own instrument in hand will carry forth, with great ignition, your most inner thoughts to manifest forth for all mankind. In those days it will be the work of these two children to go forth in the darkness, among the greatest suffering all around. It will be the work of these children, with focussed minds, to carry on. It is for this reason, in these days, that such mental strength also be ripened. Worry not, Vishnu Swami, for all that is soon to come is beyond the intellect, beyond the gross mind and perceptions. I am here."

July 16, 1978

A number of students have come to me in hopes of solving physical problems. Some of these, according to Master, are due to the *pranas* going forth at this time.

"Time is greatly measured. Know well, Vishnu Swami, many children going forth in these days are going forth in a manner of great, great purification and a process of inner ripening. You will come to witness many, children, coming forth to your feet with unexplainable problems at hand."

(Yes, Gurudev, today also we have eight or ten children here; I don't know what to do.)

"Know well, Vishnu Swami, ripening process is increasing in many of my children. Understand well as strengthening comes forth from within, areas of weakness bring forth symptoms of complication. Worry not, Vishnu Swami, all in slow time passes away. It is of paramount importance to understand signs, in going forth, of Sadhana from day to day. Sadhana intunes children greatly to ripening process, to those areas of weakness gaining much, much strength. Let *all* children heed these signs. Pranas going forth will manifest problems at hand as this continues on. Children in slow process more and more are greatly being affected by currents in the atmosphere of that place. Also, in slow time process of ripening increases more and more. As all goes forth problems will come, will manifest forth and also Sadhanas going forth, ones directly bringing forth direct result symptoms and problems. Let children take great, great notice of these efforts causing direct problems. As this goes forth, let these children change Sadhanas from one area to another, that all in slow time pass away."

(Gurudev, this was not clear, what type of *sadhana* should they change?)

"If gross actions produce direct problems at hand let this be a sign to that child to change those actions. It is not prepared to continue forth actions causing more and more complication, but rather go forth in action causing direct fruits, go forth in action where all continues on in purpose, in result with little or no complications. Remember well, Vishnu Swami, explanation already given to you. Those children going forth in these days in profession following knowledges of medicine are ones engrossed greatly in darkness. These children understand not integrated systems of subtle body's connection with the gross sheath. As these children go forth in efforts to change symptoms of problem at hand, know well, Vishnu Swami, in their actions they go forth causing more and more complication to children going forth in Sadhanas, for introduced to the system will be medications of greatest poison to the gross sheath as well as the subtle bodies. This *must* be prevented in these days, Vishnu Swami."

(Yes, Gurudev, I understood that.)

"Poisoning of systems takes great, great efforts and greatest time to heal and rejuvenate back to proper balance. All complication of this manner must be by-passed, for in days ahead Children of Light must go forth in works at hand greatly intuned to the subtle bodies. It is of paramount importance that these bodies *not* go forth in a polluted manner."

(Gurudev, I didn't understand what is meant by polluted manner)

"Introduction of poisons [medicines, chemicals] from those children who go forth changing symptoms of problems at hand. Know well, Vishnu Swami, in ignorance the children go forth, through their own actions. Medications, poisons of this manner, go forth into the gross sheath and in slow time pollute the subtle bodies as well. This must be by-passed."

(Yes, I understand that now, Gurudev.)

"Vishnu Swami, it is of paramount importance, and your duty as well, to instruct these children to go forth relying greatly on Sadhanas, on inner strength, focussing greatly within to this higher Source."

(Yes, Gurudev should guide them, and they are having tremendous faith in Gurudev; I'm sure they will more and more come to thy lotus feet to get help.)

"Let not these children at your feet worry greatly of small complications at hand in the gross sheath, for in these days, and in many days ahead, more and more complications will manifest forth before all.

"This is all my work going forth, for these children are greatly being ripened. Let each and every one continue on, let these children with innermost faith know well each and every complication will but in time pass away.

"You understand well, Vishnu Swami, Sadhanas go forth from greatest varying types. If complication goes forth from the physical actions, change then Sadhanas to mental efforts. If mental complication comes forth, let children change to actions external. You understand well this point, Vishnu Swami."
(Yes, Gurudev)

"Change of Sadhanas can go forth and in this way. Changing from one type of Sadhana, directly producing great inner complications, to another type of Sadhana can easily go forth. In this manner many, many complications can be directly lessened and easily by-passed."

August 24, 1978

"Blessed children, it is my work unfolding more and more to all lost sheep going forth in darkness. From within many-fold experiences come forth manifesting great, most profound, confusions to those minds of those lost children. Each and every lost sheep will in time go forth in most great great effort for help, for understanding of problem at hand. These lost sheep will walk through thy gates, will come beckoning at each door. It is your duties, my children, to welcome these lost sheep; bring forth with greatest love and understanding these lost ones, welcoming greatly into your great family of light. You will come to witness these lost sheep gaining immense, great great, most great immense help. You will come to witness all problem at hand soon but vanishing away as these lost children enter purified area of pranas from this place. This is exactly prepared."

CRYSTALS: THEIR USE AND PURPOSE

November 3, 1977

"Vishnu Swami, you must learn the secret power lying within the crystals. You have now met one child already learning the secret [Mr. Marcel Vogel]. You must learn this, for hidden within you are powers to help humanity."

November 9, 1977 — Partial Manifestation

Master Sivananda has occasionally given information that

could not be understood except through time and experience. This is one such message where the significance really cannot be understood as yet.

"A third crystal must be obtained for my three-fold power to manifest. Tell Vishnu Swami it belongs to the one chosen as my link, the one he knows as my voice. He will understand. The purpose of this crystal is to connect to the four-sided altar in the celestial Garden of Truth and Justice."

November 21, 1977

"Vishnu Swami, your external actions at this time are of less importance. It is your thoughts, it is the power of your thoughts connected to the crystal which affect the Earth plane."

(How can I do this, Master?)

"A sign has already been given. By your connection with me and by the power of your thoughts focussed, you can change whatever you wish. All what is meant to be, all, ignites through the crystal. This is its secret. Your thoughts, chanelled *only* at the proper moment, take ignition and manifest at that time. Your thoughts *cannot* manifest through the crystal at the improper time."

December 2, 1977

The significance of the crystals was not fully understood until some time after the first one was received. It was only through the constant pain of Swami Sri Dharananda and Swami Gokulananda that I was brought to realize how great a part they played in Master's plan.

(What is this tremendous energy that moved into my body when I touched Swami Sri Dharananda?)

"This child, her work like many of the others is one of great great difficulty. She is being prepared in another time, in another place. She is being guided to connect to places of energy far greater than can be understood. She is having great difficulty in the process of moving from one of great great prana, of great light and energy, to that which the gross body is able to contain. You are acting as an intermediary source, taking that which cannot enter into her own body."

(Why can't it enter into her body?)

"Vishnu Swami, I am guiding all. When you connect to her, you are able to contain that excess that she is not able to contain. A time will come when even *you* cannot contain that excess."

(What shall I do at that time, Master?)

*Quartz crystals, silicon dioxide, cut by Marcel Vogel. The smaller one,
on the right, was presented to the author on November 3, 1977. The
larger crystal was received on March 2, 1978.*

"You must connect with the crystal."

(Still I have not learned how to use it properly, Master.)

"Vishnu Swami, the crystal is only an instrument that transfers thought that transfers energy and prana from one level to another. All manifestation is only levels and degrees of vibrating prana, vibrating light. The crystal is an instrument that can stop, that can interfere, that can change the pattern of prana."

(Master has said that the crystal must be ignited. Has it actually happened yet?)

"The power behind the instrument will be the power that flows through when you connect to me. For I am guiding, I am protecting."

December 7, 1977

From the very beginning, exact instructions were given by Master on how to use the instrument. All through the month of December, the messages continued to emphasize that the crystal was the only answer to help the two children in times of difficulties manifesting in the gross body.

"Vishnu Swami, use the instrument on this child, for soon she will be released."

(Please guide me to use it properly.)

"Focus the instrument on the sahasrara."

(Yes, Master. Now what shall I do?)

"Absorb in me. Synchronize the breath with the child before you. All the power contained in the human gross sheath will be expelled, for if this excess comes into this human gross sheath it can cause havoc.

"Vishnu Swami, to send forth a powerful thought, to ignite the crystal with the breath, and then to absorb the being deeply deeply within. This is the process."

December 10, 1977

(Master has said that Mr. Vogel is making a larger, more powerful instrument for me. What will be the difference between this crystal and the one yet to come?)

"Vishnu Swami, the instrument is only as good as the connection to an energy source. Ultimately, an instrument is only as good as it has been ignited."

December 12, 1977

"Vishnu Swami. At this time you must help this child [Swami Sri Dharananda]. When the power goes beyond her ability to contain it, her physical gross body goes into reverse bandhas [in which the energy from the higher Source becomes locked in one nadi]. The locks protect her physical sheath. But the child is caught. Without your help she will be unable to breathe. You will learn the signs, for even now her body is reacting to that which she has endured."

(Yes, Master. I can see the lock. The abdomen is swollen and hard as a rock.)

"Feel the diaphragm, Vishnu Swami."

(Yes, Master. It is very tight. What shall I do?)

"At the top of the diaphragm you feel a sensation of the pranas. This is the energy hitting on the lock in reverse. I am here guiding, Vishnu Swami, worry not. You must use the crystal. Use the instrument, for I will ignite its power. The body has a built-in mechanism to shield and protect itself; when the power gets to a level beyond that which the physical sheath can contain, the locks will automatically go on for protection. Use the instrument to draw out the excess from the gross physical sheath."

December 28, 1977

"Vishnu Swami; at this time set forth a schedule in use of the instrument."

(How many times a day should we meet, Master?)

"Vishnu Swami, the instrument works, but yet it only comes forth in a very subtle way. You will see the benefits and fruits coming forth as it is properly ignited; but at this time, it is meant to be used regularly. Regularly, that the children will not bear an unnecessary struggle. On a regular basis the instrument not only expels energy absorbed from that higher Source, but also neutralizes the electrical system in the gross body that it may function properly without disturbance during this learning situation that is unfolding."

(Is once a day sufficient?)

"Minimum usage of the instrument at this time is the times of the movement change of light, of exchange of the moon and sun. For all this time on Earth the psychic and physical energies are subjected to a great exchange and movement. To prepare the system from undergoing a situation out of control, use the instrument at these times when the energies tend to move at its greatest rate."

(When I use the instrument, exactly what type of breathing should I do mostly?)

"Vishnu Swami, the instrument is ignited, but its connection, its source of energy, its power to go through to connect with the systems where you wish it to be part of, this also is a mental process as well as connection with breath. Take the instrument; use the great power of thought; connect the instrument where you wish it to unfold its work. Coordinate the breath through the instrument and finally then redirect your complete absorption to me. This is the process for you."

(And what is the process for the children?)

"The children must receive properly. They must coordinate the breath with yours, for this connects their energy with that of the instrument. This is a psychic phenomenon which at this time is *not* understood. The subtler bodies are directly affected by the power of the instrument.

"Vishnu Swami, the instrument in your custody will be ignited in a way that any intellect can never understand. This is because the Source from which the ignition comes forth is far beyond that which can be grasped by the human intellect."

February 6, 1978

"Vishnu Swami, take notice of three properties you can feel directly through the instrument you possess. In the areas of high high energy, collected as it is magnetized and drawn out, you will feel great pulsation in your instrument. There is a second property which you must take notice, in areas of blocks in the nadis [nerves of the astral body] which hold the pranas. As these areas unlock, the instrument draws out the energy that was causing blockage and you feel the direct experience of pulsation and warmth. However, intune yourself to the third property of the instrument which is one of coolness. As you pass over an area which is blocked, the area of the physical sheath which has little or no pranas yields forth a sensation of coolness. For this has great great significance. For in the future, as you learn this well with a great instrument, you will be able to heal."

February 12, 1978

The following is an example of the typical exchange that went on during the period that Master was giving specific instructions on the various properties of the crystal.

"I am manifest, Vishnu Swami. Intune yourself with the instrument at this time."

(I feel the pulsation, now.)

"More and more the pulsation will manifest through the instruments."

(Yes, Gurudev. I can feel it.)

"At this time, the energy flowing back is one of an intense

nature. This will connect to your instrument, Vishnu Swami."

(Should I move the crystal to the solar plexus area, Gurudev?)

"Throughout the system readily you can feel the different vibrations going forth."

(The vibrations are more on the right side. Is this correct, Master?)

"Vishnu Swami, you are learning well. Continue, continue the instrument. It is of great and paramount importance before the new instrument soon to come that you learn certain properties and understand better the movements and functions of the instrument. Intune yourself, for at this time the gross manifestation of energy is changing now to one of a more subtle level. Intune yourself, intune yourself, Vishnu Swami."

(Yes, Gurudev. Pulsation is felt at the tip of the instrument instead of more on the finger tip.)

"Vishnu Swami, more and more changes will take place. As the lessons change from one of a gross manner to one of a more subtle level, continue the intunement."

(I feel intense energy.)

"Yes. More and more through the instrument you will understand this intensity, this great level of manifestation. As you become more and more intuned, this manifestation will become greater and greater, that you may be able to understand."

(Will I be able to distinquish these subtler levels, Gurudev? What are the signs?)

"Vishnu Swami, understanding the different rates of vibrations going forth, learning parts from other parts, distinquishing contrast from one area to another, slowly you can become more and more intuned. First ignite the connection with the greater more manifest energies flowing forth. This you already now understand well, from the diaphragm when the instrument is pulsating greatly. This is a sign that your instrument has connected well. However, movement of the instrument and the ability to connect to lesser rates of energy flowing forth and understanding one area differently vibrating from another, this you must concentrate on at this time. You will come to understand. Strive on. Learn well. I am here, guiding you, bringing forth more and more that you may be able to understand well. Vishnu Swami, before you is but another child [Swami Gokulananda]. At this time use the instrument to draw out the energies before complications manifest. You must understand the contrast flowing forth from one child to another."

(Yes. I could not feel so much energy coming from the other

child. Am I correct?)

"At this time the gross manifestation of energies is flowing forth from one, while directly in contrast in a subtle way, the energies are flowing forth from the other."

(I could feel it. Now Sri Dharananda's sahasrara is vibrating. She is connected to her also?)

"Vishnu Swami, the energies flowing forth and manifesting now can be connected to mentally by this child sitting from the other side [Swami Gokulananda]. This child which is laying down [Swami Sri Dhararnanda] is connected in another way. This is all my work going forth. You must understand well, Vishnu Swami. You can feel the energies now coming forth from the other child known as Gokulananda Swami. Energies coming very greatly in a gross way. As the instrument connects, you will notice the vibrations going down. Energy will be drawn off. When the instrument comes to a halt, when vibrations seem to stop, again reconnect to this child that you may be able to understand the contrasting energies.

"Vishnu Swami, there is a field of energy going forth at this time. It is one of a subtler nature, vibrating at a different rate than one of a gross nature. Feel this in the instrument now to understand the energies are more finer, vibrating as a quicker rate, going forth at an extreme rate seeming almost as if it is not there."

(Yes, Gurudev, I can understand that.)

"Feel now. Intune yourself. You will understand."

February 24, 1978

"Vishnu Swami, that which you are experiencing through the instrument is a pulsation type of more high intensity prana from this place. It is this prana that flows forth and fills the child [Swami Sri Dharananda] that this manifestation [his messages] is made possible."

February 25, 1978

It was about this time that Master indicated that the preliminary lessons had been learned, and that it was time to learn intunement with the crystal to more subtle pranas.

"At this time this child [Swami Sri Dharananda] is greatly and deeply absorbed in a higher level. Due to this only those great great subtle pranas from this place are flowing forth at this time. Intune yourself, Vishnu Swami, with great great inner concentration. You will in time come to understand even these pranas. Connect the instrument to the sahasrara. In this place vibrations are going forth more intensely. You can readily understand now the difficulties, the problems upon which you are faced to understand well these pranas flowing forth from such a high high frequency of movement. Vibrations at this frequency are so so rapid, perceptibly it can barely be understood. All that appears at this time is due to a frequency moving beyond your perception, so so quickly that it appears not at all to exist. In later days you will become greatly familiar, greatly intuned with these more subtle pranas, and will remember back to this time that you seemed not to understand."

February 27, 1978

(Gurudev, one of my students presented me with a small crystal today. Is this for some purpose? What shall I do with this?)

"Vishnu Swami, understand well. There are infinite instruments upon the Earth. However, only those chosen to be properly ignited will be of use. You understand well the property of these instruments are as mere particles from the earth with insignificant value alone. Only properties coming forth bring value when these instruments are properly intuned and ignited from this higher Source."

"Vishnu Swami, this day past marks the beginning of a new era to unfold on the Earth plane. Through these days past you and your brother [Marcel Vogel] as well as many incarnated on the Earth plane now have been learning the properties of the instruments. Until this day both you and your brother, as well as a few other links who now possess instruments, have undergone an exact learning process. This process for each is exact and has been greatly prepared that each one ripen properly. Each one, day by day, step by step, will go forth in inner unfoldment until *each one receives exactly the frequency from this place.* When the Earth is finally immersed in great great darkness, in that time, each one will come to know this particular frequency directly intuned from the Earth plane to this place."

(This new crystal I received from my brother Marcel Vogel, I am not able to feel the same vibration as from the old one. What is the cause for this?)

"Vishnu Swami, understand well. To the degree upon you focussing and properly connecting to the instrument and to the degree that the instrument becomes properly intuned to your own vibration, together, and in time, the instrument will gain its power. As you saw past in the other instrument, only in time and to the degree that you became one with it, did it ignite greater and greater."

(The crystals and stones I bought as we were leaving Calcutta, I felt compelled to buy them. Can you give me some direct advice on how to start experimenting with them?) This question was posed by Marcel Vogel. Aside from him, only Swami Gokulananda has asked questions of Master.

"For you, much of this ripening process to proper understanding of the varying types of frequencies and pranas which are ignited through many instruments will come to you through these small insignificant channels. It is only for your ripening process in the efforts to help you understand the variations and differences of frequencies on Earth. Understand these subtle differences well. In time as you gain these knowledges, more will come to you that you further understand what you must do. Vishnu Swami is endowed with these two Children of Light which enable him also to gain the exact experiences through these children. Though each are different, the gained knowledge is but the same."

March 29, 1978

Many healing sessions were held with Gaurishankar. This is a small excerpt from a typical hour-long session where exact details are given.

"Move on now, Vishnu Swami, to the other child [Gaurishankar] who has come for your own help. Connect your instrument to that spot you know well on the diaphragm. As proper connection takes place, only then move on to the lumbar region. Connect your instrument to the spinal column first, then move on. In this time emphasis will be upon breaking the blockage over the left hip area. First move the instrument between the area of the spinal column and the hip bone, for in this area many many nerve endings are greatly greatly blocked."

(Slowly the energy is building up, Gurudev.)

"Only upon bombardment of great great pranas to the areas that are these days greatly blocked, can these nerve endings be healed. Understand well the powers you are following. As you first connected to the lumbar region, you were greatly greatly connected into the spinal column where great great pranas flow forth throughout the entire being. As you connected there, much much went forth into and through your instrument. As you reconnected your instrument to areas where pranas are blocked, where problems manifest forth, you have greatly magnetized and drawn forth great pranas to those areas of weakness."

June 4, 1978

(Gurudev, can you explain to me the phenomenon of the instruction book for my new watch disappearing? I was sitting in the airplane with the quartz crystal watch which I had just received, and the instruction book just disappeared off my lap.)

"Vishnu Swami, much will manifest forth before your own sense perceptions that cannot be properly understood. Know well the instrument you now possess has the great great properties within to change quickly energies, pranas, from one plane quickly to another, and back again. It is for this reason that you are greatly guided, that control be maintained. However, in some times as ignition goes forth in a greatly subtle way beyond your own comprehension, at these times many properties manifest forth within your own instrument, beyond your knowledge. This is reality. This is going forth though much of mental perception cannot perceive."

June 7, 1978

In this message, Master mentions for the first time the "pranic field" that was being built up in the small room where the sessions were held twice daily. This was mentioned several times later, including the last message to come before completion of this book. In that message, of August 24, Master said that a pranic field would also be built wherever his children gathered regularly to meditate.

(Gurudev, I feel intense energy all over my body. It's as if the crystal has disappeared. I feel only energy; there is no sensation of holding a gross object in my hand. It is so wonderful to feel this energy throughout my whole body and everywhere.)

"Understand all that which is going forth. As your own instrument becomes one with your own being and through your own efforts, connecting day by day to these most subtle pranas as these pranas flow into and become magnified greatly with your own instrument, in that hour you will be filled. Already given has been this promise in great days past. However, in that time you were not able to comprehend. More and more as you intune yourself to these greatest pranas flowing, as you release these pranas from within these two children, you will be causing an intense pranic field. As you then take forth your own instrument in hand and connect to those pranas going forth all around filling the environment, only then you can yourself be immersed greatly in that field."

(Gurudev, this is the first time that I can feel the energy all around me.)

"Understand well this energy. These pranas you are now experiencing through the instrument have been held within these two children. It is for this reason that intense pain manifests forth."

June 8, 1978

As the summer of 1978 progressed, Master began to empha-size frequently the importance of the "pranic field" which was being built up in the room where the sessions were held.

"For as pranas connect to your own instrument [crystal] being drawn out upon blockage from within these two children, these pranas will but add to greater and greater becoming this pranic field. It is of importance to you, Vishnu Swami, that this field go forth remaining undisturbed, pure; for it is within this field that intense growth will go forth in days ahead. More and more, as you remain in this place, as this field becomes greater and greater, many new phenomena will but bloom forth before you as you take this instru-ment in hand and connect with this place; for beyond these children, pranas within the atmosphere also take important types of action. This field also has great effect on your own instrument. Remember also, this pranic field is of a most most subtle nature and has effect on all who partake, on all who but enter into it. It is of importance that these fields go forth, be not disturbed. Day by day you will come to experience the intensity of these pranas but lingering forth in this place, and in ratio upon the intensity growing more and more will be your own ability to use your instrument in its most subtle manner."

June 12, 1978

The next message refers to the electrical storm that took place while I was using the crystal on Swami Sri Dharananda. At that time the energy of the storm was magnified through the crystal causing great difficulty to the two Children of Light. Master immediately gave instructions to immerse them in water and baking soda.

"Vishnu Swami, given to you in these moments is but a brief summary of that which has taken place. Understand well, within your own instrument is the property of transference of pranas from one level to another and back again. Understand well; as this process [of connecting into the two children] goes forth, protective mech-anism is but shielded from these two children. It is for this reason, as you but connected to this child, opening of the gross sheath and opening of the subtlest bodies went forth in but a prepared way. However, due to the situation of electrical disturbance in that atmo-sphere, the natural protection which is but built into the gross sheath and into the subtle bodies in that plane was but removed through the property of your own instrument. This going forth but allows the currents in that atmosphere of a great but subtle nature to enter in, causing great great disturbance. It is for this reason, instruction be given you causing but mechanical effect, in a mechanical way going forth creating that process of natural protection. It was for this reason instructed to you was immersion of each hand in water. It is for this reason that the electromagnetic systems be *grounded* in a natural way, shielding off these subtle currents from entering back through the physical sheath, passing forth into the subtle bodies."

June 16, 1978

The smaller of the two crystals was received in October of 1977; the larger one, in March of 1978. Here Master clarifies their use. No further word has been given regarding the third crystal, or when it will be received.

"Vishnu Swami, for this smaller instrument ignition passes only the reflection of that which goes forth in the gross sheath. Not only gross pranas but subtle pranas in many levels can come forth to your experience from this smaller instrument. Ignition to the great great instrument goes forth only to the subtle bodies. As the ignition of the smaller instrument only reflects that which passes through the gross sheath, the larger one only reflects that which passes through the subtler sheaths."

THE ANCIENT LOST KNOWLEDGE TO BE RESTORED ON THE EARTH PLANE

Quite often Master Sivananda makes reference to knowledge and communication with higher sources that were once available to mankind and which are soon to be rediscovered. Specifically he has spoken of Atlantis as well as an ancient civilization near Ponnambalam Medu in India. And, through the automatic writings and drawings of Swami Sri Dharananda, as well as her experiences while out of the body, it seems that there is also knowledge hidden in the pyramids of Egypt, soon to be brought to light.

It has been indicated by Master Sivananda that as man is prepared for what is to come, the ancient scriptures and spiritual truths will again be made known. Science and medicine, at odds with religion during the recent "age of reason", will become a part of this spiritual quest. The crystal is an example of this truth, although Master has indicated that we are just beginning to learn.

October 30, 1977 — Automatic writing

In many of Swami Sri Dharananda's out-of-body experiences she is taken to ancient civilizations where people have knowledge and abilities that present-day man does not have. In the following, the first paragraph is an automatic writing; while it was being written she had an inner experience of learning. The second paragraph she wrote was her immediate reaction to what she perceived while the automatic writing was coming through her.

"All the old forms [she believes this refers to the Pyramids, Stonehenge, etc.] from ancient days are storehouses of information never to be lost. All contain vibrations within the rock forms itself. The writings on the outside give instruction where and what is contained within — a type of index. When the time is right, the knowledge will come to decipher the vibrations contained within."

"I somehow feel I *know* what to do — an old deep memory is trying to emerge. I feel it strongly. The memory of ancient deciphering is contained within my *samskaras*. They have to emerge to help mankind somehow. This will again repeat in history. The records will again be transmitted into a form to transcend time. No history will be lost. The voice, 'Yes, yes,' is thundering within loudly." [Often when Swami Sri Dharananda hears Master's voice, this confirmation is given after she repeats or writes what she has heard.]

December 18, 1977

A few days before this message came, I saw a light hovering for about fifteen minutes above the hill across from the Winnebago where I was staying at our Ashram in Grass Valley, California. It seemed to be a U.F.O.

(The experience I saw at Grass Valley, I still can't understand it. Can Master guide us about what happened that night?)

"Vishnu Swami, much comes forth, much beyond your understanding, but all will unfold that you will understand."

(But still, was it illusion or imagination, or something for the future? Only that much guidance I need.)

"Your vision was reality Vishnu Swami. Many people also are seeing these same.... [words not audible]. They are in truth a reality coming more and more to the Earth plane. There children in darkness *must* must come to a new level. But few are prepared to accept that which must come."

(Is there any way we will come to that experience where direct contact will happen?)

"Many things will unfold to determine whether higher entities can come, will be accepted on the Earth plane. For now children who are open, children who are but instruments will receive the information, the knowledge from the higher Source. In time Earth can evolve to a state where it will be receptor to a gross manifestation of higher entities. For now is not ripe. The time now is one of great darkness, one of great fear and emotions. Higher entities to manifest at this time will cause great *chaos,* greater darkness, more upheavel on the Earth. The children must be ripened, must be made receptors for this to manifest."

(So that night it was just a symbolic event which took place?)

"Vishnu Swami, what you saw that night was in reality a gross manifestation. These manifested ....[inaudible].... of higher beings are reality on Earth, but few, few are receptive."

January 2, 1978

Man is being gradually prepared. Different parts of the whole knowledge are being given to different people. When the time is right, according to Master, all the links will be brought together.

"When the time is ripe, a team of many, many people from all over the globe will unite, and will come together to understand and receive the great, great instruments that are soon to be discovered from the ancient times, from the ancient civilizations buried in history."

(From where will most of the crystals be coming?)

"Many instruments, Vishnu Swami, will come forth from the ruins, from the civilization of Atlantis. But many, many instruments also were secretly scattered beyond this civilization from this main land form for protection when knowledge came of the final destruction. And even these will be identified and come forth in a time beyond the first discoveries of the immediate ruins of this lost civilization. In time, Vishnu Swami, those that are meant to be discovered will come forth, not by coincidence, but almost by force, for the power already going forth from these instruments are leading as keys, are leading as significant messages that will link the intellect to lead mankind to their place that they lay waiting to be found. Vishnu Swami, follow well the subtle incidents coming forth on the Earth plane that cannot be understood. For these are signs of that which is coming forth."

(What types of signs, Master?)

"Many unexplainable events, many unexplainable disappearances, many unexplainable situations coming forth from within mankind, on an individual level as well as a great level of humanity itself are blooming forth at this time, Vishnu Swami. For the instruments are sending powerful, powerful currents throughout the atmosphere, and more and more taking a manifest direct form, a direct manifest reaction. This will continue."

(How can humanity be protected from such dangers?)

"The only protection there is, is inner strength, inner faith, and direct connection from within to the higher Source.

"Of your own efforts you cannot help these children with this crude instrument for these children are greatly blocked by ignorance, by emotions, by their own experience lacking, being one in the darkness. These children are but afraid as energies surge and lock into this frequency. You must understand, Vishnu Swami, *the reason these children can connect to this frequency going forth is only due to the opening of these children by the current going forth.* This current is of a lesser frequency but also you must understand it is opening these children even before they are ripe and ready to become opened."

(Is this energy coming from the higher Source, or manmade, or from the crystals buried in the Earth?)

"Vishnu Swami, it is coming from a dual source. As the instruments are being ignited and used in a way for gaining experience to bring forth understanding and knowledge, these currents go forth and reignite ancient great crystals increasing frequency and intensity of currents going forth. However, many who are in possession of such instruments know not and understand not that which is going forth. Much, much current is flowing forth in an undirected way and thus becoming more and more connected to these frequencies, when they are not yet ready. Vishnu Swami, more and more great, great children, links from this place to the higher Source through proper devotion to their Masters, are properly learning well in a directed and exact way. As they understand proper, the ancient lost truth more and more, the currents will go forth directed rather than scattered, causing in later days less and less chaos within these children scattered over the face of the Earth. However, in these days much is unfolding in a way that most cannot properly understand. For this reason, Vishnu Swami, you and many brothers who are learning now will have a Karma to fulfill, one of helping these children who understand not what is happening to them. Through the use of the instruments which come to your posession you will easily be able to help them by restoring back proper balance of prana. And in days ahead you also will gain experiences in a way that you can properly seal off these children that they may again dwell in peace, not being bothered by pranas that indirectly cause havoc within the children who understand not what is going forth."

February 9, 1978

A good portion of the information on lost knowledge was given in relation to visits made to the ancient temple site at Ponnambalam Medu where, Master explained, a crystal from very early days was buried. I had an intuition that this is related to the "Garden" to which Swami Sri Dharananda would sometimes travel.

"Vishnu Swami, a greater amount of connection to a higher intensity of energy, from a greater source is going forth. Until this child is able to understand and learn proper balance, an intense amount of energy will flow back.

(How is this child going to learn this, Master?)

"This is part of what is going forth in the place which is known as the Garden of Truth and Justice."

(Gurudev, can you give me a little bit of description of this Garden. Is it on the physical or astral plane?)

"Vishnu Swami, this place does exist, but it is *not* part of the gross manifest plane. However, in days past, many, many children who were greatly intuned to the higher source were able to become part of this place. And many events did take place that brought gross manifestations that represented closely a type of replica of this place.

"Vishnu Swami, there are signs in that place, as you have already witnessed on that rock carved, still remains. This has great significance, but cannot at this moment be given forth. Other remains also exist, but may take great time and effort to bring forth properly. Know well, Vishnu Swami, that these symbols are of great value and have great deep deep meaning that holds within hidden truth from those days. Some of those people who existed in Truth in those times knew well of the coming destruction, and therefore were of great instruments, having these signs made permanent that all the knowledge would not go in vain in days ahead. Only at the right moment, Vishnu Swami, will this truth that is hidden be again revealed. It will come only when the experience matches the truth that lies there to be again told that it will make full sense, full understanding when it is revealed at that time."

February 11, 1978

(Is it Master's advice whether I should take this child [Swami Sri Dharananda] to India to this special place, Ponnambalam Medu, where I am going with Marcel Vogel? Will it help to understand the crystals and the ancient temple?)

"Vishnu Swami, at this time you now are being introduced to this whole new concept of lost truth that step by step will again come back to the Earth plane. Many, many lessons lay waiting before you that you may properly understand that which will come soon to manifest forth. To reveal parts of great mystery before your experiences manifest that you can readily understand, will go forth in vain, Vishnu Swami, for the mind without proper experience will not accept and will not understand properly. Therefore you will start to find places that do manifest great, great and powerful energies where in days past the great truth manifested. Many many symbols, remnants do remain in these places. But only at the exact time will all be revealed before you. Vishnu Swami, at this time you are greatly learning, you are being made to understand in a way that others will be made to understand. This manifestation, Vishnu Swami, is one more of a gross manner, for this, too, is of great importance in days to come. However, for proper information, for proper knowledge to come forth, many chosen children on a subtler level must go forth, and learn in a different way. Each is very significant, Vishnu Swami, that all may manifest properly back to the Earth plane. Vishnu Swami, for this child to be brought to such a place will not be of necessity at this time, for much is ongoing in this higher place. However, for you to experience and learn the intunement of the instrument, this would be of value to you. However, Vishnu Swami, go at a time that is in balance. Go when you can be intuned, for much can be learned on a subtle level."

One of the themes that has been repeated in Master's messages is that the ancient civilizations misused their knowledge and powers, causing their own destruction. During the second trip to Ponnambalam Medu, Marcel Vogel and Swami Brahmananda, who accompanied me, had a joint experience that seemed to underline this point.

After exploring the site of the carvings at Ponnambalam Medu, they decided to meditate and attempt to tune into the past of that area. Marcel Vogel asked the question, "What is our purpose in coming here?" Moments later Swami Brahmananda clearly heard a voice in his head: "To ignite the flame." Then, each had a separate vision of the temple that had stood at that site many, many years ago. Marcel Vogel's vision was of the destruction of the temple, of which he has since made drawings. In Swami Brahmananda's vision, he found himself looking down over the temple from above, and began to move in closer in order to see more. Despite a general disinclination towards "psychic" things and the definite feeling that something was attempting to stop him from entering, he asserted his will and entered the temple. The moment he was inside, he felt a great darkness and negativity, and a powerful presence seemed to compel him to leave.

For some time after our return from India, Marcel Vogel, Swami Brahmananda and I experienced high fevers and a general disorientation. Swami Brahmananda, in particular, experienced great amounts of negativity such as he had never known, which "seemed to come from a source outside of myself." The remainder of the February 11 message that follows and that of March 19 received after our return (given later in this section), indicate how the crystal may have opened the channels for the visions and for intunement with the negativity that was once there.

(Marcel Vogel says he has crystals and he wants to install them at all our Ashrams. Also, he has one to put at Ponnambalam Medu, so it will once again become an important pilgrim's place. Master's advice and guidance would be very important at this time.)

"Vishnu Swami, it is one of error to leave such an instrument where one is left alone, one not in tune to this place. For they can easily fall again into a negative path due to the great curiosity in the mind of man at this time. It should be one of great, great caution that only instruments be held and kept guarded, greatly guarded by those who do understand."

(Yes, Gurudev, I am very happy Master gave me these instructions. I will follow Master's advice.)

"Vishnu Swami, instruments, even lowly vibrating ones not ignited through this source, can still through a powerful mind, through great concentration, through powerful thought, any human being can send forth negative thoughts and if connected through any instruments, this will go forth. Vishnu Swami, this must be prevented. Help your brother to understand this point well, He already knows there is a quality of great mystery about these instruments. Let him know that all instruments to come forth must be greatly protected and guarded from those who understand not, Vishnu Swami."

(Yes, Gurudev)

"Your instrument gains great power in these places that still are in tune from days past. You can learn very great and subtle lessons by holding the instrument and learning well the subtle patterns of energy flowing forth from within it."

(Can I apply this to various places like I do to the child, to get this same experience, Master?)

"Vishnu Swami, in these places that remain you can learn greater and greater lessons, for the energy going forth remains there connected and caught that used to be from this Source. By connecting into the field of energy that is in this place, it is like being connected to this Source. It will be of interest for you to connect into such an energy, for you can ultimately learn much of what was going forth from these instruments. Vishnu Swami, you were intuned to the energy source in that place. Ultimately, all who pass through this place are subconsciously connected. You did notice a reaction of fever. This was not a common reaction, but was in fact caused by the electrical systems of all who pass through this place to be thrown greatly out of balance temporarily, due to the magnetic forces in this place.

"This will go on and on. It is this mysterious reason others in the past learned and understood something going on that they could not fully comprehend. And in time, because of this, this place was shielded by ignorance from anyone to visit. You understand this from the experience you had going there. Many, many souls come to fear this place due to ignorance.

"Vishnu Swami, you can and will learn much from this place on your own, which ultimately will be again relearned through this child with my guidance. As you find other places from days of yore, again and again you will repeat this learning experience from within in silence. Vishnu Swami, from deep inner experiences at these times, along with these other physical manifestations and gross lessons, you will come to understand and verify within your own self the truth that is coming forth."

February 15, 1978

"Vishnu Swami, in this time the Earth plane is greatly immersed in darkness. To stand firm, and go against such darkness is a great and impossible task, at this time and much, much injustice is manifesting forth and appears to be just for the eyes of the multitudes. *Vishnu Swami, actions that go forth directly against truth and justice in the areas concerning religion, in the areas concerning the ancient written truth, these must be maintained pure in days ahead.*

"This must manifest from a higher Source. Vishnu Swami, you are one of many that will come together, will unite to stand strong, stand firm and together will go forth amidst the darkness and shed great great light."

(But why is help not coming from the higher Source? Why are we struggling so greatly to correct all these false statements and distortions of our ancient truths?)

"Vishnu Swami, you know well the signs of the Kali Yuga age. You know well which unfolds in this time. However, all darkness must end in light. Through great strife, through great struggling, great suffering does negativity change back to one of positive great light."

February 21, 1978

"More and more you will gain proper experiences to understand the multitudes of properties that are held as qualities of these types of instruments. For this reason, Vishnu Swami, step by step you must learn well."

(Am I experiencing these properties now, Gurudev? I can feel a little sensation like a drawing from the crystal to the body. Am I correct?)

"Vishnu Swami, this experience is one of magnetizing pranas through the crystal from one area of great great stress, of energy, to one of a lesser area. You can move pranas, Vishnu Swami, with proper intunement of the instrument, through a great and pure, a powerful instrument held in your possession. In later days this property will be known as *pranic healing*. In a great, great and powerful sense you will be able to greatly help others when you finally understand and can use readily the instrument properly."

(Gurudev's Grace.)

"For this reason, Vishnu Swami, experiences must come forth in a lesser way that you properly understand. These two Children of Light before you are but mere instruments before your feet, intuned and struggling that you may learn properly.

"Vishnu Swami, already brought before you has been an explanation of currents flowing more and more upon the Earth plane. These currents as days progress on become subtlely stronger and stronger. As these currents flow forth, understand well, in a finer and subtler manner many Children of Light are being affected. For this reason, Vishnu Swami, the ripening process that has gone forth in a subconscious way even without knowledge going forth within these children, as these children connect to this manifestation of a higher frequency of energies flowing forth, these children too become connected. It is for this reason that at that time days ago before many children when manifestation came forth, so many had a great inner experience. It is not one of a psychic nature in a way previously understood. Vishnu Swami, understand well and know in your heart of these currents always going forth, day by day, hour by hour, moment by moment, continually bombarding the atmosphere of the Earth plane. More and more the currents go forth taking great effect beyond the knowledge of the children."

(What name can we give to these currents or energy. Master

has said it is not psychic phenomenon or experience. What can we call this to more easily explain it to the masses of people to make them aware of it?)

"Vishnu Swami, only in the great, great past has intunement through these properties in these instruments gone forth in such a way as again they are going forth now. More and more instruments are becoming connected to this higher place, and more and more incarnating back at this time are souls again flowing forth all in great numbers from the ancient days of Atlantis when this happened again, and is repeating now. It is in the great samskaras (latent impressions from past incarnations) deep, deep within these children that much, much intunement once known before again is reopening now due to these currents. There is no name, for it is only a phenomenon ongoing."

(Why at this particular time of this century are the souls reincarnating and the currents flowing so strongly?)

"Vishnu Swami, you know well cycles of history repeat again and again over and over. Much moves in darkness and then once again is restored to light, only to become dimmed back to darkness, only again to be restored to light. This is always known and repeats over and over. You understand this point well, Vishnu Swami. All these children coming forth with a combination of great and deep samskaras, from past intunements and past experiences with these subtle experiences of a nature concerning more subtle pranas, are again reawakening forth into a manifest way as currents become stronger. Many of these children have been greatly lost and in their struggles to find their inner way have gained many impurities and for this reason, Vishnu Swami, as the pranas flow forth from intunement and ripening in a way that necessarily these children are not ready for, many blocks will come forth. Blocks and more blocks due to impurities of past as well as functions blocking for protection coming together, the energies become so so great. You have experienced this with a few children a few days ago.

"However, you must understand your experience and knowledge is truth. But in these days, through the instrument you now possess, only your intunement goes forth and cannot necessarily help these children in these days as will your efforts that will manifest in days to come. You must remember, your instrument you now possess is only meant for your learning from this child, these two Children of Light before you; for you intunement and direct experience from this guidance from this place . . . [inaudible] . . . forth before you on such a large scale. For this is not psychic phenomenon of itself. Understand well, Vishnu Swami, that phenomenon which is taking place. These children, these children before you are greatly, greatly being affected by these currents, by the power going forth in a scattered undirected way, by many who are testing and who are trying to understand those instruments which they have come to possess. These people understand not the havoc, nor the unfoldment that has been caused to take place."

(Why are only a few children being affected now, Master?)

"Vishnu Swami, few now, but many, many more, for as the currents grow stronger and stronger, they take a greater and greater effect. As this effect comes forth into manifestation these children unfold direct conscious experience that they understand not. For this opening to the past samskaras, to the subtler bodies and levels, they once were in control and once lived comfortably in, has been shielded and due to this, these children still remain in a gross manner, in chaos, in darkness, in an unfocussed way. Lead them well, Vishnu Swami, teach them to focus, to focus and to refocus to the higher Source, to surrender. This will be their protecting link until their strength from within is once again restored. Vishnu Swami, many children of a weak nature are vulnerable to psychic phenomenon at this time of inner unfoldment. Many are not ready to open to the more subtle bodies. However, because of the current going forth these children are opened before they are ripened to do so and are caught in a very dangerous situation. For this reason, you must stress the importance of mental focus, of surrender, and of regular Sadhana. For this is their protection. This will be their inner strength."

February 24, 1978

(Gurudev, what is the purpose of learning to distinguish these different types of energies with the crystal?)

"Vishnu Swami, these changes of prana are of great, great importance. For in later days you will come to understand and intune yourself through more powerful instruments to other systems greatly in distress, in sickness and disease. You will in days to come gain proper knowledge to manifest such a higher frequency of pranas within disturbed systems that healing and proper balance be once again restored. This is one great property of the instruments which is of significant value for all mankind."

(Gurudev, how is it possible to help innummerable human beings with this knowledge as I am only one person and my time is so limited?)

"Vishnu Swami, in days ahead all science, by great, great meetings will come to understand, will be made to see the truth of these pranas as a great means of proper healing, for proper balance of the systems. For these scientists, the whole, whole of medicine will be changed. For now they grope in darkness. In days ahead, with all that must manifest forth that is in great preparation, many will come to understand these higher truths. Not only for you, Vishnu Swami, for your work now is only a foundation of proper understanding. This will link together with other brothers that in the proper moment in time all will unite to go forth."

February 27, 1978

Not all of the ancient knowledge to be revived is about crystals. The realm of science and medicine will also undergo change.

"Vishnu Swami, in later days these truths will greatly awaken scientists and those in the field called medicine. For direct, these truths will prove how crude the philosophies and understanding are, that these professional children, ones considered of great knowledge, will understand how crude their understanding really is. These higher truths will fill in the areas considered unknown, that more and more all children will benefit. All mankind will again dwell in higher Truth. Vishnu Swami, energies, pranas, spirituality, all these are still considered phenomena not yet known in general to mankind. More and more, those closed will be ripened by inner struggle to see these thoughts that do greatly exist and will greatly benefit all."

(Will scientists ever be able to prove the manifestations of energies through the crystals with their scientific instruments?)

"Vishnu Swami, at the exact prepared moment, disciplined circles of great, great fields of science and medicine, much will be revealed they will greatly understand. These will be significant times, that time will go forth to change and ripen the multitudes to a higher understanding. In time, as scientists and those in the profession of medicine receive truths that come forth in later day, in time, all mankind will greatly benefit, as they too, from either error or inner great lessons, all will manifest and ripen properly in each child through each field. More and more, one affects another, until knowledge ripens again on earth. This work is not through only a few but through many, many, many children in this stage, as the ignition of Truth back on Earth. A *few links have been chosen to be taught directly.* It will be their efforts both directly and indirectly that start a chain reaction; for these knowledges are of great great value and will come forth, and will be properly received. Worry not, Vishnu

Swami, for this goes forth. You will not be alone. All is exactly prepared. I am here witnessing all that comes forth."

(Gurudev's advice please, is there any scientist I should contact when I go for the expedition with Marcel Vogel to Ponnambalam Medu; or should I keep as quiet as possible?)

Vishnu Swami, go forth in a way that you gain valuable lessons with your brother. For in the place you wish to visit, your experiences will be one of a subtle nature. In these days as you ripen forth, much cannot yet be properly proved before other scientists who can only see through the gross manner. Rather, wait until you are properly ripened, then you will come to understand; methods and situations will come that all may see properly, that all may understand well. Go forth now and connect greater and greater to this brother. For each together will bring more and more strength. For in days to come these great links together will prove to many the great and most value of this that is coming."

(Gurudev, can you shed some slight light please on the subject of Ponnambalam Medu? At this place there is the mandala of the Devi [A mandala in the shape of a Star of David]. Is it very ancient? And second, the pond, the spring pond; is there anything underneath? Is that the place where the ancient temple was located? Third, in that forest area in Ponnambalam Medu, is there anything there? Gurudev's light on these subjects and guidance will greatly help me.)

"Vishnu Swami, it is not one of coincidence that a pond seems to manifest in a place there. It is a great reason, exactly prepared, that this water manifest forth. For through the powers of water, the vibrations going forth from the great instrument buried there, much, much of the power is directly absorbed; much, much is brought to a little that cannot bring harm. For the instrument buried there is one of great, great power and is still intuned at this time. Vishnu Swami, for this reason the power can still be directly experienced coming to this place. But with the water that surrounds and protects, much of that power going forth is directly absorbed through that water, that destruction to others who visit this place cannot manifest. Already you experience the effect of such energy upon your systems as well as others. Even at this rate, the power emanating going beyond the source of the water still creates havoc in those who visit. You experienced what is known as fever. As a direct result of the high, high frequency changing and interrupting your electro-magnetic system within your own systems. This, too, manifests in others. As days pass, Vishnu Swami, more and more others will come to fear this place as rumors and experiences bring forth more confusion, for those who visit this place are greatly affected and understand not. It will be of great time, much, much time before these fears can be dispelled and in these days your experiences will be one from within, one of a subtle nature and therefore you cannot prove to others in this time that which is truth. For this reason your journey will be of value to only you and your brother, who will learn much. But to others who understand not, the experience will cause but more havoc and serves as more and more reason for fear within as these children understand not, as they are being affected by coming to this place."

(Is there any way by going to this place I can help humanity understand that great energy there? Is that my Karma?)

"Vishnu Swami, It is not in these direct days that this purpose can be fulfilled. It is only one of a significant nature for you to visit such a place and learn [about that which,] in a powerful way, is buried greatly, greatly within the earth. Such cannot be proved to those who dwell in fear and darkness. Your work and efforts to bring forth truth about such a place will seem futile in the end, for fear is great among peoples who live near. Go forth and learn well for all is greatly and exactly prepared step by step that you may learn and understand well. Vishnu Swami, concern yourself not with external symbols in this place, for long long lost is that temple. Rather go forth and intune yourself with your instrument that you may learn and gain experience from the power emanating from the higher and greater instruments in that place buried. These pranas will be of value to you to experience. Go with an open heart; go greatly intuned that you may learn well."

March 19, 1978 — Addressed to Marcel Vogel

"Understand well the properties of the instruments you come to possess. For each has the capacity for intunement both within the Earth plane as well as to these higher realms. You know well from your own unfoldment how to intune to vibrations and frequencies held from past times in the Earth plane. From this time onwards let your focus *not* be with intunement to that which remains from the past on the Earth plane, but rather with one-pointed focus to these higher realms. For only these intunements coming forth again will manifest to help all mankind. Your reaction has been exactly prepared that you may exhibit before your brother the problems that can manifest by intunement to ancient, ancient frequencies that led to final destruction of those who misused those instruments. Those frequencies, those vibrations of destruction, intuned more and more through the magnification of the instrument from this plane passed back into your own being. *Intune not within,* intune not to the Earth plane vibrations. For this in days past has been the great ruin of mankind. For you to intune to these vibrations passed magnifies greatly these vibrations once again on this plane. This brings great, great havoc and inteference to many and in time will bring havoc upon all mankind. Take this warning well."

Master Sivananda is not the first to communicate from the higher planes regarding the ancient lost knowledge. Among others, Edgar Cayce, "the sleeping prophet", was well known for his reincarnation readings. While in a semitrance state he would give accounts of people's past lives, during which great amounts of information on the early advanced civilizations was revealed.

According to Cayce, Atlantis was destroyed over a period of many, many years. In its early days its citizens were greatly intuned to higher sources. But in time, man began to ignore the Teachers and abuse the power he had been given. This eventually destroyed even the continent itself. Those who remained intuned were given instructions for leaving Atlantis and preserving its knowledge.

In the book *Edgar Cayce on Atlantis* by his son Edgar Evans Cayce, there are an uncanny number of references similar to those of Master Sivananda. In particular, note his readings regarding the present-day reincarnation of many Atlantean souls, the discussions of crystals, and the information on the "sealed room" yet to be discovered which coincides with Swami Sri Dharananda's experiences.

"While the destruction of this continent and the peoples was far beyond any of that as has been kept as an absolute record, that record in the rocks still remains. Also their influence extended to the lives of the people to whose lands they escaped. Even today, either through the direct influence of being reincarnated in the Earth, or through mental effects on individual's thoughts, they may influence individuals, groups and nations in the present.   (364-3)"

"In Atlantean land at time of development of electrical forces that dealt with transportation of craft from place to place, photographing at a distance, reading inscriptions through walls even at a distance, overcoming gravity itself, preparation of the crystal, the terrible mighty crystal; much of this brought destruction.   (519-1; Feb. 20, 1934)"

"...in Atlantean land before the second destruction when there was the dividing of islands, when the temptations were begun in activities of Sons of Belial and children of Law of One. Entity [or person for whom the reading was being given] *among those that interpreted the messages received through the crystals and the fires*

that were to be the eternal fires of nature. New developments in air and water travel are no surprise to this entity as these were beginning development at that period for escape.   (3004-1; May 15, 1943)"

"These [air and water crafts], *then, were impelled by the concentration of rays from the stone* [crystal] *which was centered in the middle of the power station, or powerhouse (as would be the term in the present).*

"In the active forces of these, the entity [or person for whom the reading was being given] *brought destructive forces by setting up — in various portions of the land — the kind that was to act in producing powers for the various forms of the people's activities in the cities, the towns and the countries surrounding same. These, not intentionally, were tuned too high; and brought the second period of destructive forces to the people in the land — and broke up the land into those isles which later became the scene of further destructive forces in the land.*   (440-5; Dec. 20, 1933)"

"As the time draws nigh when the changes are to come about, there may be the opening of those three places where the records are one, to those that are the initiates in the knowledge of the One God.

"The temple by Iltar will then rise again. Also there will be the opening of the temple or hall of records in Egypt, and those records that were put into the heart of the Atlantean land may also be found there — that have been kept, for those that are of that group. The records are One.   (5750-1; Nov. 12, 1933)"

"...those records of the activities of individuals were preserved — the one in the Atlantean land, that sank, which will rise and is rising again; another in the place of the records that leadeth from the Sphinx to the hall of records, in the Egyptian land; and another in the Aryan or Yucatan land, where the temple there is overshadowing same.   (2012-1; Sept. 25, 1939)"

"[The sealed room contains] *a record of Atlantis from the beginning of those periods when the Spirit took form, or began the encasements in that land; and the developments of the peoples throughout their sojourn; together with the record of the first destruction, and the changes that took place in the land; with the record of the sojournings of the peoples and their varied activities in other lands, and a record of the meetings of all nations or lands, for the activities in the destruction of Atlantis; and the building of the Pyramid of Initiation, together with whom, what and where the opening of the records would come, that are as copies from the*

sunken Atlantis. For with the change, it [Atlantis] *must rise again.*
(378-16; Oct. 29, 1933)"

MESSAGES OF INSPIRATION

Despite the amazing amount of technical information given in Master Sivananda's messages, the most striking aspect about them is their inspirational nature. They are such that they can be read, reread, and read again. They remain ever uplifting, an infinite source of wisdom.

November 11, 1977

"Know I am manifest, Oh Children of Light. Time is growing very, very short. Waste not a moment of your precious time. You must do Sadhana. More and more Sadhana. Dive deep, deep within. There I am waiting. You are all stars shining in the darkness. The way is prepared. All is laid waiting. Do not waste one precious moment lost in sensual pastures. You must dive deep within. There the light will be kindled. All lights must shine on the Earth for time is growing short. Darkness is covering the Earth. All my children must shed light. I am with you all. I am manifest to save humanity. Do not doubt, for all that is prepared is beyond human understanding. Do your Sadhana; focus within. There I am waiting. All that comes is meant to be. All must unfold at the proper time. Fear not. Lose all doubts. Do not tarry in human emotions for this will cloud your inner light. All my children, shine, shine bright. All must shed bright, bright light. Oh Children of Light, be bold, be brave, struggle on for I am with you."

December 18, 1977

This message was given before the Winnepeg Yoga Teachers Association of approximately 80 people.

"Learn your lessons well, for you must at all costs abide in Truth. For the Earth is dwelling in darkness. Be bold, be brave. Regulate your lives with Sadhana; purify. Go forth, my children. Help others, lead them well; but to lead others you yourself must be perfect examples for others to follow. Learn well my children, strive on, struggle hard. You must abide in Truth at all costs. Do Sadhana, Sadhana, and more Sadhana. For this will give you inner strength. You will gain inner peace. This peace will radiate out like a great light to others. This light of peace will draw others to you.

Teach them, lead them well. Help them to also abide in Truth. For all the Children of Light must once again come together. Must once again shed their light. Go now."

January 5, 1978

"I am manifest. Know, all my children are greatly, greatly protected. For I am here protecting all. I am here witnessing and guiding at every moment. Let it be known that in the hours of darkness before all my children stands the great, great light. Worry not, for I am here with you all. Worry not, for I am protecting all my children. Go forth, walk like lions, for I am your guiding shield. I will remain with my children until the last moment through their departure from this place. Know always, I am here. I am with you. I am witnessing and guiding at every step. Worry not.

"All darkness in the hearts of my children must at once be dispelled, for there only light, only joy shall remain. Focus at my feet whenever you feel darkness for there I am always waiting to serve my children."

January 9, 1978

"I am manifest, blessed Children of Light. At all costs lose not your regular routine of Sadhana. In days to come much will unfold. Much, much will manifest to utilize your energies and strength. In days to come you will be leading and helping others. But in this effort lose not sight of your goals, nor lose your regular pattern of Sadhana at any cost. Sadhana is your only strength in days to come. Prepare yourself from this very moment. March on boldly. You must, you must learn to balance your days, your time in each day, with all that manifests outwardly. Balance, balance. Always set apart time for Sadhana, for your only strength lies in your deep, deep connection to the silence within. You must come to know the secret of inner strength. All my children must learn to become flexible. To learn balance. For both your efforts in days to come, helping those lost in darkness, can only become an effective effort only by your constant, constant connection within.

"Those who become rigid, dealing only outwardly and forget their time to go within, surely will become consumed in darkness. Oh, Children of Light, beware, for now is the time to learn this balance. At all cost learn, at all cost. Be flexible with that which manifests within each day, to search and find; make the time. Go off, find the short time to be alone, to dive within, to once again connect and reconnect and reconnect day by day to that inner silence. For this will be your saving shield in days to come. Practice now; days will come soon, more and more difficult day by day to keep up this daily routine. You must understand the importance for continuing, no matter what comes, to keep this routine for this will be your saving shield. March on my children. You must learn to distinguish that which is important from that which *seems* important. For your inner strength comes only from Sadhana. Sadhana, day by day continued. You must continue.

"Leave not even one day without such peace. For one day missed surely leads to another and another and another until you become finally immersed also in the darkness. Therefore my children miss not even one day, for the mind is greatly weak and you surely will fall. Therefore stand strong. This strength comes by practice, by practice, by continuing day by day. Find the time, fit yourself within that which manifests, for events will come more and more and more overlapping, drawing you outward and outward, immersing you more and more, until time has slipped away and you have but forgotten. At this time you will fall in darkness. For the more you become immersed outwardly, the greater difficulty it will be to go within. The longer you wait, the more days that slip by, the farther you fall away from your true strength. Therefore, my children do not allow yourself even one day amiss. You will find your strength. I am here waiting. I am manifest to guide and protect you all.

"Step by step, you all will march on to fulfill that which has been prepared. Oh, my children, without this inner strength you walk blind in darkness. You are but weak sheep innocent going forth among the wolves. Dive deep, dive deep, deep within. Each day you will emanate a shield that cannot be broken by the forces, by the darkness where you must ultimately tread to fulfill your work. Start your work protected and you will not fall. March on boldly for I am here guiding and protecting you all."

February 13, 1978

The crystal was used on Swami Sri Dharanandaji as usual. She lost body consciousness and entered an absorbed state with no perception of the external world. It was about 8:10 p.m. when this occurred and I was waiting for a message from Master. I was not going to meditation. Then I decided to bring Swami Sri Dharananda to the temple so that the message could manifest before all. Six men carried her to the temple on a mattress. There were about 175 people in the temple. After a while her arms went up in the *mudras* and the following message came from Gurudev Sivananda.

"Vishnu Swami."

(Yes, Gurudev.)

"At this time there are many children sitting and watching in great disbelief. For these children, one may come forth to verify the gross manifestation of this movement of energies in this child."

(Which child would Master like to come forth? Any one child?)

"This does not make a difference."

(Okay, the psychologist, please come here.)

"Have this child lay the hands upon the feet at this time. Have this child now move from place to place up the physical sheath."

(Feel the currents, move your hands up slowly. Master, give us more instructions.)

"Let any child come forth, any child who wishes to experience this energy. Let them lay hands upon the thigh area of this child. Let others move on, that all who wish may gain this experience."

After a number of guests and students had felt the *pranas* moving within Swami Sri Dharanandaji's body, Master instructed them to sit and meditate, and the following message was given.

"Blessed Children of Light, learn well that which is being brought before you from this great Child of Light. Learn well. Open yourself to that higher Truth soon, the days before you are numbered but short. Great and highest Truth will be revealed before you. Learn well. It is my wish that I lay before your feet, that each and every one go forth beyond these days of learning and walk in Truth. Bend not, fall not by the wayside. But stand strong! Walk boldly! with truth in your hearts. In these days you will be marching in great darkness, and times will come when it seems impossible to stand firm in Truth. It is these times that your only strength will be Sadhana. For this will be your great strength, your foundation which will remain strong to support you always.

"Great Children of Light! Learn well. Understand, your missions in life will unfold. But it is your choice to either walk on the path of Truth or bend and fall, becoming immersed also in darkness. It is your choice. Know each one has a great and wonderful mission to fulfill in this incarnation. It is for this reason that you have come to this place. Open yourselves, become fulfilled, that you may leave with an inner light that will not go out, no matter how much, how far you walk amidst the darkness. Each one walk *boldly, stand strong, be brave like lions*. Radiate your inner light that all may see, that all may become again walking in Truth, that they may use you as perfect examples to help others. In this way your mission, wherever it may unfold, may properly be fulfilled. I am at your feet — to help you and guide you when time seems so great and difficult. I am manifest to serve you all. Therefore, my children, I must go now. Learn well. Know always, I am manifest that you may find me always within."

(Bolo Sat Guru Sivananda Maharj Ki Jai)

About three dozen people in the temple, either just after the message, during the night or next day, reported inner experiences and inner awakenings. Some manifested externally as great blocks of energy or automatic breathing. Swami Vishnuji had to physically help a few people by releasing excess energy. Master later said in subsequent messages that what happened in the temple that night was greatly prepared so that I could see the ripening process going on in many children which for the most part they themselves are not aware of. Master also said that the crystal could not help these children much at this time as the present instrument (the smaller crystal) was very crude and it requires great intunement and ignition to be effective.

April 3, 1978

A student who was having difficulties with mental negativity came for help. Master gave words of encouragement.

"Like others you are greatly burdened with great and difficult thoughts that manifest again and again into your mind. Recognize these as only but clouds that darken your vision to once again see the sun shining bright. Know this to be a sign to help your own growth. Rather than going forth and bending, becoming weaker with identification to these clouds, rather *stand firm, stand forth* with Mantra in the mind. *Greatly roar like a lion. Stand strong.* Know well these thoughts will but vanish, take to their heels and go forth lifting off this burden from you. Again and again this will come to help in your own path of growth. Worry not, for these are of great benefit. Instead of identification with these as problems, rather know well they are of but great benefit for your own learning.

"Go forth then again and again with mind greatly focussed on your own Mantra. Go forth and stand strong in the face of these difficulties. You will notice with your own efforts these burdens more and more quickly will but vanish before you. Worry not as these small, small incidents come forth, only come forth for your own great evolution. In time you will see these coming forth and will come to know, your own self, strength that comes forth as you meet on these burdens again and again, only with proper focus of mind, with your own will and strength.

"Continue on day by day with great, great vigor and you will but in time come to know its own great benefits. You, like many others, have a great task laid before your feet that you may walk forth and help many other children who are but immersed in darkness. Therefore, go forth and find your own light first. And in those days, as your own struggles become smaller and smaller, as your own strength from within builds greater and greater, know as your foundation becomes solid like a great rock from efforts in Sadhana, only then you can become a great and fit instrument to go forth in the darkness helping others. Go forth my child. Continue on fervently with your great Sadhana. You will greatly ripen."

Finally, one of the most interesting aspects of the phenomenon of the messages from Master Sivananda is the fact that so much of what is now coming through from him is similar in many ways to his style of speaking and writing when he was still in the body. Often even the very words themselves are the same. Not only are they of a greatly inspirational nature, but they encourage the aspirant to forge on ahead fearlessly in his spiritual endeavors. Given here are several quotes culled from the volumes of his writing that show the parallels in theme and wording between his works on Earth and those beyond:

"Stand up. Be bold. Be cheerful. Be strong. Rely on your own Self. Get the power and strength from within."

"No Sadhana ever goes in vain. Every bit of it is credited toward your evolution. This is the law. Think not negative thoughts, but calmly go on with Sadhana. Be regular at it. Without missing a single day, proceed onward with your spiritual practice. Little by little the power accumulates and it will grow."

"Withdraw. Meditate. Dive deep into the recesses of your heart."

"Tarry not. Falter not. March onward, forward, and Godward."

"Be always cheerful and bold. Take recourse to God's name. Face all problems boldly; they will melt away. Be regular in your Sadhana."

"Practice intense Sadhana. Keep your spirits high, for you are the Lord's Child!"

"March boldly on the spiritual path. Be not troubled. Be a brave lion: roar *Om Namah Sivaya* in happiness and sorrow."

About the Author

In 1957 Swami Vishnu Devananda set out from the foothills of the Himalayas to carry out the bidding of his Guru: "Spread the seeds of Yoga in the West." And he has done precisely that. For the past twenty years, he has been one of the most active and dedicated spiritual leaders to come from the East. In that time he has travelled many times around the world, from one continent to another, teaching Yoga and establishing centers where his Master's work could be carried out.

He was born Swamy Kuttan Nair on December 31, 1927. After completing school, he spent some months teaching, then entered the Corps of Engineers of the Indian Army. It was while he was in the Army that he first met his Guru; and no sooner was he discharged than he joined the Ashram of his Master, Swami Sivananda, considered to be India's greatest modern saint. Within a year he renounced all things of the world, and embraced the life of spiritual study and service of humanity. He was given the name Swami Vishnu Devananda. For twelve years he remained in the service of his Guru. There he acted as the professor of Hatha Yoga at the Vedanta Forest Academy, and was General Secretary of the Sivananda Ashram as well as personal secretary for two years to Swami Sivananda.

Upon leaving India for the West, Swami Vishnu Devananda spent a year travelling, lecturing and demonstrating Yoga in Ceylon, Singapore, Hong Kong, Indonesia, Australia and Hawaii. When he finally arrived in San Francisco, he quickly taught himself to drive and spent another year travelling throughout North America.

It soon became apparent that Westerners were so caught up in the whirlwind of their lives that they neither knew how to relax nor how to live a healthy life. He immediately devised the concept of a Yoga vacation, and set about to establish places where people could go to bring into practice the five main points of Yoga: proper exercise, proper breathing, proper diet, proper relaxation, and positive thinking and meditation.

Within a few years, the Sivananda Yoga Vedanta Centers and Ashrams were established. This is a network of over two dozen teaching centers located in major cities around the world, and five Ashrams, or retreats, where people can find an atmosphere of peace and quiet, away from the tensions and anxieties of everyday life.

In 1969 the True World Order was established. It grew from a vision which Swamiji had in which hundreds of people were tearing down the walls and barriers that exist between nations. In a massive cooperative effort, all of humanity was suddenly united. The True World Order, TWO, is dedicated to this purpose of unity and understanding between peoples of the world. Its main functions include the sponsoring of various conferences, symposiums and festivals, and the offering of the Teachers' Training Course. This is a unique course aimed at bringing about harmony in the world through training leaders for the age to come in the basics of Yoga discipline. This purpose has begun to manifest as an increasing number of professionals, politicians, and students from all parts of the world participate in the course.

In 1971 he made headlines by flying around the world in his Piper Apache, painted by Peter Max, "bombing" the trouble spots of the world with flowers and leaflets of peace. At that time he braved a flight from Tel Aviv to Cairo flying directly over the Suez Canal, with his Jewish co-pilot where he was almost shot down, in an effort to help bring about peace in the Middle East. He also marched through the streets of Belfast with actor Peter Sellers, chanting and praying for peace.

His other projects have included: A World Conference of Religions, 1969; Yoga Peace and Music Festival, 1970; the White House March for Peace, 1974; the International Yoga Teachers Conference, in Nassau, 1975; World Parliament of Religions — All Gurus Festival, 1975; Symposium on Yoga and Psychic Discoveries, 1976; Symposium on Yoga: Man and his Future, in Spain, 1976; Symposium on Yoga and Psychic Discoveries, in India, 1977; and the Symposiums on Physics and Metaphysics, in Los Angeles and New York, 1977.

Swami Vishnu Devananda is well known for his outstanding work *The Complete Illustrated Book of Yoga,* often referred to as the "Bible of Yogis".

If you are interested in knowing more about the Sivananda Yoga Centers and Ashrams, Please contact:

Sivananda Ashram Yoga Camp Headquarters, 8th Avenue, Val Morin, Quebec, J0T 2R0, Canada. (819) 322-3226